Politics and Public Policy
in Latin America

About the Book and Authors

POLITICS AND PUBLIC POLICY IN LATIN AMERICA
Steven W. Hughes and Kenneth J. Mijeski

This innovative textbook focuses on the policy approach as a systematic tool for understanding Latin American political life and then outlines policymaking variations among the Latin American regimes.

The authors introduce the student to the study of policymaking by examining various theoretical perspectives and then grounding those perspectives in the practice of Latin American politics. Rather than endorse one approach over another, they encourage students to critically examine the methods of making policy.

The book then discusses the main groups and institutions involved in Latin American politics and shows how those institutions interact in the policy process. The text offers penetrating case studies of policy formation in six countries that represent three types of regimes. The final chapters consider the impact of policy. The authors assess the principal tendencies of economic, social, political, and civil rights policies and challenge the student to consider whether these policies have had an impact on the social systems of the six countries analyzed. These chapters point out the utility, as well as the limits, of the policy approach as a means of understanding Latin American politics.

STEVEN W. HUGHES is a professor in the Department of Politics and Public Administration at California State College, Stanislaus. KENNETH J. MIJESKI is an associate professor of political science at East Tennessee State University. They are the coauthors of *Legislative-Executive Policy-Making: The Cases of Chile and Costa Rica* (1973).

Politics and Public Policy in Latin America

STEVEN W. HUGHES

&

KENNETH J. MIJESKI

WITH CASE STUDIES BY STEPHEN G. BUNKER,
JUAN M. DEL AGUILA, MERILEE S. GRINDLE, JOHN D. MARTZ,
CYNTHIA McCLINTOCK, & MARK B. ROSENBERG

WESTVIEW PRESS * BOULDER AND LONDON

To
Kris, Lisa, Jonathan,
Kendra, Keith, and Kara

Copyright © 1984 by WESTVIEW PRESS, INC.

Published in 1984 in the United States of America by WESTVIEW PRESS, INC.,
5500 Central Avenue, Boulder, Colorado 80301; FREDERICK A. PRAEGER, Publisher

Library of Congress Cataloging in Publication Data
Hughes, Steven W.
  Politics and public policy in Latin America.
  Bibliography: p.
  Includes index.
  1. Latin America—Politics and government—1948–
2. Political planning—Latin America. 3. Policy sciences.
I. Mijeski, Kenneth J. II. Title.
JL960.H83 1984   320.98   84-11835
ISBN 0-8133-0040-1
ISBN 0-8133-0041-X (pbk.)

Printed and bound in the United States of America

10   9   8   7   6   5   4   3   2   1

Contents

Preface

Searching for the appropriate textbook for a course in Latin American politics preoccupies scholars often as much as the search for the appropriate theoretical perspective through which one can gain an understanding of the political life of that region. As students of Latin American politics, we have seen various textbook trends come and go and, sometimes, return again in new forms: texts that focus on the pathological state of democracy in various Latin American countries; those that urge the student to perceive Latin America's options as either reform or revolution, development or decay, dependence or independence, socialist or capitalist; still others that, eschewing theoretical alternatives, offer the student the option of learning about Latin American politics via either a "country-by-country" approach or a more general approach to the common experiences, problems, and possibilities of Latin America "as a whole."

What we offer in this book is not "the" answer to these intellectual and pedagogical dilemmas. Instead, we more humbly suggest that many of the perspectives expressed by other observers of Latin American politics might usefully be considered by focusing on a characteristic common to all political systems and their governments: the effort to formulate, promulgate, and implement public policy. If politics and political actors make a difference in Latin American countries, it should somehow be reflected in the process by which policies are made, the substance of those policies, and their impact.

To examine the public policymaking process in all the Latin American republics would, of course, be a task of monumental proportions. We have not sought such an undertaking. Instead, we suggest (tentatively) that it is helpful to think of many of the Latin American nations as belonging to one of three categories based on government structure and the nature of the policy process: democratic, military, or postrevolutionary. For each of these three categories, we have selected two countries that we believe represent interesting variations of the general type. Venezuela is a democracy of quite recent vintage and also one blessed with valuable natural resources. Costa Rica is a somewhat older democracy (though not greatly so) and one not so well endowed; moreover, Costa Rica is tiny, both in land mass and population, and for all practical purposes an agricultural society, while Venezuela is substantially larger and more industrialized.

Brazil and Peru have been selected to represent the military category. In the case of Peru we have chosen to focus our analysis on an earlier period of time—1968–1975—because during those years Peru experienced rule by a "leftist" military government; since military regimes tend to be quite conservative, at least insofar as social policy and economic redistribution are concerned, 1968–1975 Peru provides a very exciting case study. Brazil, since the military coup of 1964, is an example of a country containing a government that seeks rapid economic growth while behaving in a typically authoritarian and conservative fashion.

Finally, our postrevolutionary category contains two very interesting types. Mexico is a country that experienced a revolution in the early twentieth century, while Cuba's revolution occurred in mid-century. What is instructive in the contrast between the two lies in the interests that successfully captured the revolution and dominated the country's reconstruction. In the Mexican case, urban bourgeois interests came to control the revolutionary outcome while in Cuba the revolution came to be dominated by socialist interests.

Through both general overviews and detailed case studies, we seek to provide you with a thorough familiarization of the contours of policymaking and policy impact in six countries and, by generalization, of three common types of regime. We do not suggest that this exercise will provide you with a thorough understanding of all of Latin America. That will require many years and a good many books.

Our debts to others, intellectual and otherwise, would take another book to outline adequately. By his early encouragement and continuing support for the project, John D. Martz of Pennsylvania State University has been a sustaining force. Glen T. Broach, chairman of the Political Science Department at East Tennessee State University, and William Neeley and John Wold of the Department of Politics and Public Administration of California State College, Stanislaus, offered insightful comments on various drafts. For typing and retyping and for their general skill in juggling numerous and often conflicting obligations to see that this manuscript eventually got to the publishers, Jean Haskell and Jean Wright of the CSCS Department of Politics and Public Administration and Betty Wagner of the ETSU political science department have been invaluable; thanks are due also to the several student workers who added much by way of typing at different stages of manuscript preparation. A special thank you is owed to the Department of Politics and Public Administration at Stanislaus State and to its chairman, Professor Kenneth Entin, for encouragement, hand holding, criticism, and other, more tangible, forms of support. We are deeply indebted to Lynne Rienner, formerly of Westview Press, for her commitment to the project; thanks also to her staff, especially

Caren Dickstein and Byron Schneider, for their help and kindness; and to Jeanne Remington, Kathy Streckfus, Marian Safran, and Holly Arrow for a superb job of polishing and improving the readability of the book. Finally, we thank our families, particularly Kris and Kendra, for an unlimited amount of patience and understanding, and for some very helpful critiques. Of course, any sins committed in this enterprise (such as errors of fact or misinterpretations) belong solely to us.

STEVEN W. HUGHES
KENNETH J. MIJESKI

[1]
Approaches to the Study of Policymaking

Politics, and thus the study of politics, involves a wide range of activity. Particularly on a national scale, politics includes individuals and groups and conflict and power and leadership. It sometimes involves speeches and coups d'état and revolutions. But eventually all these people and all these activities are about getting something done or preventing something from getting done. Whether we are interested in understanding politics in the United States or Mexico or Brazil or Cuba, politics ultimately leads to the making of choices about things like the printing of money, the building of houses, the growing of wheat, the taxing of income, the paving of roads, and the shooting of guns. All these choices and actions are referred to as public policy. The making of public policy thus can be said to be at the heart of the political process.

The chapters of this book deal with several aspects of public policy in Latin America. In particular, they focus on the question of how governments make decisions. Chapters 2 through 5 provide various kinds of information that address this question. Besides the making of policy, the other major area of concern for students of public policy is the impact (consequences) of policy. Chapters 6 and 7 provide some information on this subject. Before we turn to the substance of our discussion, however, it is necessary to spend a bit more effort exploring the meaning of the term *public policy* and some of the ways by which policy analysts study the making of policy.

Go to the university library and pick up ten books on the study of public policy and the odds are that you will find at least eight different definitions of public policy. Some of the definitions are long and some are short. Some are very carefully worded and seem to make a lot of sense. Others seem to be an exercise in "mumbo jumbo." Although some of the more elaborate definitions offer helpful hints about what to look for in the study of policy, in the end we must agree with political scientist Thomas Dye, who wrote that discussions of definitions of policy tend to be exasperating, often divert us

1

from the primary task at hand, and, "upon close examination, seem to boil down to the same thing. . . ."—"public policy is whatever governments choose to do or not to do" (1981:1). Although it would not be too difficult to quibble with Professor Dye's definition, including some things he left unsaid, we accept the wisdom of this straightforward definition and employ it in this book.

The two points made by Dye's definition need some emphasizing. First, public policy consists of what government does, not simply what it says it is going to do. We are all familiar with the phenomenon of government officials making promises and then actually doing nothing. Only somewhat less frequent is the phenomenon of government passing a law but failing to act. When this is the case, we cannot say the law constitutes policy. Policy certainly includes promises and laws, but it especially includes what government actually does. Let us consider two examples of situations where governments made promises that were intended to convey a particular policy, but where inaction or subsequent modification of the initial promises rendered them meaningless.

In the early 1970s, President Luís Echeverría of Mexico announced a policy of electoral reforms to make the Mexican system more democratic; the policy became known as the democratic opening (*apertura democrática*). Though some modifications were made—the voting age was lowered to 18, for instance (Johnson 1978:150)—the same dominant party, the Institutional Revolutionary Party (PRI), remained in control of the party and electoral systems, and authoritarian policymaking continued as the norm (Eckstein 1977:24). Statements by the Mexican president and other officials notwithstanding, it clearly was not the policy of the government to allow more democracy.

A similar series of events seems to have occurred in Brazil in the early 1980s. In November 1981 the military government of Brazil announced a package of reforms of the electoral system to allow for the direct, popular election of several officials, including state governors, congress, and members of an electoral college for choosing the next president in 1984. Through these reforms of the military's accepted way of controlling political institutions, Brazil appeared to be on a direct road back to democracy. However, in the first real test of its democratic inclinations, the military failed. When the congress refused to pass a bill lowering workers' wages, the executive ignored that legislative body and enacted the bill through decree. As of early 1984, one must still wonder when Brazil will return to a more democratic political system.

The second part of the definition of public policy consists of what government chooses not to do. What the Cuban government chooses not to do about creating political competition is just as important an indicator of Cuban public policy as what it chooses to do to repress dissent. This part of the concept of public policy gets a little tricky. We must realize that it is not always easy to determine whether something is *not* done because of conscious choice or because of insufficient power to get it done. For instance, Fidel

Castro on numerous occasions has spoken of the need for greater sexual equality in Cuba. But, as in the United States, the rhetoric of equality and its practice are quite different. It may very well be that the Cuban government (which is more than Fidel) simply is not yet prepared to bring about full-scale sexual equality. It also may be that sexism (particularly in the form of machismo) is so ingrained in Cuban society that no government effort could achieve sexual equality. Even though it is not always easy to determine exactly what government chooses to do, it is even more difficult to determine what it chooses not to do. Nevertheless, to understand fully the nature of a government's policy, one must do both.

Models for Policymaking

In order to cope with some of the complexities of political life and make the study of it more meaningful, academicians have developed a number of analytic approaches and models. Because several of these have been found to be of particular help in the study of public policy, we briefly review them here. The first three models to be reviewed, the stages approach, the rational model, and incrementalism, are used commonly in analyzing decisionmaking. The language and insights of these three models are so common, in fact, that most of the policy literature makes little sense without at least a brief introduction to them. The fourth model reviewed, the policy perception model, has been employed on a comparative basis and found quite useful (Smith 1975). Of even greater importance for our purposes, the model has been utilized in the study of a Latin American country, Mexico (Purcell and Purcell 1977). The final two models, corporatism and dependency, are not ones you will find in the literature on public policy in the United States. In fact, as will be noted later, neither corporatism nor dependency were designed as tools for the study of public policy. We offer them because they are used frequently in the study of Latin American politics and suggest potentially important characteristics of the Latin American policy process.

The Stages Approach

One of the most common approaches used in the study of public policy is to view the policy process as a series of sequential steps or stages. Although different scholars use different forms of the stages approach, in general they employ something similar to the following six stages. First, people must recognize that they have a problem and that government can do something about it. Policy is always a response to something, and that something is the expression of needs or demands. Until a problem is expressed, it simply does not exist. However, the mere expression of a problem is insufficient. If I tell my wife that I don't think the government is spending enough resources on education, I have not exactly created a public problem. But if my wife can convince me to express that complaint to my representative in congress, I am closer to creating a public problem. Better yet, if I can get my wife and a number of other people to support my complaint, the odds are even higher that I will have formed a public problem. Thus, this first step, usually called *problem formation* or *issue formation*, involves the expression of a need or demand to government, usually by a number of people. Several important questions in the study of public policy are suggested by this notion of problem formation. Who makes demands? How are demands made? What demands are being made?

Two fairly typical characteristics of problem formation in Latin America can be noted at this point. A significant percentage of the population in most countries, notably the rural poor, rarely get involved (or are allowed to get involved) in making demands. When they do, their involvement often takes the form either of supplication to a local official (to ameliorate some limited problem) or of poorly organized but large-scale protest, including land seizures and, in extremis, guerrilla warfare. Conversely, those problems that are articulated in a well-organized fashion tend to come most frequently from individuals and groups representing urban upper- and middle-class interests. In other words, one way in which the powerful remain powerful (and keep the weak powerless) is by dominating the very beginning of the policy process. Moreover, and this is the second characteristic, in many countries and particularly in the more authoritarian ones, government officials constitute one of the most important sets of demand makers. For instance, most of the policy initiatives in Costa Rica to expand and reform the Social Security System in the 1970s came not from interest groups but from government officials—especially the technocrats within the Social Insurance Institute (Rosenberg 1979:126–130). A classic case of government demand making has been provided by Merilee Grindle in her study of CONASUPO (National Company of Popular Subsistence—a staple goods distribution system), the Mexican agency responsible for a wide variety of programs of direct relevance to the poor and to rural development. As she notes in her study, many of the changes in agricultural policy in Mexico in the 1970s occurred not so much because of demands by farmers but because of government officials' concern about declining agricultural productivity and the potential for rural violence (Grindle 1977:70–90).

Simply because demands are made, there is no guarantee that decision-makers will pay attention to them. Getting the attention of government is the next step in the policy process. This may be accomplished by a variety of means, including personal contact with government officials, newspaper articles, demonstrations—in other words, by the utilization of power resources. When a policy demand has received government notice, we say that it has been placed on the *government agenda*. Anyone who has ever participated on committees, such as a student council or a personnel or budget committee, will recognize the importance of setting the agenda. To control the agenda is to control the problems or demands to be considered.

Why the government considers some demands and not others, then, is an important question in the study of public policy. The leaders of all the countries of Latin America are interested, to some extent, in the economic growth of their countries. Because businesspeople and industrialists play such crucial roles in the economic systems of these countries, except of course in Cuba, their demands usually get on the government's agenda. There is another reason that upper- and middle-class demands frequently receive government attention. Much that is accomplished in Latin America, as, to some extent, everywhere else, is done so via personal contacts. These are very important, far more so than, for instance, in the United States. Obviously, the ability to establish personal contact is greatly aided by such factors as kinship, friendship, or, at the least, similarity of behavior and speech, which, in turn, is often a function of similarity of class and locale of residence. Since most decisionmakers are of the upper and middle classes, citizens from these classes are much more likely to be able to establish personal contact with them. Though certainly not the only reasons, government desire for economic growth and the opportunities for personal contact go a long way toward explaining why some demands are attended to and others are not.

The fact that government, or more accurately certain government officials, takes note of a demand and pays some attention to it does not mean that anything concrete necessarily will occur. For the policy process to continue it is necessary for government to consider ways to deal with the problem. This stage is called *policy formulation*. In Latin America, in contrast with the United States, virtually all policy formulation activity occurs somewhere within the executive branch; the legislature plays no meaningful role. Of course, there are exceptions. Costa Rica and, to some extent, Venezuela possess legislative bodies that do engage in the consideration of alternative solutions to problems. More typical are Brazil and Mexico, where the legislatures do not play a significant part in offering and debating policy alternatives.

Another fairly common feature of the policy formulation stage in Latin America is that it tends to be based upon limited and distorted information. As Charles Anderson noted (1967:111–119), the political process in Latin America tends to "constrict and distort" information from society as it winds its way to policymakers. This problem is particularly acute when decisionmakers are considering a problem of a community quite different from the ones with which they have some personal familiarity. As a consequence, government policies for such areas as impoverished rural communities or urban squatter settlements often have little relevance to actual conditions.

Policy adoption, the fourth stage, refers to the process of getting goverment to choose one of the options it is considering. Why governments select one course of action and not an alternative is the question with which we are concerned at this point. Many of the answers to our questions about the earlier stages help provide answers to the question of why one proposal is adopted over another. Personal contact, similarity of viewpoint between those making the demands and the decisionmaker, and government concern for economic growth are all factors that help explain policy adoption. In highly centralized and authoritarian systems like Cuba and Mexico, much of the answer has to do with the personal preference of top-level government leaders, such as Fidel Castro in Cuba or the president in Mexico. Finally, several of the other models we review below seek to provide answers to why some options are adopted and not others. For instance, the rationality model argues that the option with the highest ratio of benefits to costs should be chosen, and the incremental model suggests that options offering only marginal change from past decisions should be chosen.

Public policies rarely are self-executing. The government's choice of a policy option means nothing unless that decision can be put into effect. So, for the policy process to continue, the adoption stage must be followed by *policy execution* or *implementation*. One dismaying characteristic of many Latin American governments is their frequent inability to carry out policy decisions. From the collection of income taxes to attempts to direct business investments, from policies designed to eliminate corruption in government to policies to improve agricultural production, executives and bureaucrats in Latin America have not been very effective in implementing policy. Even military regimes, often brought into existence in part because of the administrative shortcomings of civilian regimes, find there are policies that cannot be implemented. Peru's attempt, under General Juan Velasco Alvarado, to restructure its institutions of participation, specifically, to create a new organ of mobilization and participation, SINAMOS (National Social Mobilization Support System), met with far more failure than success (Philip 1978:127–131 and Collier 1976:106–116).

Many factors that are responsible for the problem of implementation are certainly not unique to Latin America. Difficulties in the collection of income taxes, for instance, are universal and are just as acute in France or Italy as in Brazil or Mexico. However, in comparison to the United States, the problem of policy execution is noteworthy. Fundamentally, the causes of the problem are two. First, the agencies responsible for execution usually possess an insufficient number of well-trained personnel and inadequate financial and information resources to get the job done. The second factor has to do with the existence in so many Latin American countries of a bifurcated, or dual, culture. According to one prominent scholar, "the most critical barrier to policy penetration in much of Latin America must be seen against the background of that universally felt clash of culture, the gulf of values that separates traditional and modern society" (Anderson 1967:153). In other words, the differences between the values and behavioral patterns of middle- and upper-class, urban-based government officials and those of the poor of the countryside or the newly arrived urban immigrants are so vast that the gap often impedes the ability (and desire) of government agents to implement a policy.

According to most stages models of the policy process, one additional stage, beyond policy implementation, occurs. This stage is *policy evaluation*. Presumably, any group of decisionmakers desires to know what has been the impact of its decisions. Is the policy doing what it is supposed to do? Are there negative consequences of the policy that necessitate a reconsideration of the policy? Some evidence of the use of fairly systematic evaluations of policy does exist. For instance, the redirection of much agricultural policy in Mexico under President Luís Echeverría (1970–1976) occurred, in part, because of a systematic evaluation of previous agrarian programs (Grindle 1977a:81–89).

A more typical form of policy evaluation is what one group of political scientists called "seat-of-the-pants" evaluation. "In general there are two types of policy evaluation: (1) seat-of-the-pants or political evaluation and (2) systematic evaluation. Seat-of-the-pants evaluation is impressionistic in nature. At best, such judgments are based on fragmentary evidence and are often strongly ideological or biased" (Anderson, Brady, and Bullock 1978:11). For instance, when the military came to power in Brazil in 1964, it proceeded to criticize the social and economic policies of previous regimes, claiming that they had failed to generate sufficient development in Brazil. Although some of the criticism was based on analytic evaluations, most stemmed from ideology and personal feelings about the previous regime.

In general, though, few governments possess the resources needed to analyze effectively the impact of policies. Rather than analyzing a policy's effects, most regimes rely on some form of "feedback." Policy evaluation in this context takes the form of government decisionmakers interpreting the reaction of those affected by the policy. However, when governments do not use policy evaluation as such, and when channels for reaction (feedback) are severely restricted (as in highly authoritarian governments), then the ability to correct policy mistakes is greatly reduced. Such has been the case with most social policy in Brazil and most economic policy in Cuba.

Problem formation, agenda setting, formulation, adoption, implementation, and evaluation are the various stages of the policy process. At least, this is what many scholars would have us believe. But are governmental decisions really made in such a conveniently ordered and sequential fashion? Many other scholars think not and have created other models and theories of policymaking based on that view. Even if it is true that virtually no governmental decision of any importance follows in precise timing the process model set out above, it is our belief that the concepts of problem formation, agenda setting, etc., are quite useful in analyzing who is doing what to whom and why in the making of public decisions. Most likely what occurs is a series of forward, backward, and sideways steps in which any number of "stages" take place simultaneously. Whatever the exact ordering, the stages model does provide some conceptual utility to aid us in raising questions about public policy.

The Rational Model

One of the oldest, and most heavily criticized, models of policymaking is the rational, or rational comprehensive model, as some call it. Two fundamental assumptions are the heart of the model. First, it is assumed that decisionmakers are purposive and goal oriented. They know what they want and they go after it. Second, the model assumes that decisionmakers always want to achieve their goal in the most informed, analytic, thorough, and efficient manner. To accomplish all this, the rational model posits a process of decisionmaking that bears many similarities to the stages approach. First, the problem is carefully defined. The decisionmakers list their goals and rank these from most to least important. Then all possible alternative solutions are listed, with a thorough analysis of the costs and benefits of each solution. By this point, the "decision" becomes automatic. It is simply the alternative that best meets the decision-makers' goals and has the highest ratio of benefits to costs.

For a student of politics, or for anyone who has ever attempted to make a difficult decision, all this must sound very idealistic. And, indeed, that is the basis of all the criticisms of the model. At every point, the rational model can be attacked for positing behavior that, at least most of the time, seems impossible to attain. Most people are not sure what many of their goals are, and to try to get them to rank goals with any confidence usually is out of the question. To get a group of decisionmakers to agree on a ranking of goals seems especially difficult. To expect people, particularly government deci-sionmakers, to consider all possible alternatives is to ignore abundant pressures of time, power, and ideology. Finally, to perform extensive cost-benefit analyses is not only to ignore political and time pressures but to assume access to an amount of information (not to mention quality of information) typically not available. Therefore, if there are so many faults with the model, why bother with it?

Like most models, the rational model abstracts from actual behavior certain features believed to be most characteristic of the behavior being studied. These characteristics usually do not totally define, but rather, typify that behavior. The process of modeling thus inevitably distorts the extent to which those highlighted features adequately represent the total behavior. Consequently, it is not necessary to find that decisionmaking be fully "rational" to accept the utility of the model; it is sufficient that decisionmaking be more like the model than not. In other words, if we accept the basic idea of the rational model, but apply it in a somewhat less stringent manner, then we may discover more decisions made entirely, or at least in significant part, according to the rational model. Some, though certainly not all, Supreme Court decisionmaking in the United States could be accounted for in rational model terms (cf. Frohock 1979:58). During the mid-1960s in Brazil, the development of antiinflationary policy seems to fit a rational model.

Under the civilian and highly trained minister of finance, Roberto Campos, a group of university-educated technocrats set about analyzing the problems of stable economic growth in Brazil. They concluded that inflation and industrial inefficiency were two key factors blocking attainment of the long-term goal of stable growth. Decisions such as reduction in wages and revision of tariff policies were made to drive down inflation and to reduce the likelihood that government policies were serving as incentives for inefficient businesses. Moreover, many of these technocrats argued for a centralized and authoritarian regime as a mechanism to reduce the need for decisionmakers to respond to political, i.e., "nonrational," factors (cf. Skidmore 1973:19–21).

There is another reason to spend time considering the characteristics of the rational model. Whether or not public policies are made in accordance with the model, we often speak as if they were (or should be). To say that "the government decided to" or the "military regime determined to" or "the agency has decided that" is to impute to these organizations a unity of value, purpose, and behavior that rarely exists (Allison 1971:28–38). Admittedly, sometimes we use such phrases simply for brevity and ease of discourse. At other times, we use such phrases because we do actually wish to imply unity and a "cold," calculating behavior on the part of some group of decisionmakers. What we must realize is that when we infer calculating behavior, we may be inferring that the group behaved according to the rational model. Understanding the model allows us to decide whether or not we want to make that inference.

Finally, if indeed we find that few, if any, decisions are made according to the principles of the rational model, we have made an interesting discovery about public decisionmaking. After all, the rational model as a prescriptive theory, that is, as a statement of what should be done, makes a good deal of sense. If decisions are not being made this way, then why not? Awareness of the model "helps identify barriers to rationality. It assists in posing the question: Why is policy making not a more rational process?" (Dye 1981:34).

For students of Latin American politics, the question of rationality is of particular interest, given the recurrence of military takeovers and the justifications for the takeovers. One of the constant criticisms held by the military of civilian rule is that the standard political game distorts and denies rationality in the process of decisionmaking. This viewpoint has led to a strong emphasis on teaching rational techniques like budgetary planning in some of the military training schools, such as the *Escola Superior de Guerra* in Brazil (ESG—Superior War College). "A basic commitment of all ESG thinking was to rational planning and organization of all aspects of national life" (Flynn 1978a:323). In enumerating the basic changes the new military regime would bring about in Peru, a manifesto from the junta began as follows: "The action of the Revolutionary Government will be shaped by the necessity of transforming the structure of the state in such a manner as to permit efficient governmental operation . . ." (Loveman and Davies 1978:209). Thus, the military, as a rule, claims an ability to impose a more rational and efficient form of policymaking. The rational model provides us with the criteria by which to judge the military's claims.

Incrementalism

Because the rational model fails to explain most decisionmaking processes, scholars have devised other models in the hope of finding something with greater explanatory power. In recent years, the incremental model, more commonly known as incrementalism, has come to be one of the most popular descriptions and explanations of policymaking. The incremental theory is essentially a rejoinder to the rational theory; it builds on the critique of rationality. According to incrementalism, decisionmakers face tremendous pressures of time, ideology, and conflict and therefore cannot afford the luxuries of strict adherence to the rational model. We quote political scientist James Anderson's succinct listing of the main characteristics of incrementalism.

1. The selection of goals or objectives and the empirical analysis of the action needed to attain them are closely intertwined with, rather than distinct from, one another.
2. The decision-maker considers only some of the alternatives for dealing with a problem, and these will differ only incrementally (i.e., marginally) from existing policies.
3. For each alternative only a limited number of "important" consequences are evaluated.
4. The problem confronting the decision-maker is continually redefined. Incrementalism allows for countless ends-means and means-ends adjustments that have the effect of making the problem more manageable.
5. There is no single decision or "right" solution for a problem. The test of a good decision is that various analysts find themselves directly agreeing

on it, without agreeing that the decision is the most appropriate means
to an agreed objective.

6. Incremental decision-making is essentially remedial and is geared more
to the amelioration of present, concrete social imperfections than to the
promotion of future social goals (1979:11).

This process will lead to conservative policymaking. We use conservative
in the sense "that existing programs, policies, and expenditures are considered
as a base, and attention is concentrated on new programs and policies and
on increases, decreases, or modifications of current programs" (Dye 1981:36).
Incrementalism gets its name from the notion that, given the process as
described above, a decision will differ from previous decisions only marginally,
or incrementally. An agency's budget for next year will be this year's, plus
or minus a relatively small increment. Thus the incremental model not only
describes and explains a process but also predicts an outcome.

Unfortunately, there are several problems with the model. First, the theory
fails to specify any boundaries for what constitutes an incremental change.
We have to answer the question: How much change must occur before a
decision is no longer incremental? Is a 5 percent increase in the military budget
incremental? What about a 20 percent increase or a 30 percent increase?

Moreover, when we are dealing with policies that cannot very easily be
reduced to quantitative measurement, or can be so measured only in part, it
becomes even more difficult to determine an increment. Political philosopher
Fred Frohock, for instance, argued that any one of four definitions would be
consistent with an intuitive understanding of incremental: (1) An increment
is a small departure from previous policy. (2) An increment represents a
middle-range compromise of conflicting demands. (3) An increment is any
policy that is modest in resources and scope. (4) An increment is any policy
that accords with the more modest of claims made on any policy issue (1979:55).

Another problem with incrementalism has to do with the relationship among
power, conflict, the process of choosing a policy alternative, and the policy
outcome. Given the environment in which the incremental theory has been
developed, and given the setting to which it seems to refer, it appears that
the incremental theory argues that an incremental process exists because
significant conflict, caused by a fairly wide-spread distribution of political
power, forces the decisionmakers to a particular style of decisionmaking that
leads to incremental adjustments in policies. Put more directly, one could say,
based on the theory, that incrementalism exists in the United States because
of pluralism (a type of democracy).

Evidence from Latin America, however, suggests that an essentially incremental style of decisionmaking can exist without pluralism. For instance, one
study of educational and defense spending in the various Latin American
countries found that the best predictor of next year's education budget was

the current year's budget (Ames and Goff 1975:181–183). In other words, changes in educational spending were so consistently incremental that one could predict the ensuing year's budget fairly accurately by merely adding a small amount to what was currently being spent.

In Latin America, not only are many outcomes incremental, but also a fair number of decisions seem to be made according to the characteristics of incrementalism. However, this has less to do with the pluralistic distribution of power than with the values of the members of the policy elite, lack of information, and insufficient resources. Conflict, primarily within the policy elite rather than in a broader base, is also involved. What this suggests is that most decisions, most of the time, will be made largely in an incremental fashion regardless of the type of regime. This is true because ideology, at least as much as pluralism, can lead decisionmakers to consider only limited alternatives, to accept the basic legitimacy of previous decisions, and to concentrate on patching and mending rather than fundamental change. A nonincremental style is most likely to occur when a large number of top-level decisionmakers are replaced suddenly and when the new group holds values quite different than the former group's. This was the case in Cuba in 1959 when the Castro-led revolutionaries came to power. It occurred again in Peru in 1968 when a group of reform-oriented officers came to power in a coup d'état.

Finally, we should realize that incremental features of a policy may mask other aspects of a policy that are not incremental. Much of the work done by researchers in applying the incremental theory has dealt with budget expenditures, particularly the size of the budget. However, the total amount of money an agency has to spend may be less important as an indicator of policy than the way in which the agency spends the money.

The Policy Perception Model

A different kind of model of the policy process has been offered by Theodore Lowi. Lowi's model originally was built upon American experiences; subsequently, it was modified by T. A. Smith to fit a broader, comparative context (1975:5–8). Because Smith's version goes beyond the U.S. experience, our discussion will be based largely on his modification.

This model, in contrast to the first two, is concerned with explaining amounts and types of policy conflict, rather than with individual behavior. The model states that the nature of political conflict is determined by the participant's perception of the likely policy outcome. Additionally, the way in which an issue is resolved can be explained by the anticipated outcome.

In Smith's version, there are four types of policy, i.e., four different perceptions about the type of policy outcome. *Distributive* policies provide benefits to certain individuals or groups in a way that avoids any feelings that others have lost something. Policy problems are cut up into small pieces (disaggregated) and "solved" by distributing benefits to particular individuals or groups. Conflict in this situation is kept to a minimum, and policy decisions are made easily. Typical examples of distributive policies include patronage (in the broadest sense), the location of a new school building or a post office, and laws that provide immediate, limited benefits to a particular individual or family.

Sectorally fragmented policies are those that respond to demands in a particular policy area (or sector), such as education or industrial expansion, and are seen by at least some groups in the area as harmful to their interests. High school teacher groups might be pitted against elementary school teachers, or urban teachers against those teaching in rural areas, in a policy dispute over how best to expand the educational system. These policies result in significantly more conflict than distributive issues and require a more "delicate" process of decisionmaking.

Emotive symbolic policies consist of "way of life" issues such as church-state relations, family planning, or capital punishment. Governments' attempts to clear urban slums often become an emotive symbolic issue for slum dwellers. These issues arouse deeply held views and values and thus potentially are quite disruptive.

The fourth type of policy is *redistributive*. Put simply, redistributive issues involve taking away something from one group to benefit another. Commonly, redistributive issues are class conflict issues. In Latin America, many issues may be considered redistributive because limited economic growth, which most countries have been experiencing, means it is difficult to help the poor without taking away from the rich. Because they engender so much conflict, redistributive issues can be resolved only at the highest level of government, or by large scale social upheaval, as in the case of Cuba.

A Mexican Variation

Political scientists John Purcell and Susan Purcell have suggested another variation of the model originally developed by Theodore Lowi. The Purcells' model is offered tentatively, since it is based on only a limited number of cases of Mexican public policy and these solely in the realm of government-business relations. Three principal policy types are defined: (1) regulatory distribution; (2) indirect, piecemeal regulation; (3) regulatory redistribution (1977:201–217).

As the name implies, regulatory distribution policies in Mexico contain features similar to both distributive and regulatory policies in the United

States. They are like Lowi's notion of regulation in that their apparent impact is to regulate, and they tend to have a scope of impact like regulatory policies in the United States. Prima facie, these policies are regulatory. However, the decisionmaking process resembles what one would expect to find for distributive policies. Conflict is low; the decisions are cut up into many small pieces; and the participants perceive the outcome in distributive terms, i.e., there are winners but no immediately obvious losers. Typical examples of this type of policy would include exemption of a business from a particular import license, privileged access to loans from one of the development banks, and price supports. Although some of these appear to be typical government mechanisms to regulate the private sector, in Mexico business tends to perceive these as direct benefits in a distributive sense.

The second type of policy, indirect, piecemeal regulation, in essence is similar to regulatory policies in the United States, and its outcome is perceived as regulatory. There is a relatively extensive amount of interest-group activity directed at preventing or limiting the impact of the intended regulation. Conflict is higher than in the case of distributive policies. However, according to the Purcells, regulatory policies in Mexico differ from their U.S. counterparts in two important ways. First, regulation of business in Mexico is done in a much more indirect manner. Government regulation of pricing is a good example. Rarely will the Mexican government announce a particular price level, e.g., for food, and then attempt directly to control prices charged by retail stores. Instead, because the government itself buys and sells food through a chain of government-owned stores, it can indirectly influence prices by its own pricing levels. Given the Mexican government's ownership of so many businesses and industries, this indirect means of regulation can be effective. The government will utilize direct price controls, however, when it feels the situation is critical.

The second characteristic of much regulatory policy in Mexico is that it is piecemeal. A particular regulatory action tends to arise in response to short-term or immediate causes and not as the result of a commitment to long-range goals or plans. "In Mexico there is an oftnoted lack of coordination between one regulatory decision and another, with the result that while particular, fairly narrow or short-term policies can be implemented, long-range or large-scale policies, including various kinds of economic planning, run into serious difficulties" (Purcell and Purcell 1977:210).

Regulatory redistribution, the third type of policy, like much of distributive policy in Mexico, presents one face that simply masks another, truer face. Some policies, like the decisions in the 1961–1963 period requiring certain businesses to establish profit-sharing plans for their workers, clearly appear to be of a redistributive nature. On their face, these decisions would take a percentage of the firm's profits away from the owners and make them available to the workers. During the decisionmaking process, however, the government reassured business that various redistributive provisions would be modified. Given the fact that the profit-sharing decisions were harder on the less modern businesses than the more modern ones, it appears that a redistributive policy was being used for largely regulatory purposes (Purcell and Purcell 1977:213–214).

In addition to these three policy types, the Purcells state that a more pure form of distributive policies also exists. Given the vast networks of patronage and the highly personal nature of so many political relationships in Mexico, it would be extremely surprising not to find a classical form of distributive policies. If we add this to the three types discussed in detail by the Purcells' analysis, we then have four basic types of policy in Mexico: distributive; regulatory distributive; indirect, piecemeal regulation; and regulatory redistributive. Since this typology is based on a Latin American case, it may have more applicability to the rest of Latin America than either the original Lowi typology or the one developed by Smith.

Corporatist Policymaking

Properly speaking, corporatism is not a theory or model of policymaking. Rather, "corporatism should be understood as a set of structures which link society with the state" (O'Donnell 1977:47). It is, then, essentially a model of representation and group behavior. In fact, corporatism is one of the very few fully developed alternatives to pluralism or interest-group liberalism, theories of representation and group behavior far more familiar to citizens and students of the United States. Nevertheless, most theorists of contemporary corporatism, particularly as it applies to Latin America, attribute to it a range of characteristics that allows it to be used as a descriptive model of policymaking without unduly distorting the basic notion of corporatism (cf. Collier and Collier 1979; Malloy 1974; Pike and Stritch 1974; Wiarda 1973).

In contemporary usage, the basic features of corporatism are as follows: (1) The right to associate and to engage in politics is granted by the state. (2) Corporations (i.e., organized groups) are given wide latitude and autonomy within spheres of action. (3) Boundaries between groups are strictly kept and regulated by the state. (4) Groups are defined functionally—not geographically or ethnically (Schwartzman 1977:93). The essence of corporatism, at least its justificatory essence, lies in the notion of occupational groups as the basis of social life. "Since one's occupation is the major component of his adult life, this is the individual's major area of concern. Thus, one's work not only represents interests but also orders and regulates a large part of his individual life. For him, it is more than a group; it is a community with consummatory as well as instrumental dimensions" (Malloy 1974:57). Occupationally derived group loyalties form the basis of organizing people, not only for the purposes of making demands upon the public, decisionmaking institutions. The groups exist also for broader social purposes.

In this brief summary of the corporatist model, you can see an outline of policymaking emerge. Demands are made by groups that are organized along occupational lines. Individual demand making would be considered illegitimate. Only those groups sanctioned by the state can assume that they would be heard and given access to the government's agenda.

Contemporary theories of corporatism go beyond characterizing the demandmaking phase and suggest features of later policymaking stages. As most theorists note, corporatism tends to an authoritarian style of politics, though in theory corporatism could exist in a democratic society. Writing of Brazil and Mexico, one scholar noted the following: "The decision-making bureaucracy is . . . susceptible to . . . a *técnico*-centered decision-making style, in which major policy initiatives flow from 'nonpolitical' groups of development-oriented experts and specialists who have become entrenched in various administrative sectors and are relatively insulated from either group or clientelist pressures" (Kaufman 1977a:136).

This statement captures the essence of decisionmaking in many Latin American countries and seems to be a logical corollary of corporatism, or at least of a particular variant of corporatism often called the bureaucratic-authoritarian state (cf. Malloy 1974). Many demands come from groups created or accepted by the state. These demands are fairly well controlled by the state because of the state's ability to control (by withholding acceptance of) the groups. But in addition, officials within the government itself comprise a major group of demand makers. These development-oriented *técnicos* also constitute a significant portion of the decisionmaking elite. Of course, major decisions are controlled by the highest officials within the government; middle- and upper-level technocrats within the bureaucracy, however, play some role in making major decisions while largely controlling the more routine decisions.

Technocratic and authoritarian decisionmaking are logical, if not inevitable, corollaries of corporatism because it is a system that seeks to control society in highly organized and institutional ways and in which political conflict and competition are considered illegitimate. In fact, most of the literature suggests that corporatist societies seek not only to organize interests but also to process decisions in a particular way. In sum, the corporatist model is one in which (1) interests are organized primarily according to type of job; (2) the organizations (corporations) are either created by government or "licensed" by government; (3) intergroup behavior is carefully controlled by government; (4) demands are legitimate only if they emanate from a certified organization or from within the government; (5) policies are formulated within a bureaucracy dominated by technocratically oriented officials.

We offer corporatism as a model of policymaking because it appears to be more relevant to experiences in Latin America than theories (e.g., incrementalism) developed with U.S. experience in mind. We reiterate, however, that we have had to expand slightly a "classical" notion of corporatism to make it into a theory of policymaking. Moreover, the literature suggests that different styles of decisionmaking, including a democratic one, are compatible with a corporatist form of group organization and representation. If this is true, then what we have done is to focus on a particular variant of corporatism, namely an authoritarian one, and offer this as the model of corporatist policymaking. In our estimation this is proper because we believe that in practice corporatism and authoritarianism are so intertwined as to be parts of a whole. Democratic polities may well possess corporatist features, but only as rough approximations of those in more truly corporatist polities. Instead, a fully relevant model of corporatism ought to be one that links classical notions of corporatist representation with contemporary notions of a bureaucratic and authoritarian state.

Dependency Theory and Policymaking

Another theory very much based on Latin American experiences is dependency theory. Like corporatism, dependency theory was not developed to understand the particularities of public policymaking. Rather, it is a very broad theory that seeks to understand the politics and economics of one country through an understanding of international politics and economics. A full comprehension of dependency theory, however, is complicated by the existence of differing versions, or variants, of the theory. Put most simply, there is a Marxist (more accurately a neo-Marxist) and a non-Marxist variant of *dependencia* (dependency) (cf. Hughes and Mijeski 1980:22–25). Because the neo-Marxist variant (and it too contains variations) seems to be the dominant one, the following discussion will focus on it and, particularly, a work by the Brazilian Fernando Henrique Cardoso and the Chilean Enzo Faletto, *Dependency and Development in Latin America* (1979). This book has been seen by many as the central text of contemporary dependency theory (cf. Packenham 1982:131).

The essence of what dependency theory strives to be is stated succinctly by Cardoso and Faletto in the preface to the English edition of their book: "We seek a global and dynamic understanding of social structures instead of looking only at specific dimensions of the social process" (ix). And later: "We stress the socio-political nature of the economic relations of production, thus following the nineteenth-century tradition of treating economy as political economy" (ix). And finally: "From the economic point of view a system is dependent when the accumulation and expansion of capital cannot find its essential dynamic component inside the system" (xx).

What is striking to Cardoso and Faletto, and to many other students of Latin America, is the extent to which political and economic structures and practices in the region have been conditioned by forces external to the region. From Spanish colonialism to contemporary American imperialism (or "hemispheric dominance"), one is struck by the absence of much independence of action on the part of Latin America. What, in essence, dependency theory does is to say that this situation must be analyzed and understood historically if one wishes to comprehend what is going on inside any individual Latin American country. Two more quotes from Cardoso and Faletto ought to suffice to make the point.

Viewed globally: "For an understanding of the present situation of the industrialized and dependent countries in Latin America, an analysis is required of the increasing control over the economic system of nations by large multinational corporations" (174). And looking internally: "Political institutions at a given moment can only be fully understood in terms of the structures of domination because these express the class interests behind political organization" (14).

Dependency theory is, then, a kind of view from the top, a very broad and rather sweeping view of politics as it is tied to international economic structures and as the latter develop over time. By contrast, the approach taken in our book (i.e., the policy approach) is a good deal narrower. Our goal is only to learn how consequential public decisions are made; *dependencia* seeks to grasp a much wider reality. But *dependencia* is not by any means irrelevant to our endeavor. On the contrary, dependency theory offers several very useful suggestions for understanding the policy process.

First, dependency theory clearly requires us to take into account the economic bases of political power. According to this theory, based on the insights of Karl Marx, those who are most visible in policymaking may not be the most influential. Rather, power flows from one's position in the structure of the economy, that is, from one's relationship to the means of production and the accumulation of capital. Secondly, dependency theory tells us that the most critical elements of the economic system are to be found outside of the Latin American country being studied. It is not the Brazilian or Mexican or Venezuelan industrialist, but the North American, or perhaps Japanese, head of a multinational corporation who wields ultimate power. Of course, as dependency theory clearly states, the native economic elite may be tied to the external elite in a number of complex ways that provide some limited, autonomous sources of influence. Nevertheless, any analysis of policymaking that excludes international economic forces would be incomplete.

Moreover, since the external economic elite is, in turn, tied to and greatly influences, or controls, the government of its home country, that government will also serve as a force in policymaking. In other words, the dependency approach makes us aware of the role of both multinational corporations *and* major foreign governments in the policymaking process in each of the Latin American countries.

Finally, again given the Marxist basis of dependency theory, it follows that a study of policymaking must take into account the structure of social classes and the role of classes in order to determine how policy is influenced. Class analysis will also be instrumental in guiding the researcher to an understanding of who benefits from policymaking, i.e., an analysis of policy impact.

We should note, parenthetically, that because of its Marxist roots and hence its emphasis on the international capitalist system, dependency theory tends to ignore the role of noncapitalist forces in Latin America. One obvious consequence is that many scholars utilizing a dependency approach will not see Cuba as a dependent political economy. There are some good reasons to see Cuban dependence as different from the dependence of other Latin American countries, particularly with regard to the nature of economic exploitation. It is, nevertheless, dependent.

Summary

Each of the models discussed above offers a particular perspective from which to consider significant questions about the process of public policymaking. As you read, ponder, and attempt to come to terms with the material in the ensuing chapters, you should keep in mind the questions suggested by the various models. Let us conclude this chapter by recalling some of the more thought-provoking questions posed by the models.

You recall in our discussion of the stages model that we listed many of the questions posed by it. Instead of repeating all those here, let us suggest some very general points to consider. Does it appear that policies are made in accord with this model? Or does it appear that in Latin America a particular stage (or stages) consistently is bypassed or consistently occurs "out of sequence"? Are there any groups, or individuals, that seem to dominate particular stages of the policy process? What are the interests of these groups? Do these interests seem to "win out" in the making of policy?

Our discussion of the rational model indicated that many of the characteristics of this model are incompatible with many characteristics of democracy. Is it true that the requirements of democracy conflict with the requirements of rationality? Are there more instances of rational policymaking in the authoritarian countries than in the democratic ones? Are some aspects, or stages, of policymaking handled more rationally than others?

In spite of its intuitive appeal, the incremental model seems to pose more fundamental, methodological questions than do the others. Two issues in particular need to be resolved before we can proceed comfortably to apply incrementalism. First, we need to come to some consensus concerning the limits of an "increment." Until then, we always run the risk that what is an incremental change to one is a significant departure to another. Second, we must decide whether a policy must meet the requirements of incrementalism in terms of both the way in which it was made and its outcome to be called incremental, or whether one or the other is sufficient. For instance, if we find that government expenditures for education consistently increase each year by small amounts but that the process leading to these decisions is not consistent with incrementalism, do we label educational policy as incremental or not? Or we can handle this not so much as a problem of definition but as simply an empirical question. That is, we can ask whether or not incremental outcomes are always associated with incremental processes.

The policy perception model suggests to us a vantage point from which we can ask a number of related questions: To what extent does the type of issue affect the way in which the issue is decided? In the original version of the model, as developed by Lowi, different issues would be perceived in different ways that would affect the amount of conflict and the principal arena in which the issue is resolved. Additional questions are suggested by the model. Does the nature of an issue influence the sequencing of the policy stages? Are some issues more likely to be handled in a rational manner, and others more likely to be dealt with incrementally, or in a corporatist way? Are issues perceived in comparable fashion in different countries, or do similar issues lead to very different perceptions?

The primary utility of corporatism is that it provides us with a way of visualizing and conceptualizing a process of policymaking different from the frequently offered pluralist model. As we suggested above, the student of Latin America needs an alternative to pluralism, especially given political organization in countries like Chile, Mexico, and Cuba. Although corporatism may not be the ideal model through which to view the political process in all these countries, it does provide us with a beginning point that, we believe, will be more useful than pluralism. In any event, the most basic question we must ask is to what extent does the system of political organization and representation resemble the corporatist model. If corporate representation exists, can we find evidence that the remaining features of the corporatist model also exist? If we find that some countries are usefully (and fairly accurately) characterized as corporatist, then we can move to the consideration of several critical questions. What differences can we find between corporatist and noncorporatist states in terms of types of issues dealt with by policymakers? Do the interests that dominate in corporatist states differ from those in noncorporatist states? Are there significant differences in policy outcomes between corporatist and noncorporatist states?

Perhaps the single greatest advantage of a dependency perspective, compared to the other approaches, is that it draws our attention to the global environment of policymaking. A cursory glance at even journalistic accounts of politics in Latin America should suffice to convince us that representatives of major international corporations and foreign governments often play important roles. The dependency approach not only emphasizes this point but also suggests the principal mechanism through which foreign influences are exerted: the dependent condition of the economies of Latin America. An initial question suggested by dependency might be how foreign economic actors are connected to domestic actors. Some additional questions would include the following: To what extent are foreign actors more powerful than domestic actors in the policy process? Or are they equals? Do foreign actors seek to control the outcome of all policy issues, or only some? Can dependent states become economically independent and, if so, does this affect the policy process and/or policy outcomes?

These are only some of the issues that you might consider as you move through the remaining chapters. Whether you think about these or other questions, it is important that you utilize the models to ask critical questions and to work out answers for yourself.

[2]
Actors in the Policymaking Process

Generalizations about politics in Latin America are made frequently and just as frequently evaporate when carefully scrutinized. In spite of the North American's penchant for seeing Latin America as a single, massive entity, nations of the region are as different as they are similar. This does not mean that we cannot make generalizations about Latin American politics; it does mean we must be sensitive to differences and hence cautious about our generalizations. As a starting point, we can say that the student should be warned not to view all of Latin America as merely an extension of Mexico or of whatever particular country currently attracts the attention of the mass media.

It is not possible in this book to discuss all of the important differences and similarities among the nations of Latin America. (In fact, all the important differences and similarities are not known.) There are numerous books and articles that examine such areas as political history, religious developments, economic developments, and compare the experiences of various Latin American countries. The serious and committed student must be dedicated to exploring these works to begin to appreciate the points at which experiences in these countries deviate.

While we cannot explore these topics here, we have sought to provide a more limited overview of contemporary Latin American politics. Our discussion will concentrate on the six countries of this study and examine the actors involved in making policy and then look, in very general terms, at the process of policymaking.

There are various actors that play roles in the process of policymaking in Latin America. These actors are not identical in every country, nor are they of equal importance in the policy roles they play. Some actors are part of the "official" government and include the executive, legislative, and judicial branches. Other actors, while not always official, have as large or perhaps even a larger role to play in making policy than do those that are constitutionally specified. Among these actors would be the military when it acts beyond its constitutional mandate and certain key interest groups, particularly when the latter occupy critical economic and social positions in the country in question. Effective policymaking involves significant control over the resources of the state, and may involve control of the government itself as well. Moreover, the analytical distinction between governmental and nongovernmental actors does not always hold empirically. L. Vincent Padgett noted, for example, that there is considerable controversy among scholars on the exact nature of the Institutional Revolutionary Party (PRI) in Mexico. There is disagreement over whether the PRI is an autonomous, nongovernmental actor or merely an extension of the government itself (Padgett 1976:73–74).

With these caveats in mind, we will proceed to make an organizational distinction in this chapter between governmental and nongovernmental actors in the policy process.

Governmental Actors

One of the safest and most enduring generalizations about the policy process in Latin American politics concerns the extent to which the process is dominated by the executive, especially in the person of the president. Dominance of the executive over the legislative and judicial branches, and the predominance of the presidency within the executive, have a long and consistent history from the colonial period to the present. Thomas V. DiBacco lends credence to this tradition as he points out that "throughout the continent, even among military dictators, the term 'president' is widespread and revered, often as a symbol of political legitimacy" (1977:vii). Reasons for the near hegemony of the president can be found in both formal, institutional arrangements and in less formal, symbolic, and cultural sources.

Presidents in Latin America generally have been given a range of constitutional powers broader than those of the U.S. president. These constitutional grants include wide-ranging appointive powers—and removal powers—for a number of key positions including judicial personnel and regional and local administrators. Latin American presidents also have greater constitutional powers than U.S. presidents in their ability to declare martial law or suspend constitutional guarantees.

Although some of the power of the Latin American presidency is derived from formal grants of authority, significant power comes from less formal sources. Given the long tradition of executive dominance beginning with the important symbolic position of the Spanish monarchy and its various executive representatives in the New World, there has developed an aura surrounding the position of the *jefe supremo* (supreme head or leader). Moreover, hundreds of years of rural economic patterns characterized by powerful *patrones'* (landlords') domination of peasants have created a national culture where the president came to be viewed as the country's chief *patrón*. Latin American legislatures typically grant legislative powers, whether prescribed by a constitution or evolved by custom, to the chief executive, allowing him to issue decree-laws covering a very broad range of issues. The tendency among Western legislatures to cast laws in general terms, thereby facilitating considerable discretion on the part of the executive in implementation, has been greatly extended in Latin America, where presidents issue decrees on virtually any legislative matter they wish to address (Duncan 1976:147; Hughes and Mijeski 1973:7). Executive decrees are a powerful presidential tool used to short-circuit the more conventional lawmaking process; they can be particularly useful to a president in the context of an opposition-controlled legislature. Eduardo Frei Montalva, president of Chile from 1964 to 1970, facing a breakdown in his own party and an increasingly hostile opposition in both the Senate and the Chamber of Deputies, increasingly resorted to decree-laws during the first four years of his administration (Hughes and Mijeski 1973:18–19). Even in Costa Rica, where the president's power to issue decrees is not nearly so unconditional as in most other Latin American governments, one study found that in an eight-year period, about one and one-half times as many decrees as laws were issued (Hughes and Mijeski 1973:39).

Of the six countries that are the focus of this book, Costa Rica fits least well the generalization of presidential dominance; and it is reasonable to argue that the legislative and executive branches are roughly coequal. Moreover, the presidency has only partial control over numerous autonomous and semi-autonomous agencies (Mijeski 1977:61–69). Constitutional grants of authority to the president are much less extensive in Costa Rica than in most of Latin America. For instance, there are severe restraints on the executive's right to suspend constitutional guarantees. And some quasi-executive officials such as the comptroller general are appointed by the legislative branch. In fact, Costa Rica probably has the strongest legislature in relation to the executive of the six countries examined here, and indeed, throughout Latin America.

This situation, however, is not static. We have learned from the abrupt changes in Latin American politics not to exclude the possibility of alterations in the power of actors in the policy process. Had this book been written before September 11, 1973, for example, we would have included Chile in the same category as Costa Rica concerning the power of its legislature vis-à-vis the executive. But on that date, swift and drastic changes were enacted by another critical actor in the policy process, the military, which totally transformed and negated not only the power of the Chilean legislature but also the role of many formerly active participants in Chilean policymaking. At about the same time, the military transformed Uruguay from a political system with a bargaining relationship between the presidency and the congress into another authoritarian regime. In short, not only should we be cautious in our generalizations among countries but also we should be sensitive to changes within a particular country over time.

At the opposite pole from Costa Rica are Mexico and Cuba, both of which are examples of almost total executive hegemony in policymaking. Mexico was the seat of the first major political revolution in Latin America, and out of that revolution emerged a presidential system that is second to none in the power exercised by the president. Several scholars have, in fact, characterized the Mexican president as a virtual dictator (Padgett 1976; Johnson 1978; Stevens 1974; Brandenburg 1964). Historian Frank Brandenburg has said, only partly tongue-in-cheek, that Mexicans "avoid personal dictatorship by retiring their dictators every six years" (1964:141). In Mexico, therefore, the greatest check on official presidential power is the agreement, reached after years of bloody war, that no president will ever succeed himself in office.

The appointive and removal powers of the Mexican president are very extensive; the latter, especially, are almost unlimited and include both state and local, elected and administrative officials. The president's control of the budget, particularly vis-à-vis congress, is just as complete. Congress, for example, has not vetoed a presidential budget since the late 1920s. In fact, most bills proposed by the executive to congress have been approved unanimously, and the remainder receive the overwhelming majority of the legislative votes cast (González Casanova 1970:19–20; Purcell and Purcell 1977).

Most people who think of Cuba think immediately of Fidel Castro. But probably only those who keep up with current events in Latin America rather carefully will know the name of Mexico's current president, let alone the past one. While the Cuban executive is, like that of Mexico, a supremely dominant policymaking actor, there are many systemic differences. A key distinction between these two countries is that the power of the Mexican presidency has become almost wholly institutionalized and, therefore, largely depersonalized, and that presidential power in Cuba is synonymous with the personality of Fidel Castro. In fact, today in Latin America it is doubtful that any other personality dominates a society and its system of government as does Fidel. Moreover, Harvey Kline argues that before 1970 any attempt at formal institutionalization of power increased rather than detracted from the significant charismatic influence already wielded by Castro (1979:453). But Kline does suggest that since the early 1970s further efforts at institutionalization and reorganization of government and party seem to be weakening Fidel's dominance. In particular, the Council of Ministers, which is composed of Fidel as head of the Council of State, six other members of the Council of State, the president of the Central Planning Board, and the remaining government ministers, is designed to provide a more institutionalized and presumably more collegial basis for decisionmaking (Kline 1979:453–454). However, the Council of Ministers appears to be too large to operate effectively as a unit and may possibly have the effect of fragmenting rather than institutionalizing power.

If this occurs, then Fidel's personal control would once again be enhanced rather than diminished.

Venezuela lies somewhere between the extremes of the presidential dominance of Mexico and Cuba and the rough equality of legislature and executive one finds in Costa Rica. On the one hand, the constitution allows the executive to declare states of emergency and to restrict or suspend constitutional guarantees. The president is also granted rather broad decree-making powers (Kelley 1977:28). On the other hand, conditions have existed that have severely restricted presidential power. Since Venezuela is a working model of a modified two-party system, with two dominant parties—Democratic Action (AD) and the Social Christian Party (COPEI)—this is particularly the case when a chief executive's party is in the minority in the generally effective legislature. This was so when COPEI president Rafael Caldera had to deal with an opposition-dominated legislature. Franklin Tugwell, in his study of petroleum policy in Venezuela, described how Caldera decided not to seek a multiparty coalition, despite his limited electoral mandate. The AD members of the legislature, bitter over their defeat in the presidential election, took advantage of his decision and returned the initiative for oil policy changes to the congress (Tugwell 1975:242–246).

Peru between 1968 and 1980 and Brazil since 1964 offer us examples of military regimes that really developed into a kind of personalized presidential system in army garb. Both countries teach us not to assume that because the military has taken control, "presidentialism" ceases to exist. On the contrary, one could make a good case for describing the system of governance in Peru under the leader of the junta until 1975, General Juan Velasco Alvarado, as quite strongly personalistic and presidential. Similarly, the regime in Brazil has developed into a decidedly military-presidential as well as authoritarian system.

In sum, the president generally is the single most important government policy actor in Latin America. While this statement may not be true of Costa Rica in an institutional sense, it is still the case that *personalismo* continues to play an important role in that country's still very visible presidency, particularly so in the case of the "grand old man" of the contemporary presidency, José "Don Pepe" Figueres. Moreover, the generalization seems to be true of the other five nations of this study and probably is true of all other Latin American nations. However, two caveats are in order. We are not saying that Latin American presidents are dictators although under certain conditions, and usually in a finite time frame, a president may become so. Castro's position after the successful Revolution of 1959 clearly approached dictatorlike status as did the presidents of the respective juntas after military takeovers in Brazil (1964), Peru (1968), and Chile (1973). But even under these circumstances, dictator-presidents must nonetheless deal with other actors in the formulation and implementation of policy. The term *dictator* unfortunately suggests a situation where all power is monopolized by one person. Certainly, this dictator's dream is seldom, if ever, completely realized.

Second, it should be reiterated that the extent of presidential predominance varies. It is decidely very strong in contemporary Cuba and Mexico. It exists in Venezuela but is definitely less strong. In Costa Rica the president is clearly more visible than any other government official, but his power in the making of public policy is much reduced. Presidential predominance also varies over time. As pointed out above, there is even some evidence that Fidel's wide-ranging power may have been diminished during the 1970s. And while the Costa Rican president has never been the predominant actor in policymaking as is his counterpart in Mexico, there is some argument that his power is suffering further erosion in recent years at the hands of numerous semiautonomous agencies (Mijeski 1977). In short, the reader is admonished to avoid ignoring or being insensitive to variability over time as well as across space.

To the casual observer, the aspect of Latin American political life most apparent is not executive dominance in the policy process but the extensive history of coups d'état and subsequent military rule. One gets the impression when this occurs that the military plays a very important role in policymaking. Certainly, such has been the case since 1964 in Brazil, between 1968 and 1980 in Peru, and since 1973 in Chile. However, perhaps equally common has been the military coup followed by only a short interim of direct military governance, or perhaps by a countercoup, which likely signifies not policy dominance by the military but power fragmentation within the military that may rob the institution as a whole of a cohesive force in the policy process. Just as we should be alert to variability in presidential power, so should we be aware of differences among militaries in their roles as policymakers.

Perhaps a more important as well as a more intriguing question is just how strong a role does the military play when it is not directly governing? Of the six countries being studied here, only contemporary Brazil has the military directly governing. Peru, after twelve years of direct and overt military rule, returned the presidential sash to a civilian in 1980. The question about the role of the military in policymaking is difficult to answer because researchers have found it none too easy to gain complete access in their attempts to investigate the political behavior of military officers. However, some general points, which should prove enlightening, can be made. One way to proceed is to examine the military's perception of its legitimate role in the governing of the state.

General Benjamín Rattenbach of Argentina speaks for many, though not all, officers when he refers to the mission of the Latin American military as "not only exterior defense and internal security, but also contributing to the development of the nation in the economic and social aspects as well as the cultural and political" (Corbett 1972:5). This rather expansive view of the role of the military has been elaborated not only by individual officers but also by most of the major, higher level military training academies. For instance, both the Center for Higher Military Studies (CAEM) in Peru and the Superior War College (ESG) in Brazil had, for some years prior to their military coups in 1968 and 1964, respectively, been developing the notions that civilian leaders were failing to establish sound policies of national economic development. Therefore, increasing involvement by the military would be required to provide the proper policies while—not incidentally—cleaning up the moral rot the military felt was setting in (see Loveman and Davies 1978:10–11).

Even when this implicitly interventionist stance does not manifest itself directly as it has in Peru and Brazil, the mere fear of military intervention allows for indirect military influence over policy through a kind of anticipated reaction on the part of civilian policymakers. Such, in fact, occurred with the AD administration in the 1960s in Venezuela. When AD first came to power in 1945, it tried to implement a broad range of very reformist policies. As opposition to these policies mounted, the military intervened in 1948 and put an end to the AD government. When AD returned to power in 1959 with the election of Rómulo Betancourt to the presidency, it adopted a much more cautious approach to policy. In fact, AD went out of its way to create a coalition government to ensure the widest possible support (see, e.g., Martz 1977c:93–95). This example serves as a good illustration of how the military may set the boundaries of legitimate policymaking without actually taking an active role in a decision. In a sense, the military can play the role of an "invisible" interest group when it is not directly governing.

Costa Rica stands out as an exception to our general discussion. Having its army officially disbanded after the Civil War of 1948, its *Guardia Civil* is today more adept at giving parking tickets than at plotting *golpes* (coups). Nonetheless, we should not forget that Costa Rica has been one of the sites since the 1960s for U.S.-assisted antiguerrilla training, which clearly implies a beefing up of the military capability of the Costa Rican *Guardia*. So although the *Guardia* in Costa Rica is decidely subservient to civilian control and apparently plays little role in national policymaking today, we must be careful in offhandedly exempting any Latin American country from possible military intervention or its threat. After all, it was not that long ago that Chile and Uruguay, along with Costa Rica, were considered the models of permanent, civilian democratic rule. Similarly, while Mexico has seemingly solved its "military problem" after years of post-Revolutionary violence, Kenneth Johnson raises the gloomy but very real possibility of a renascent militarism in Mexico. For example, he cites former President Luís Echeverría's appointment of some military figures to positions previously considered to be reserved for civilians (1978:51).

In spite of all this emphasis on the policymaking role of the military, two cautionary points about military power should be made. First, the military itself is frequently divided and faced with internal conflict. This has been true whether the military is in power or operates under a civilian government. These conflicts may occur because of personal rivalries or differences in perspectives between the different services, or they may be a result of ideological positions within the same branch of the military (Duncan 1976:202; Williams and Wright 1975:219–221). The point is that rarely is the military a completely unified entity, either when it is directly governing, as the recurrent splits in the Peruvian military government have demonstrated, or when it is one among several actors in the political process. The second point involves the following question: If the military commands such power and influence, why does it feel the need to engage in *golpes* and directly govern? One could go too far with this line of thinking and conclude that much of the time the military is relatively powerless. Such a conclusion would not be warranted. Nevertheless, the question is not meant to be rhetorical. Indeed, one does wonder how much control the military exercises over policymaking if it feels the need to intervene and monopolize or directly control the policy process.

In addition to the president and the higher military officers, upper-level bureaucrats fill out the last of the major, governmental policy actors. Even more so than the military, the bureaucracy is a somewhat misleading term in that it may convey an impression of unity, of singleness of purpose, which does not exist. Certain units within the bureaucracy, such as a bureau or an agency, may very well act as a unit, but the entire bureaucracy does not. An example of this is the struggle that took place in Mexico between two agencies and a state-owned corporation concerning the pricing of raw materials used in drug manufacture (Evans 1979:304–305). Nevertheless, upper-level positions within the bureaucracy as well as certain agencies almost inevitably grant to the incumbents significant policy influence.

In Mexico the minister of finance (*ministro de hacienda*) and the directors of the Bank of Mexico and Nacional Financiera (state development banks) have played very important roles in the formulation and implementation of a wide range of policies (Bennett and Sharpe 1980). In general, bureaucratic power is heightened in Mexico by the fact that control over the bureaucracy tends to be weak, thus allowing bureaucrats to engage in more autonomous action. For example, Raymond Vernon pointed out the president's difficulty in controlling the momentum of the semiautonomous agencies such as those that administer the government-owned petroleum and electric power industries (1963:127).

This phenomenon of bureaucratic intransigence toward other government actors in the policy process is certainly not unique to Mexico. In virtually all of Latin America—and the six countries under study here are no exception— the bureaucracy has experienced rapid and sizable growth in the twentieth century as a concomitant to the increasing scope of activities subsumed under the state's aegis. In fact, the sheer volume of activities either directly or indirectly run by the state necessarily means that bureaucrats are significant forces in the policy process. For instance, both in a highly centralized and totally executive-dominated system like Mexico and in a more democratic and pluralistic system like Venezuela there are hundreds of government agencies and enterprises in addition to the traditional cabinet ministries (see, e.g., Sloan 1981:24). Even in a smaller country with a less penetrating state like Costa Rica, there has been substantial growth in the number and functions of autonomous and semiautonomous agencies with a consequent decrease in the ability of either the president or legislative branch to have significant control over the policy areas with respect to each agency (see, e.g., Mijeski 1977).

This increasing activism of the state and the growing belief that progress can best be achieved through an emphasis on technical, rather than political, issues has helped to elevate the policy position of bureaucrats and especially of the *técnicos*—the university graduates of a technical or specialized training. This is true of both civilian and military regimes; for example, in the military regimes of Brazil and, until 1980, Peru, the *técnicos* were given key roles in the development of economic policy.

It is more difficult to speak with much confidence about the role of the bureaucrat and the *técnico*-bureaucrat in contemporary Cuba. The apparent strengthening of the Council of Ministers referred to earlier would suggest the growing importance of high-level executive officials other than Fidel. It would also suggest the potential for those other officials to rely much more on *técnico*-bureaucrats, particularly if Cuba becomes bureaucratized along the lines of the socialist countries of Eastern Europe (see Gonzalez 1974). However, we have evidence of earlier attempts at *técnico*-inspired policy directions that were either ignored or blatantly overruled by Castro (Dumont 1970).

It should not be assumed that the role of the bureaucracy in policymaking is a purely neutral one, that it is a significant actor but only because it must respond to higher-level requests for assistance in drafting a law, or because it is necessarily involved in implementing laws. Even though they do perform these functions, bureaucracies in Latin America—and likely in most countries—are highly politicized in at least two ways. Individuals and offices develop their own particular interests and will frequently use their positions to forward those interests. In this sense, the bureaucracy operates as its own interest group and often does so quite effectively. Secondly, individuals and offices may have very strong ties to forces outside the bureaucracy. In Venezuela these ties are often with a political clique (*camarilla*). In this case, the bureaucrats may serve as a kind of "inside" interest group or may actually modify a policy to meet the desires of those with whom they have contacts.

In the case of Mexico, Merilee Grindle accentuates the importance of the bureaucracy in her study of bureaucratic policymaking. She argues that given the complete dominance of the presidency over the legislature and the essential control function of the PRI in the hands of top political elites, public policy in Mexico "is an end product of elite bureaucratic and political interaction which occurs beyond the purview of the general public and the rank and file adherents of the official party. Individuals who do regularly participate in policy making, in addition to the President and top party leadership, are usually identified in some way with the bureaucracy" (Grindle 1977a:7). William Stewart points out the somewhat different situation in Venezuela where patron-client relationships that characterize the political parties of that country also describe relationships of the party to the bureaucracy. Party members, through a patronage system, are appointed to bureaucratic agencies where they, in turn, provide leverage to encourage the agency to meet the policy goals favored by their party. Stewart argues that this sort of party-bureaucracy tie was the main thing that accounted for what little the common people received during the dictatorial Pérez Jiménez regime. Acción Democrática, operating underground during the years of the military dictator, exerted pressure on its clients in the various bureaucratic agencies to act upon its party's policy objectives (1977:220–221).

In sum, because of the tremendous involvement of the state in society, bureaucrats have a great influence over public policy, either on their own or in concert with other important individuals and groups.

Nongovernmental Actors

Students of United States and especially of European politics are accustomed to the notion that political parties play a significant role in politics, including acting sometimes as shapers of public policy. In Latin America, by contrast, parties have generally not faired well. Though organizations calling themselves parties have existed in Latin America for about as long as anywhere else, the well-organized, institutionalized, long-lived party has been a rare species. Rather, parties are often "coalitions of elites loosely tied together by personal interests and immediate short-run goals (spoils, patronage) rather than by discipline and organized institutions with long-range objectives" (Duncan 1976:181). These characteristics have served to reduce the potential policy influence of parties as institutions. As a result of this personalistic nature and emphasis on short-term goals, it is typical for parties to arise for electoral purposes and then fade.

Another factor acting against parties becoming important policymakers is the frequent takeovers by the military. Whatever dissimilarities there may be in the various forms of military rule in Latin America, one common trait is the military's decided antipathy toward "politics." Military leaders are more accustomed to getting things done by command. They feel comfortable with discipline, hierarchy and strict superior-subordinate relationships. Politics in general and parties in particular do not operate this way. Rather, the compromise and the deal rather than command and discipline are the hallmarks of party politics. Consequently, when the military assumes direct control of the government, almost without exception it either bans or suspends all political parties.

If the military decides to stay in power for some time, the officers may attempt to create "parties" of their own. But these parties are formed more for purposes of control and mobilization than for organizing competitive electoral behavior or for providing alternative expressions of policy demands. Thus, for instance, both the Brazilian military in 1964 and the Peruvian junta in 1968 banned political parties. Subsequently, the Brazilian regime created two new parties: One, the National Renovating Alliance (ARENA), was to be the voice of those supporting the regime; the other, the Brazilian Democratic Movement (MDB), was to be a kind of castrated opposition composed of a ragtag mixture of old opposition parties. The charade became even more apparent when these two parties were later disbanded only to be replaced by another military-created "party" that was named, with perfect Orwellian logic, the Social Democratic Party (PSD).

The Peruvian military took a somewhat different tack. Rather than create a party, the Velasco administration formed one massive corporatist organization to fulfill the major function of hierarchically directed mobilization. The organization, commonly known by its acronym SINAMOS, turned out to be a failure. In fact, only after the military decided to turn the reins of government back to civilians in 1980 did Peruvian politics experience some revival of party activity.

While the norm in Latin America seems to be political parties with a limited or nonexistent policymaking role, there are still countries where parties do play some role in the policy process. Though they have different kinds of parties and party systems, Colombia, Costa Rica, Mexico, Cuba, and Venezuela are all examples of countries in which parties assist government in policymaking (Duncan 1976:195).

Venezuela is the country with a party system most understandable to North Americans. That is, the system is characterized by true party competition between two major parties that are well organized and "permanent." Although there are many parties in Venezuela with representation in the national legislature, only two parties have held the presidency since Venezuela's "return" to democratic processes in 1958. These same two parties—AD and COPEI— also dominate the congress, as Table 2.1 demonstrates. Venezuelan parties are certainly not free of the weakening effects of personalism and factionalism. In fact, many of the smaller parties listed in Table 2.1 are spin-offs from the larger ones (especially AD), led by individuals disgruntled with their inability to dominate the party (Martz 1977c:96–97). Nevertheless, Venezuela's political parties, at least the major ones, stand out impressively as actors in the policy process. As Ronald McDonald concludes: "With the most modest of historical

Politics and Public Policy in Latin America

TABLE 2.1

Party Representation in the Venezuelan Legislature

	Number of Seats	
Party	Senate (1974-1977)	Chamber of Deputies (1978)
AD	60	86
COPEI	28	86
MEP	4	4
MAS	4	11
URD	2	1
PCV	–	1

Source: Adapted from Duncan, 1976: p. 189; Venezuela at the Polls, 1980: pp. 272-273.

credentials, Venezuela has evolved a system of modern political parties, sensitive to public demands and basic issues, and functionally significant to government decision-making" (1971:55).

Along with Venezuela and perhaps Colombia, Costa Rica is at this moment one of the very few Latin American countries where meaningful party competition takes place and where parties have some impact on policymaking. There are, however, some very real differences between Costa Rica's parties and those of Venezuela. Both Costa Rica and Venezuela have two major parties, but only one of the Costa Rican parties, the National Liberation Party (PLN), is a well-organized institution. It too, however, is not free from personalism. The PLN was created by José Figueres in 1952 and although it is the more ideologically structured of the two parties, there is evidence that Figueres still exerts substantial influence in its operations (Fitzgibbon and Fernandez 1981:84). The other party, the National Unification Party (PUN), is essentially a coalition of a variety of groups and interests whose cohesion derives from the desire to win elections at the expense of the PLN.

There is honest controversy among observers of Mexican politics concerning the role of political parties in the policy process. Despite the consensus about the virtually nonexistent policymaking punch of all opposition parties, there is disagreement over the role of the PRI as a party. Kenneth Johnson eschews the term *party*, arguing that by the 1970s "it was more accurate to call the PRI an organized dominant class, having at its apex an official family or coterie of privileged elites" (1978:77). Other scholars suggest that the PRI may be a more pluralistic organization, allowing for significant representation of many public interests (Scott 1964). Whatever the case may be, it seems safe to say that the historically evolved intimate connections between the PRI and the Mexican presidency have guaranteed to the former at least a symbolic role as the "institutionalized" vehicle for the achievement of the goals of the 1910 Revolution. In practice, it appears quite difficult to separate the policymaking role of the president from that of the official party.

In the case of Cuba, given the ideological authoritarianism of the regime and the dominating role of Castro, the Cuban Communist Party (PCC) does not seem to play a policymaking role. Rather, its purposes are to build support, to disseminate the ideology, and to help maintain the regime's political security (McDonald 1971:222). In light of our previous comments concerning the possibility of the increasing institutionalization and depersonalization of Castro's rule, it may be that the party in Cuba will begin to take on a more autonomous role—at least vis-à-vis Fidel—in the policy process. In fact, Edward Gonzalez suggests that a strong tendency is emerging in Cuba toward the institutionalization of the regime along the lines of a more Sovietized bureaucratic order. This tendency, he argues, would result in the growing ascendancy of the PCC as a viable policymaking body (1974:226–230). It might also signify the increasing role of the Soviet Union not only as a bankroller of the Cuban state but also as a key external actor in the policy process, a point we will address briefly in the next section.

Another nongovernmental actor in the policy process is the interest group. Widely known and widely studied as key policy actors in the United States, interest groups function in a very different political context in most of Latin America. Whereas group politics takes place in the United States within the framework of a generally liberal-pluralist ideology, interest groups in Latin America operate with only the trappings of liberalism in a political culture burdened by centuries of authoritarian, patrimonial, and corporatist tradition. And there is a set of unwritten "rules of the game" that results in group action taking place without the normal procedural limits and safeguards usually found in more completely liberal-democratic political systems.

These contextual factors imply several differences between the ability of interest groups to influence public policy in the United States and their ability to do so in Latin America: (1) The authoritarian and patrimonial traditions of Latin America lead to an emphasis on a stable administrative state above the politics of parties and interest groups. (2) The corporatist tradition implies less autonomy and independence of Latin American interest groups from the state apparatus. (3) The absence of rules of the game that specify a single legitimate source of authority, such as do election outcomes in the United States, results in groups (and the government itself) resorting to a wide range of activities, including violence, as a method to get their demands met or as a way to repress and even eliminate competing groups from the policy process altogether.

Brazil is a good example of a regime whose actions reflect the traditional Hispanic values of hierarchy, corporatism, and authoritarianism. Kenneth Erickson argues that "corporative controls have conditioned the political activity and limited the autonomy of every major associated interest group in Brazil. The controls have correspondingly increased the autonomy of state policymaking elites" (1977:161). Corporatist policies, essentially unchanged since the labor laws decreed by President Getúlio Vargas in the 1930s, have also enabled the military regime to control, by cooptation or repression, the Brazilian labor movement. Erickson points out that even in the four-year period preceding the 1964 coup, the military set limits upon labor activities: "Of the seventeen major political strikes and strike threats in the period . . . a unified officer corps opposed ten. Six of them never went beyond the level of threat, and three others the military undermined, crushed, or ended by forcing an unfavorable settlement upon the workers" (1977:162). If the labor organizations are ineffectual actors in the Brazilian policy process, which groups have been most successful in reaping policy rewards under the military regime? Two major beneficiaries are the industrialists and the landed elite. One scholar has claimed that the success of these two interests does not necessarily result from their independent efforts to influence policy. Instead, he argues, technocrats in key positions in the government bureaucracy formulated and implemented policies favorable to them because the groups' goals—industrialization, economic modernization, agricultural production—were consonant with the regime's own objectives (Erickson 1977:165, 167–168). This may be so, yet it begs the question of how the regime arrived at its objectives in the first place. If industrialists and landed elites played a key role in early stages of the policy process, such as issue formation and agenda setting, then to suggest that a policy was implemented essentially because the regime wanted to ignores the need to consider how agendas get arranged to begin with.

We do not wish to suggest that industrial and landed elite interest groups are totally independent from and eminently influential over the regime's policy choices. On the contrary, the tentative picture of group politics in Brazil that emerges is a classic case of corporative governmental controls that severely restrict interest-group autonomy. It may still be the case, as Peter Flynn suggests, that a limited number of informal groups of economically powerful people do have real, relatively autonomous influence on some issues. For example, a group of bankers was apparently instrumental in convincing President Geisel to remove one of his cabinet members because the bankers disliked that minister's proposed policies of expanding the internal market and raising wages (Flynn 1978a:507). For the most part, however, a valid generalization would be that in Brazil interest groups do exist and operate, and some of them are effective, particularly those representing capital and highly sought technical skills. All of these groups are subordinated to the state and do not operate in the open, autonomous fashion described by the liberal-pluralist model.

Our discussion of Brazilian interest groups is applicable in general terms to Cuba, Mexico, and Peru. That is, groups in these countries are largely subordinated to and coopted by the state. Their activities are tolerated—even encouraged—when their goals are consonant with the government's overall policy objectives. In contrast, groups that attempt to act independently of the state and/or espouse policy aims perceived by the regime as antithetical to its goals are discouraged and sometimes severely repressed.

Historically, interest groups have never been particularly strong in Peru (Palmer 1979:205). As in Brazil, the Peruvian military government sought to weaken and directly control the labor unions. It allowed for worker participation but only in a corporatist, nonindependent way. In one observer's words, "The government's dealings with labor and peasant organizations, business lobbies, and other groups suggest that the regime distrusts any autonomous organizations and wishes to deal only with units established or legitimized by the regime" (Lowenthal 1975:10). At the same time, some labor unions, especially those that were Communist controlled, retained a limited influence by exerting pressure through demonstrations and strikes (Knight 1975:395; Lowenthal 1975:9, 14, 16; Cotler 1975:60, 73). Even the organizations of the previously economically powerful groups, especially the old, landed oligarchy, were severely weakened and in some cases eliminated altogether, as in the case of the once powerful National Agrarian Society. The exceptions to this scenario have been those groups that are Peruvian, development oriented, and tied to urban-industrial rather than rural-agrarian interests. Such organizations were often allowed to play an active role in policymaking during the Velasco administration. This seems to have been the case of ADEX, the Association of Exporters, whose activities were strongly supported by the regime (Cotler 1975:74–75).

Cuba, while fitting the generalizations stated above, must also be seen as distinct in that a successful, Marxist-Leninist revolution has been layered over the generally corporatist, authoritarian tendencies that existed previously. There are many groups in Cuba; some, such as the Committees for the Defense of the Revolution (CDR), have been important in generating regime support and in extending ideology. But are these interest groups in the North American sense? Harvey Kline (1979:456–457) expresses the well-accepted view that the groups exist for the purposes of control, of political education, of regime support, and the like, but that they do not really serve to make demands upon the regime.

In general, we are inclined to agree with this assessment. Marxist regimes typically define their nature in such a way as to delegitimize the concept of interest groups. Nevertheless, to treat the policy process in Cuba as if no demand making of any importance occurs is to take an extreme and inaccurate position. For example, the CDRs, which certainly have regime legitimization and policy implementation as major functions, also provide for inputs of public opinion and for people to make policy demands upon the government. Moreover, another group, the Federation of Cuban Women, has actively attacked the traditional notions of "women's place" in Cuban society and has been instrumental in getting the government to establish a countrywide network of day-care centers, enabling women to pursue activities outside the home (Bray and Harding 1974:672–674). However, sufficient evidence is available to demonstrate the ideological limits of the Cuban regime's tolerance of activist interest groups, such as the number of political prisoners and the general suppression of "inappropriate" dissent (see, for example, Ripoll 1982). Demand making by interest groups clearly occurs in Cuba and is sometimes successful. Not unlike the case in Brazil and in Peru, however, the most successful groups are those tolerated by the regime itself.

Mexico is definitely not an exception to the general rules of state-dominated interest associations. Purcell and Purcell characterize the Mexican system as one of "limited pluralism": "Interest groups in Mexico are less numerous and varied than in the United States, and their autonomy is severely circumscribed by government power. Business groups are the *most* autonomous because they are the only segment of society with independent resources and organizational skills. Nevertheless the government has various ways of controlling business groups" (1977:194).

Mexico's incorporation of groups is perhaps the most systematic and thoroughgoing of all Latin America. Even though the business interests are the most autonomous, they must, under penalty of law, opt to join either the National Confederation of Chambers of Commerce (CONCANACO) or the Confederation of Mexican Chambers of Industry (CONCAMIN). Pablo González Casanova points out that private enterprise forms a network of interest groups "which the government cannot ignore," but it is clear that the government determines the context within which it pays attention to them (1970:50). Moreover, the government also constrains the business sector through its control of labor organizations, occasionally encouraging strikes to bring business interests into line. Finally, Purcell and Purcell point out that business groups seldom initiate or propose policies. Rather, they may be asked to react to government initiated proposals (1977:195). Nonbusiness groups in Mexico, of course, are even less powerful actors in the policy process. Peasants, urban labor, and middle-class groups such as teachers and bureaucrats are kept under control and are official members of the PRI (see González Casanova 1970:14–17, 169–178).

In contrast to the four countries just discussed, we find in Venezuela a large number of interest groups, most of which operate as autonomous groups without direct, incorporating linkages to the state. As in the case of its political parties, Venezuela's interest groups appear readily understandable to North Americans familiar with the liberal-pluralist model. The major and generally most influential groups in Venezuela are those that represent the interests of the industrialists, urban labor, and new urban middle-class groups. Of less influence, but nevertheless often active, are the Catholic Church, peasant organizations, and university student groups (Ieda Wiarda 1974:228). However, one should not exaggerate the picture of Venezuela as teeming with interest groups effectively representing all values in the society. The vast majority of citizens, like their U.S. counterparts, do not participate politically except to vote occasionally. Moreover, in most of the interest groups the relationship between leaders and followers has been highly paternalistic (Lott 1972:250). This suggests a decided bias in group activity in Venezuela with consequent muting of other than elite interests in the group's efforts.

Of the various interest groups, those representing business and industrial concerns seem the most active and powerful. One of the better known and most active of the peak-type associations is FEDECAMARAS, the Federation of Chambers of Commerce and Production. In contrast to the corporatist, state-created and controlled CONCAMIN and CONCANACO of Mexico, FEDECAMARAS was independently created and is fairly autonomously operated. Similar organizations in Venezuela include the rather large National Council of Industry (CONINDUSTRIA), the National Federation of Livestock Raisers (FENAGAN), and many local and regional groups. Does this relatively high level of autonomy and independence from the state apparatus inevitably result in a more influential policymaking role for these business and industrial groups? Some available case study material suggests that the policymaking role of these groups can be exaggerated.

In a discussion of business entrepreneurs and their successful efforts in support of import substitution policies, José Antonio Gil concludes that the policies were promulgated "not so much because entrepreneurs pressured for them (which they did) but rather because government leaders considered them intrinsically beneficial. Businessmen seem to have had marginal influence on deciding which policy issues would be addressed, moderate influence on formulating programs to deal with the chosen policy issues, and substantial influence on program implementation" (1977:152). Gil suggests that an examination of the export promotion policy leads to a similar conclusion. Tugwell's study of oil policy in Venezuela similarly shows that although FEDECAMARAS and multinational corporations have had significant influence on policymaking, they also have experienced real limits to that influence (1975). A general summary of the role of private business enterprise in Venezuela, which differentiates it from corporatist Mexico and Brazil yet points out Venezuela's deviance from the liberal-pluralist model, is expressed by Gil: "Can business freely pursue its interests and successfully influence public policy? The answer is a qualified yes. . . . The basic orientations and conditions under which the economy and private enterprise system operate are decided by bureaucracy and the political parties. . . . The end results are policies which allow business to operate, but under conditions designed to keep the potential influence of entrepreneurs in check" (1977:152–153).

Labor unions in Venezuela offer us another example of the variation of workers' organizations and their policy roles in Latin America. There are many local and regional labor unions in Venezuela, most of which are brought together under the national peak association, the Venezuelan Workers Confederation (CTV). Although the autonomy of Venezuelan unions has been weakened by their reliance on political parties, especially the unions connected with AD, they behave more independently than most Mexican unions, which are virtually "owned" by the PRI and the Mexican government. Even though labor groups in the United States have been traditionally allied with the Democratic Party, many elections, most recently the McGovern-Nixon contest of 1972, have demonstrated the ability of organized labor to act not only independently of but even antithetically to the Democratic Party's interests. This kind of autonomy, while not the rule in the United States, is much less likely in Venezuela.

Because of its small size and lack of economic diversity, Costa Rica has fewer interest groups than any of the other five countries in our study. Nevertheless, the general form of interest-group behavior is more like that of Venezuela than of the other countries. Among the major and sometimes influential interest groups are those dominated by landowners. Costa Rica, to some extent, is still characterized as a "banana and coffee republic," albeit one that is free of military-inspired coups or military-civilian dictators. Consequently, organizations such as the Chamber of Coffee Growers and the Chamber of Banana Growers are key policy influencers. The Cattlemen's Association has also been successful in getting the government to press for increases in the United States beef importation quota (Denton 1979:384). One of the most important interest groups in Costa Rica is the group of entrepreneurs that owns La Nación, the nation's largest newspaper. The paper, private-enterprise oriented, is consistently at odds with the major party, the PLN. The Catholic Church, in a more limited context, and the U.S. government through the State Department's Agency for International Development (AID) also play roles in the policy process.

International Actors

Our task here would be incomplete without considering the role of other than strictly national actors, either governmental or nongovernmental, in the Latin American policy process. Certainly, for example, it would be inappropriate to consider policymaking in Cuba without any reference to the estimated several billion dollars in subsidies that the Soviet Union has invested in the domestic political economy of Fidel's empire (Sigmund 1980:120). Nor would our description of the policy process that has led to the creation of what many observers have called an "economic miracle" in Brazil be complete if we did not take into account the part played by the investment activities of a large number of multinational corporations. And it is likely that domestic economic policymaking in Costa Rica is not isolated from the provisions and decisions of regional organizations, such as the Central American Common Market (CACM). It is also clear that an adequate appraisal of the recent agrarian reform policymaking process in war-ravaged El Salvador necessitates a full appreciation of the "advisory" role played by one or more agencies of the government of the United States. The so-called Phase Three or "Land to the Tiller" program of the now aborted reform, for instance, was a policy designed and instigated by the United States (Deere 1982). Therefore, we shall, in this section, briefly discuss the policymaking roles of foreign governments, multinational corporations, international lending agencies, and Latin American regional organizations.

For the greater part of the twentieth century, the U.S. government has been widely recognized as a key policy influencer in the politics of Latin America. Indeed, it has been said that before Fidel Castro came to power, the U.S. ambassador to Cuba was at least the second and often the first most powerful policymaker in that country. Prime Minister Pierre Trudeau of Canada added to the mystique of the United States as a key policy actor when he suggested that living near this country was "like sleeping with an elephant. No matter how friendly and even-tempered is the beast . . . , one is affected by every twitch and grunt" (Williams 1971:14). Another in a long list of animal metaphors is represented by Juan José Arévalo's book, *The Shark and the Sardines*. The polemic intent of the metaphor is obvious.

Besides these metaphoric tales and aphorisms, can anything be said systematically about the dynamics and effects of U.S. government involvement in the Latin American policy process? Is the United States a leading actor in all policymaking within the countries of Latin America? Or are there only certain policy areas in which the United States plays a significant role? One major area of U.S. concern, particularly since Castro's successful revolution in Cuba, has been the role of international communism in Latin America. While there is considerable debate over U.S. intent, there is good evidence linking the instrumental role played by the United States in the policy process that culminated in the creation of a number of so-called counterinsurgency programs throughout the region during the 1960s and 1970s (Klare and Arnson 1974:146–158). Even before Castro, the U.S. government, more or less covertly, played key roles by intervening in and, in some cases, thoroughly transforming the policymaking agenda in several countries. The classic case

was the Central Intelligence Agency (CIA) overthrow of the regime in Guatemala in 1954. The 1965 invasion by U.S. marines of the Dominican Republic,
the controversially successful "destabilization" of the Allende government in
Chile in the early 1970s, the above-mentioned "Land to the Tiller" program
in El Salvador in the beginning of the 1980s and recent support for the
"contras" in Nicaragua are all examples of what appear to be significant policy
initiatives carried out, at least in part, in the cause of anticommunism.

The Alliance for Progress, launched by President Kennedy in 1961, was
perhaps the most systematic effort to exert U.S. influence on Latin American
states. The Alliance has mixed reviews (see Levinson and deOnís 1970), but
it probably demonstrated both the effectiveness and the relative ineffectiveness
of U.S. efforts at shaping the domestic politics of Latin America.

The limits to the United States as a policy influencer can also be seen in
an examination of the dispute between Peru and the International Petroleum
Company (IPC—a Standard Oil subsidiary) in the 1960s. There was very
strong Peruvian governmental movement toward the nationalization of the
IPC. In the mid-1960s the president, Fernando Belaunde Terry, and the
congress initiated legislation to that end. The U.S. government got into the
act at that point and, by delaying economic assistance and reducing aid
commitments from $30 million for fiscal 1964 to $2 million for fiscal 1966,
apparently tried to pressure Peru to back down from its position (Sigmund
1980). This action on the part of the United States was never publicly linked
to the settlement of the IPC dispute, but, according to one U.S. official, "The
idea was to put on a freeze, talk about red tape and bureaucracy, and they'd
soon get the message" (Sigmund 1980:364). The ultimate response by Peru
was the military's ousting of Belaunde, followed by an immediate and complete
nationalization of the IPC.

Another, and quite different, issue that the U.S. government has taken an
interest in is that of population policy. In the 1960s and 1970s, many foreign
actors, public and private, engaged in campaigns to induce Latin American
governments to formulate policies designed to curb their countries' population
growth rates. The U.S. government and private U.S.-based institutions were
a part of this international campaign. In fact, one analyst has found that the
U.S. role has been a dominant one. Through statistical analysis, Terry McCoy
found a significant relationship between foreign actors' activities and domestic
Latin American population policies. He concluded: "Without the relatively
massive combination of external imports . . . Latin American population
policies would not have changed as rapidly and extensively as they have"
(1974:84).

The role played by multinational corporations (MNC) in the Latin American
policy process has been a subject of considerable heated debate. Some have
argued that MNCs have become the logical next step in international economic
imperialism, essentially "taking over" the domestic politics of a particular

country to suit their own profitmaking ends. Others have argued that MNCs' abilities to influence domestic policymakers is quite limited, particularly in the context of growing nationalistic sentiments in the region. Certainly a large part of the so-called "economic miracle" of Brazil in the late 1960s and 1970s is attributable to the extensive investments of MNCs in that country. But do those same multinationals necessarily call the shots in the policy game? In an excellent study of these questions in the Brazilian context, Peter Evans has suggested that Brazil is a good case of what he calls dependent development, which "is a special instance of dependency, characterized by the association or alliance of international and local capital. The state also joins the alliance as an active partner, and the resulting triple alliance is a fundamental factor in the emergence of dependent development" (1979:32). In an interesting analysis of the MNC-controlled Brazilian pharmaceutical industry, Evans concluded that the power of the MNC in influencing policy is variable, and domestic government attempts at shaping MNC activity are more successful the closer those attempts adhere to the profitability model (1979:191–193).

For example, when policies were proposed and enacted that would encourage the pharmaceutical companies to engage in more research and development within Brazil, most companies responded only incrementally and even symbolically. This was so even though the government used the carrot-and-stick approach, with emphasis on the former (Evans 1979:188–189). Moreover, the position of foreign-controlled pharmaceuticals was relatively weak at the time, seemingly making them more vulnerable to political pressure. In contrast, the state was more successful in pushing the pharmaceuticals into the production of raw materials locally since that action put their profits less clearly in jeopardy than did research and development activity. Also, a positive advantage of complying with the state's urging to produce raw materials locally derived from the state's offer of total tariff protection for those firms in compliance (Evans 1979:191–193).

More direct MNC investment, especially from MNCs based in the United States, has taken place in Mexico than in Brazil, which might lead one to conclude that MNCs are more independent policy influencers in the former than in the latter. Evans argues that this is not the case, due largely to Mexico's longer success with stabilizing and centralizing political control. As he points out, while Brazil was looking for a political formula in the forties, fifties, and sixties, Mexico's PRI quickly developed a central apparatus for organizing and channeling political-economic access (1979:300). Nonetheless, MNCs, backed by powerful domestic allies, are still a force to bargain with, particularly when the mammoth Mexican bureaucracy is at odds with itself. A good example of such a case is the steroid hormone industry where the MNCs, in alliance with the National Industrial Confederation and the National Chamber of Chemical Pharmaceutical Firms, defeated the state-owned corporation, Proquivemex, in its efforts to force a substantial increase in the price paid by the multinationals for a locally grown raw material (Gereffi 1978).

Some of the debate over the role played by MNCs in Latin American policymaking concerns the degree of collusion between U.S.-based multinationals and the U.S. government. Scholars who work from the point of view of the imperialism or dependency schools of thought argue strongly that the cooperation between U.S. governmental agencies and powerful MNCs is close and harmonious. A favorite contemporary example is the alleged collusion between the CIA and International Telephone and Telegraph (ITT) in joint "destabilizing" activities in Chile (NACLA 1973).

More recently, some observers have suggested that having a U.S. base may be a hindrance to the domestic influence of the MNCs operating in Latin America. One analyst, speaking about Brazil, has argued that "the political advantages of American 'citizenship' have become much more ambiguous than they were ten years ago. For one company, Westinghouse, American 'citizenship' was an insurmountable obstacle to winning a multibillion dollar nuclear reactor contract for which they would otherwise have been by far the strongest competitor" (Evans 1974:331). Furthermore, he argues, U.S. congressional subsidization of MNC activities, reflected by the activities of agencies such as the Overseas Private Investment Corporation (OPIC), have diminished over the last decade, in part due to negative congressional reaction to the kinds of "development" projects subsidized by OPIC: fast-food chains in Brazil, ITT-Sheraton Hotels in India, Safari Lodges in Kenya, and Avis Rent-a-Car services for Malaysia (1974:329).

However, it is premature to conclude that MNCs and international and bilateral lending agencies are playing a weaker role in influencing policymaking in Latin America. Peru is a good example. After a wave of nationalizations of the IPC and a number of other MNCs in the late 1960s and early 1970s, Peru has found itself reversing many of those policies, welcoming back some MNC activity, and even submitting its public expenditures to the monitoring of foreign banks and the U.S.-dominated International Monetary Fund (IMF) (Sigmund 1980:217–218).

The United States dominates the IMF in the sense that it contributes more money than any other country to the fund and to other international lending agencies such as the World Bank and the Inter-American Development Bank (IADB). The United States also controls the majority of the votes concerning any action taken by these so-called multilateral lending agencies. Some observers have concluded, with good evidence, that U.S. domination of these lending organizations can either make possible or devastate a recipient country's ability to formulate economic policy.

Loans to Brazil, for example, multiplied during the 1970s, adding in no small way to Brazil's "economic miracle." Today Brazil, along with several other major Latin American countries, is on the verge of bankruptcy due to its inability to repay those debts from the 1970s. The same IMF and IADB that opened their coffers during the previous decade are now threatening to close them unless Brazilian domestic policy conforms to the lending agencies' model of frugality.

Some critics of the role played by these agencies in the domestic policy process of Latin American countries have also charged that U.S. control of most of the votes is often used to punish regimes it perceives to be hostile and reward those that it sees as friendly. Recent loans and loan proposals to El Salvador (a "friendly" government) and Nicaragua (a "hostile" government) may illustrate this contention. Although the United States controls 35.7 percent of the vote on loan proposals of the IADB, that bank's Fund for Special Operations (FSO) requires a two-thirds majority vote—and therefore U.S. approval—for loan disbursements. Recently, the other forty-two IADB member nations, ironically including El Salvador, voted for an FSO loan of $2.2 million for Nicaragua for the completion of a road construction project. The United States cast the sole negative vote, thereby blocking the necessary two-thirds majority (*Washington Report on the Hemisphere*, September 6, 1983, 1). Comparing the loans received from the IADB by El Salvador and Nicaragua in a recent two-year period (1981–1982) is also enlightening. "Friendly" El Salvador received a total of $180.8 million; Nicaragua obtained only $43 million (*Washington Report on the Hemisphere*, 6).

Some final comments should be made concerning the linkages between privately controlled banks and international lending agencies. As of 1970, private commercial banks accounted for about 20 percent of all loans to developing nations, the rest coming from agencies like the World Bank. By 1980, developing nations (mostly major Latin American countries) owed commercial banks 60 percent of their staggering $315 billion debt. Peru alone, by the beginning of this decade, was more than $8 billion in debt, and 53 percent of her export earnings were going into debt repayment. Increasingly, the international lending agencies are lending money not to finance development projects but simply to help Latin American and other developing countries repay loans to private banks (Gamer 1982:383–384). Overall, this international financial situation highlights the fragility of Latin American countries' economic policymaking as well as those countries' dependence on economic and financial actors and processes outside their national borders.

Finally, let us briefly discuss the policy role of regional organizations. We limit our discussion to three regional economic organizations: the Central American Common Market (CACM), the Latin American Free Trade Association (LAFTA), and the so-called Andean Group. In a controversial analysis, Royce Q. Shaw suggests that while the CACM does, in fact, have policy-limiting influence on domestic political decisionmakers, the regional organization has also been highly vulnerable to manipulation by those same local elites (1978). An example of CACM's policy-limiting influence occurred in

1966 when President Trejos of Costa Rica applied emergency economic measures that discriminated against trade with the other four member countries. The ministers of the Common Market responded quickly, threatening to expel Costa Rica from the CACM within forty-eight hours unless it exempted Common Market members from its emergency measures. After a few days, Costa Rica agreed to exempt the member nations (1978:86). The CACM's vulnerability was demonstrated when the opposition-controlled Costa Rican legislature, mainly for the "political" purpose of embarrassing the Trejos administration, engineered the defeat of the San José Protocol, a CACM effort at solving balance-of-payments problems regionally. Only a year before, the PLN-controlled legislature had allowed the Trejos government to impose sales taxes similar to those embodied in the Protocol. Yet the PLN then claimed that the taxes in the San José Protocol were taxes on the poor, and they refused to ratify it (Shaw 1978:100).

Moreover, the CACM has continued to undergo changes that have led to its weakening as a dominant regional policymaking body. Honduras withdrew de facto in June 1971 and Costa Rica, making charges of "dumping" against certain of her neighbors' industries, unilaterally imposed discriminatory exchange rates on certain imported products (Shaw 1978:179). This action spurred a proliferation of bilateral treaties among CACM members, further weakening the organization's policymaking power.

In a more generally negative evaluation of the role played by both LAFTA and CACM, Miguel Wionczek claims that both organizations have "crash-landed" (1972:507). And though the Andean Group and the Caribbean Free Trade Area (CARIFTA) are in some sense spin-offs from LAFTA, Wionczek is not optimistic about their future role. We suspect that, given the continued turmoil in Central America, the immediate future does not bode well for the policymaking efficacy of the Central American Common Market.

The Latin American Free Trade Association is apparently an even less effective influencer of policy than is the CACM. According to one observer, "by 1968 LAFTA had virtually ceased to function, deadlocked over the free trade versus regional planning issue" (Atkins 1977:291–292).

The Andean Group nations of Peru, Bolivia, Ecuador, Chile, Colombia, and Venezuela may be the most influential of the regional organizations. The Andean Group Statute of Foreign Capital ("Decision 24"), adopted in 1971 and later modified, represents the only multilateral Latin American attempt to control investment in the region. Decision 24 calls for step-by-step redirection of foreign-controlled investment. By 1986 (1991 in Ecuador and Bolivia), it mandates a minimum 51 percent local ownership. Decision 24 certainly appears to represent a significant intrusion of an extranational actor in the domestic policymaking process. However, as in the splintering and disputes that have plagued LAFTA and CACM, though perhaps not quite so devastating, numerous waivers and exceptions to Decision 24 have been applied, especially in the cases of Chile and Peru. As a consequence, according to one scholar, the Industrial Code of the statute has become virtually ineffective (Atkins 1977:295).

Before concluding this section, let us take a brief look at Cuba as a special case. Of the six countries that constitute the focus of this work, Cuba alone is strongly tied to the Soviet Union and is not a member of any of the regional organizations just discussed. There is no question that the Cuban economy relies heavily on Soviet assistance. But does this dependence virtually guarantee to the Soviet Union untrammeled influence, if not outright control, of Cuban policymaking? As you might have expected, there is no general consensus among scholars in this regard. Some analysts argue that the increasingly bureaucratized and centralist model to which Cuba has conformed since about 1970 resulted largely from Soviet pressure (Domínguez 1979:159; Gonzalez 1979; Mesa-Lago 1978:105). Others have argued that the changes in the 1970s can be explained apart from any Soviet pressure (Valdes 1976; LeoGrande 1979).

However, William M. LeoGrande found that there is a virtual consensus among scholars that Cuban foreign policy is made in Havana, not in Moscow. "Even those scholars," he points out, "who argue that Cuba's domestic policy changes came at Soviet initiative reject the idea that Cuba acts as a Soviet puppet in Africa" (1981:202). Instead, it is argued, the Cuban venture into Angola, while supportive of Soviet interests in Southern Africa, was undertaken in pursuit of Cuba's own Third World interests. Clearly, we are dealing here with questions of inferential influence in an area where heat often exceeds light and where serious scholars continue to disagree seriously. Nevertheless, the uniqueness of the Soviet-Cuban connection in our understanding of the policy process is a factor that should not be dismissed. We shall pursue in somewhat more detail the issue of the Cuban policy process, historically and today, in Chapter 5.

The Policymaking Process: An Overview

Clearly, individuals and institutions that are formally part of the executive branch of government comprise a critical set of policy actors. In most countries, some individuals and a few organizations involved in private commercial, industrial, financial, and agricultural interests also play important policy roles. Most other individuals and groups, from middle-class professionals, business-men, politicians, and intellectuals to the church, urban labor, farm workers, and the very poor, play very limited roles in the policy process.

In the remainder of this chapter, we move from a discussion of individual actors to an overview of the nature of government policymaking. This discussion is of a general nature, meant to highlight the major contours and the boundaries of the process. In the following three chapters, we provide a more detailed discussion of the policy process in the six countries of this study.

Perhaps the best place to start is with a simple but important quantitative observation: A great many problems and issues are subject to public deci-sionmaking. This is true because (most of) the Latin American states typically are involved in a large number of enterprises. For instance, the government of Mexico owns or participates in over four hundred enterprises, engaging in activities from the production of steel to the distribution of milk (Sloan 1981:24). In Brazil, the activities of the various levels of government account for almost 60 percent of the Gross National Product (GNP) (Wiarda and Kline 1979:60). The most dramatic change in recent times occurred in Cuba, where, during the 1960s, a capitalist economy came to be replaced by a socialist one. As a result, the Cuban government is very actively involved in an ex-ceedingly wide range of activities. Though not quite so dramatic, Peru of the 1970s provides an illustration of great expansion of government activity within an essentially capitalist economy. Traditionally one of the weakest and most limited states in Latin America, from 1965 to 1975 the government's share of national investment rose from 13 percent to almost 50 percent (Lowenthal 1975:7–8).

Though the Latin American states, with the exception of Cuba, operate within an essentially capitalist economic environment, it is a form of state capitalism that grants to the state an involvement, especially in the economic realm, that would be considered illegitimate in the United States. We may call the typical country in Latin America an activist or interventionist state to indicate this phenomenon. As one scholar stated it: "In the 20th century, the Latin American state has become the ultimate patron, from which citizens expect everything—except justice" (Sloan 1981:18).

This picture of the interventionist state requires some qualification so as not to exaggerate the point. First, the governments in Latin America, while generally having expanded the range of issues that are legitimately the concern of public policy, have not sought to make that list all inclusive—again, with perhaps Cuba an exception. Government activism in Latin America essentially defines a relationship between government and economy. Even here, the role of government tends to be limited to such actions as the provision of investment funds or energy resources or technical advice. While governments do pe-riodically take over businesses and industries, they do so on a limited basis. In Cuba, this is not so. Instead the picture here is reversed—private ownership does exist but on a limited basis. Second, government policy in Argentina and Chile (from the mid-1970s to the present) forces us to consider the possibility that the increasing degree of state activism is reversible. In both of these countries, the governments have sought to reduce both the number of firms owned by the government and the size and expense of the government bureaucracy.

Another general characteristic of the policy process is that it is reflective of a state that is more politicized than institutionalized. Political structures and processes, that is, are seen as something less than permanent, something always on trial. "Policymaking institutions are themselves subject to active political questioning and conflict, and their reconstruction is viewed not so much as a violation of basic principles (as it would in the United States) but as the outcome of a particularly important confrontation" (Chalmers 1977:24). Recent history in Argentina, Chile, Peru, and Uruguay suggests how tentative are political arrangements. Of course, some distinctions need to be made. As of this moment the Mexican state is significantly less the topic of debate than is the Brazilian. The Cuban state is clearly becoming more institutionalized while, perhaps arguably, the Chilean or even the Costa Rican one may be becoming less so. Moreover, we can certainly add that nothing remains forever in any one, particular condition. Nevertheless, one striking feature of Latin America is that the formal process of decisionmaking commands a good deal less legitimacy and a good deal more debate than is true, for instance, of the United States.

As a corollary to the general tentativeness of the political process, the formal policy process tends to vary, often significantly, from policy to policy. This is true not only in the sense that different types of policy will generate different configurations of conflict, as predicted by the policy perception model. It is true also in the extent to which the process of decisionmaking for a policy issue tends to follow a regularized pattern or, instead, is characterized by ad hoc procedures. For instance, in fiscal and especially monetary policymaking, reasonably well-developed and defined structures through which decisions are made exist in most countries. In an area like labor relations, this is usually not the case (Anderson 1967:131).

In addition to problems of institutionalization, several other factors, previously noted, work to inject distortions and disturbances in the policy process. Although the policy process often works fairly smoothly when demands emanate from well-organized representatives of upper- and middle-class interests, the process often bogs down when demands come from lower-class groups. In the latter case, either the groups are poorly organized and thus present demands in a disorganized and often ambiguous fashion or the leadership presents the demands in ideological, grandiose, and radical terms (Anderson 1967:121–131). The labor organizations of Argentina are perhaps a classic illustration of this point. The tendency is for them to assume a confrontational stance and to present demands in such a way that decisionmakers are faced with ideologically defined redistributive or "emotive-symbolic" issues. Though there are certainly times when sweeping demands, such as an overhaul of the entire employer-employee relationship, are in order, more often than not labor's style of demand making simply turns the whole process into a giant shouting match.

When issue formation and demand making involve the rural poor an added difficulty emerges. As we pointed out in the previous chapter, the vast gap that exists in values and reference points between peasants and government officials almost inevitably means that there will be misunderstanding. The difficulties of communication frequently lead the peasant group simply to drop out of the process; less frequently the communication problem serves to radicalize the group and, as with the more common labor situation, leads to a confrontational style of decisionmaking.

The increasingly vociferous and radicalized nature of demand making by labor and peasant groups is one of the principal reasons, perhaps the principal reason, for the increasing tendency toward a corporatist style of politics and policymaking, as suggested in Chapter 1—especially a corporatist style under military control. This is likely to continue until either sufficient economic growth can be established so that labor and peasant demands do not always have to be perceived in redistributive terms, or a sudden and massive redistribution of political and economic power occurs through revolution.

Certainly, the clashes between students and police in Mexico in 1968 and 1973, the clashes between labor and government troops in Peru in 1974 and 1975, and the perpetual conflict between *peronista* labor unions and the military in Argentina, among others, can be cited as examples of the "radicalized" nature of much demand making and the breakdown of the policy process, but we should note that these are not typical of most issues. We hasten to make this point because the U.S. press portrays Latin America as a constant series of coups, revolutions, and student and worker uprisings. In fact, most issues are handled in a rather quiet and generally routine manner. Most decisionmaking occurs within the bureaucracy, particularly within the new semiautonomous agencies. Normally, this includes direct interest representation by groups and individuals expressing values of industrial, business, and other influential and "modern sector" groups (Anderson 1967:128).

Finally, it behooves us to take note of some internation differences in the policymaking process. First, let us discuss some of the more cogent differences between the authoritarian regimes and the democratic ones. In the democratic countries the extent of "independent" interest representation and demand making are more extensive. In the authoritarian states interest groups tend to be tied directly to the state. Only some of the business and industrial interests appear to have autonomy, though in Brazil this is questionable, and in Cuba group autonomy is not permitted. Moreover, in authoritarian regimes political parties are proscribed, as in the case of Chile; are part of the government, as in the case of Cuba; or are structured so that one dominant party functions much as does the party in Cuba, while others are allowed to exist but are tightly controlled. This last situation has existed in Mexico since the 1920s and has been attempted in Brazil.

Not only is demand making more complex in democratic states but so is the policy formulation stage. This is true primarily because only in the democratic states does the legislature play a meaningful role in developing and deciding upon policy options. In the authoritarian states, virtually all policy formulation takes place within the executive branch.

The last difference to be noted has to do with the different ways in which regimes react to mass demands. In general, the democratic states are more willing to listen to, or at least accept the legitimacy of, mass demands than is true of the authoritarian states. Brazilian repression of worker demands, Peru's attempts to control mass demands in a corporative organization, and Mexico's success at corporative and co-optative control, along with occasional repression, differ rather notably from the real need to court mass votes in Venezuela and Costa Rica.

Reaction to mass demands, however, suggests differences among the authoritarian regimes. In a political system like Mexico's, the government will react to mass demands if the group is well organized and can demonstrate a good deal of power. In cases where a rightist military is in control, as in Brazil and Chile, the "regime regards demand-making from below as, in principle, subversive" (Portes 1979:21). Finally, in leftist, revolutionary systems, such as Cuba, the regime will react positively to a wide range of mass needs, usually in the areas of education, medical care, housing, and agrarian reform, while controlling mass demands.

[3]
Policymaking in Military Regimes

At the purely descriptive, concrete level, it is fairly easy to identify a military government. Put in an obvious and perhaps deceptively simple fashion, a military government is one in which the military dominates the government. We say that a military government exists in an operative sense when the following two criteria are met: The presidency and most or all cabinet positions are held by members of the armed forces; members of the armed forces control appointments to governmental positions. The central notion of a military government is that the military *as an institution* governs. That the president is a military officer, for instance, is not a sufficient indicator to label a government "military." In fact, many Latin American countries (as well as the United States) have had generals or exgenerals as presidents but with little (direct) involvement in governing by the armed forces.

Although the concept of military government is not hard to identify, the broader theoretical framework for decisionmaking in such a government has been more difficult to establish. For instance, as we detail in Chapters 6 and 7, there is a vast amount of disagreement among scholars as to whether or not military governments tend to produce essentially similar policies. Likewise, there is no complete agreement about answers to the question, do military governments make policy in a similar fashion? As our discussion notes, there are some differences to be found between Brazilian policymaking since 1964 and Peruvian policymaking between 1968 and 1975. In both cases, the military governed. But in Brazil civilians have played a significant role in policymaking; in Peru they played a generally minor role. Differences in the degree of centralization of policymaking, in relations with the Left, and in the extent of repression also exist.

Yet, one might very well wish to argue that of greater import is the number of similarities among military governments. Brian Loveman and Thomas Davies, Jr., in the introductory essay to their book of readings on military government in Latin America, characterize military rule as one of "antipolitics" in which power is held by the military and a few civilians, and "normal political life" is eliminated in order to solve economic problems rationally.

One widely held assumption of Latin American military officers, and one also shared by many conservative civilian groups, was that "politics" was largely responsible for the poverty, instability, and economic backwardness of their nations. This assumption was not new, nor did it originate in all cases within military circles, but the depolitization of "politics" and the establishment of an administrative regime to forge an organic, hierarchically structured polity provided a crucial ideological link between civilian propertied interests and military modernizers.

Acceptance of this ideology of antipolitics also entailed the denial of the legitimacy of labor protest, strikes, political party claims of representing diverse interests, and, more generally, of opposition to government authority, policies, and programs. Order, obedience, authority, and stability—cherished values of the Hispanic socioeconomic elites—not only dovetailed neatly with the spirit of military training but also provided easy rationalizations for military rule (1978:4–5).

As you read the material in this chapter, and compare it with other materials you have read on the military, you can begin to determine if there is a pattern to military rule. Are military governments essentially similar or dissimilar in their policymaking behaviors? Do they have more in common with each other than with other forms of government? Can we explain the similarities and differences and do these explanations suggest an underlying theory of military rule?

To reiterate a point made in the preface: We have selected Brazil and Peru in 1968–1975 because they represent—at least on the surface—very different varieties of military rule. Military rule in Brazil has been highly repressive and completely oriented to promoting economic growth. By contrast, many referred to the Peruvian government under General Juan Velasco as "leftist" or "reformist." Therefore, if we nevertheless detect underlying commonalities, we can begin to develop a model of military governance.

Brazil

THE PRE-1964 POLICY PROCESS

For quite some time, and certainly since the early twentieth century, the Brazilian state has been an active and interventionist one. In his excellent review of modern Brazilian politics, Riordan Roett refers to the state in Brazil not only as interventionist but also as paternalistic and authoritarian (1972:51).

Within this paternalistic state, major decisions generally were controlled by an elite consisting of sugar plantation owners, cattle ranchers, and coffee growers, representing the economic side; and upper-level bureaucrats and military leaders, representing the permanent bureaucracy (cf. Roett 1972:53). To these groups, one might add church leaders, though their power seems to have been less stable and exercised more through a generalized and diffuse influence on values. A pervasive system of patronage and influence peddling served to tie the elites together—not that intraelite conflict didn't occur—and then extended the ties from the elite to the middle class. Urban populism in turn served to link middle-class politicians (and by extension the elite) to many elements of the working class and poor. In the countryside, most nonelites were effectively kept under control by the vast power wielded by the major plantation and ranch owners.

The two periods prior to the current one are worth noting, for together they illustrate both the continuities and the changes in the process of policymaking and in the participants. In the first period, from 1930 until his overthrow in 1945, Getúlio Vargas dominated an increasingly authoritarian and personalistic regime. Following his ouster, the second period began, and Brazil experimented with electoral democracy until the *golpe* of 1964.

In 1930, a series of military uprisings led to the deposition of the president, Washington Luis, and the creation of a transitional military council, or junta. A short time later, the junta was dissolved and the reins of government were presented to one of the rebel leaders, Getúlio Vargas.

Vargas moved to create a highly structured, authoritarian state along corporatist lines. (See Chapter 1 for a discussion of corporatism.) What Vargas wanted was a government, led by himself and a permanent cadre of high-level bureaucrats, that would make all major decisions. These decisions then would be transmitted to an essentially passive populace through the corporatist hierarchy. An influential spokesman for Vargas put forth the point this way: "Docile submission to the authority of the State is not repugnant and cannot be repugnant to normal individuals, for they intuitively understand that in order for a people to transform itself into a nation, it must organize itself into a hierarchical structure" (quoted in Erickson 1979:154).

The Vargas era involved more forces than just his own ego. The Vargas coup was as much a product of middle-class, urban, military officers' frustration with an outmoded, rural-based regime as it was a result of Vargas's personal frustrations at having been robbed of the presidency in rigged elections. Besides being backed by the military, Vargas also was supported by the urban industrialists who were just beginning to obtain economic wealth but who were often denied social position and political power by the rural elite. Vargas wanted to industrialize Brazil; the industrialists sought political influence. The "marriage" was successfully consummated. Ranchers and plantation owners no longer ran the government but remained almost invincible in the countryside and still exerted some influence in the capital. The old elite, in other words, was not destroyed. It was simply forced to make room for a few more participants.

In addition to the industrialists and middle-class bureaucrats and officers, Vargas eventually was tied to and supported by most of organized labor. But in this case, the relationship was clearly unequal. Certainly, organized labor benefited from Vargas, especially in wage negotiations and in the development of a social security system. Labor, however, did not directly participate in or consistently exercise influence over policymaking. Only after the demise of Vargas's *Estado Novo* (New State) in 1945 did organized labor seek to exert independent influence and come to be perceived as a real threat to elite control.

With the defeat of Hitler and Mussolini in World War II, corporatist-style governments became most unfashionable. Vargas himself recognized this and promised to reorient the political system to permit free elections. When he seemed to be reneging on his promises, his erstwhile supporters in the military moved to the opposition and Vargas was ousted.

Following the involuntary (and temporary) retirement of Vargas, Brazil embarked on its most democratic voyage. Competitive elections were held in 1945 for the presidency and were again held in 1950 (won by Vargas), 1955, and 1960. Elections were held for many other offices, including national and state legislatures and state governors. Three major parties vied for control of elections: the Social Democratic Party (PSD), Brazilian Labor Party (PTB), and the National Democratic Union (UDN).

In spite of the institutionalized appearance of Brazilian democracy from 1945–1964, the period is probably most accurately characterized as a populist democracy. Generally, this period witnessed the development of a kind of dual political system. At the local or regional level, there were a number of popular, populist politicians seeking to dominate a particular area; nevertheless, at the national level major decisions tended to be controlled by the elite network brought into existence by Vargas.

BRAZIL: POLICYMAKING SINCE 1964

In 1964, the populist system was abruptly terminated. In its place the military created a new system that has been highly authoritarian and repressive. From the takeover in 1964 until the late 1960s, the military consistently moved to increase its control over policymaking. High-ranking officials in the military chose candidates for the presidency from among themselves (see Flynn 1978:438; Schneider 1971:120–121, 298–299). Congress was controlled first by intimidation, then by utilizing indirect elections, and finally by outright closure. The military also sought to control the selection of state governors, members of state legislatures and, of course, officials of the bureaucracy.

The zenith of such blatantly repressive methods of control was reached with the invocation of Institutional Act Number Five in December 1968, which gave "authority" to the military to do whatever it wanted. The president (always a high-ranking general since 1964) could close congress and administer state and local governments. Individuals could be deprived of their political rights and habeas corpus was suspended. With this instrument in place, the military government went on a binge of arrests, tortures, expulsions, exilings, and the like. Moreover, the political parties of the populist period had been disbanded and were replaced by two military-approved parties: the government-backed National Renovating Alliance (ARENA) and a carefully watched, "umbrella" opposition group called the Brazilian Democratic Movement (MDB).

The military also came to dominate the labor movement. Virtually the entire union leadership was removed and replaced by either military officials or civilians hand-picked by the military. Kenneth Erickson put it aptly in his study of organized labor in Brazil: "The military simply decapitated the radical labor movement" (1977:158). Henceforth, the military would carefully monitor labor activity and would tolerate no attempts to disrupt the careful and well-planned efforts to place the burden of capital formation on labor.

Clearly, by the end of the 1960s, policymaking was not influenced by parties, legislatures, elections, or unions. The principal policymaking institutions were dominated by the military and military-approved civilian technocrats. The top-level policymaking bodies have become the presidency, the Chief of Staff of the Armed Forces, the National Security Council, and the National Information Service (SNI), a kind of combined CIA and FBI. Collectively, the people who sit in the top positions in each of these organizations seem to have prime responsibility for setting the direction of public policy and for monitoring the activities of other organizations. But to suggest that these high-ranking military officials alone control policymaking would be misleading.

From the beginning, the military has allied itself with industrialists and growth-oriented, civilian technocrats. The Superior War College (ESG) was not just a place for military officers; indeed, as many civilians as military personnel attended and taught at the ESG. Moreover, for high-level policymaking positions and in the middle-level bureaucracy, the military appointed many highly educated civilians, like Roberto Campos, Antônio Delfim Netto, and Mario Henrique Simonsen, to help map out and implement policy. This has been particularly true in the area of economic policy.

The technocrat-bureaucrat is not the only civilian involved in making policy. Industrialists have had significant influence over certain policy decisions. As Chapter 6 makes clear, the Brazilian military has made economic growth and industrial modernization its top priorities. To accomplish these goals, the military necessarily has had to turn to local, and especially foreign, capital. In his study of "dependent development" in Brazil, Peter Evans convincingly shows that a number of major economic decisions have been taken either in direct collaboration with important industrial firms or in order to help develop the infrastructure to permit industrial development (1979). Another study notes that in the process of making a 1974 decision to emphasize import substitution of capital goods, there were close links between certain government agencies and "major, private associations in the machine building, electrical, and heavy-industry fields" (Dye and Souza 1979:91). However, it is the state, through both its civilian and its military technocrats, which seems to dominate the relationship—at least as it applies to the making of specific, explicit policy decisions. In summarizing his study of a wide range of energy policymaking, Kenneth Erickson writes: "In setting the direction for the national economy, state policy makers have easily overshadowed the Brazilian bourgeoisie in a pattern of domination consistent with the nation's historical experience" (1981:163). Whether the Brazilian state is so powerful in its relationship with foreign, especially U.S., capital is another matter. In this regard the evidence is not so persuasive.

Although the state tends to dominate policymaking, it is important to note that it is neither a monolithic state nor a monolithic military that dominates. As the state has expanded its role in the economy, assuming not only increased control functions but also greatly extending its entrepreneurial and managerial roles, the number of state agencies has grown rapidly. According to one count, there were 571 state firms in 1976 (Hewlett 1980:110). This great expansion has had the consequence of decentralizing a good deal of decisionmaking, despite the centralized policymaking structure.

Conflicts that demonstrate that even the military is not a monolithic entity have also occurred within the military. Probably the most frequently cited case of internal military conflict occurred during the latter part of 1968. A debate of significant proportions had emerged between those seeking a short-term military rule (the moderates) and those wishing for an indefinite period of military rule (the hardliners). This debate was joined by another dispute between those who emphasized the need for economic growth based on the modern sector of the economy and those who believed that the government must develop the poorer regions of the country, especially the northeast. General Alfonso Albuquerque Lima, then minister of interior and very popular with many of the younger officers, arose as the leading spokesman for the hardline view and for the need to develop the underdeveloped areas. Albuquerque Lima's position, however, ran counter to the president's preferences, and, in January 1969, Albuquerque Lima was forced out of office (see, e.g., Flynn 1978a:419).

Conflict between so-called hardliners and moderates has, in fact, been a constant of Brazilian politics ever since the 1964 takeover. The dispute surfaces during each presidential "campaign" period and periodically during each administration. Initially, the moderates seemed to have had the upper hand, but by the close of the 1960s, the hardliners were in control—the Albuquerque Lima episode notwithstanding. More recently, the moderates have been ascendant.

In March 1979, General João Baptista de Oliveira Figueiredo became the fifth president of Brazil since the military takeover. General Figueiredo was picked by outgoing president General Ernesto Geisel to carry on the "slow, gradual, and sure" process of return to civilian, democratic politics (Sanders 1981:181). Under Geisel and Figueiredo, the party system has again been reorganized. ARENA and MDB were abolished; the former was replaced by the (inappropriately named) Social Democratic Party (PSD), and the MDB by a number of independently organized, opposition parties. Congress has been reconvened, though still emasculated. Amnesty has been granted to a large number of former political exiles and prisoners and there has been a noticeable increase in political activity. In November 1982, elections were held for congress, governors, state legislators, and a large number of mayors. While the government did engage in some fraudulent practices to limit opposition victories, the opposition was allowed to campaign and did well.

Fundamentally though, as of early 1984, the primary elements of the decisionmaking structure have not been altered. However, the march to redemocratization (probably along populist lines once again) now seems to be unstoppable; some substantial modifications in policymaking are inevitable in the near future.

Peru

THE PRE-1968 POLICY PROCESS

The state in Brazil has been an activist one for several decades at least; in contrast, the Peruvian state has become activist only in the last few decades. For most of its existence since achieving independence in 1824, the state, and especially the government, in Peru has been greatly restricted and quiescent, essentially the plaything of wealthy landowners and *caudillos* (military leaders).

During the first two decades of independence, political action was dominated by two very different types: the heads of families owning vast tracts of land in the Sierra and along the coast, and self-appointed *caudillos,* often from a lower-class background. These two frequently went their own way (see Astiz 1969:33–37). By the mid-nineteenth century, close ties were established between the landowning oligarchy and the *caudillos.* This produced a pattern in which *caudillos* (and during a later period, professionally trained generals) would serve as presidents while most of the rest of the state was dominated by the oligarchy. From independence until 1968, Peru had seventy-six presidents. Of these, fifty were either *caudillos* or modern generals. Peru did not have a civilian president until 1872 (Astiz 1969:131). In spite of this presidential history, it would be a mistake to see Peruvian policy as dominated by the military.

From the time before independence until about the second decade of the twentieth century, preponderant political power has been held by those owning the very large haciendas in the high country (the Sierra) and those owning the large cotton and sugar plantations along the coast. In his definitive study of pre-1968 Peruvian politics, François Bourricaud said: "In the nineteenth and early twentieth centuries, a small group of families took all essential decisions for the country without paying much attention to the opinions or desires of the masses" (1967:16).

Beginning in the early twentieth century, policymaking became a bit more complicated. First, a major foreign actor arrived on the scene in the form of the International Petroleum Company (IPC), a subsidiary of Standard Oil of New Jersey. Adalberto Pinelo, who documents the development and political power of the IPC, shows that IPC was effective in obtaining numerous concessions and in vetoing policies against its interests (1973).

But Standard Oil was not the only important North American actor. U.S. private capital became heavily involved in mining, land ownership, and, later, in industry and finance. By the end of the second decade of the twentieth century, U.S. involvement in Peru had become quite open. In fact, President Augusto Leguía (1908–1912, 1919–1930) appointed U.S. citizens to top government positions, including the leadership of the Ministry of Education and Air Force chief (Astiz 1969:235–237).

As time went on, close relationships developed between various representatives of the U.S. government, especially the military, and representatives of the Peruvian government. Thus, both U.S. corporations and the U.S. government played active roles in policymaking.

Following World War II, the policymaking scene was further complicated by the growing diversification of the economy and the political-economic elite (see Quijano 1971:50–55). Growth in the size of the urban population in general, and specifically in the urban middle class and blue-collar groups, led to a growth in consumer-oriented industry. The growth in industry in turn led to a broadening of the financial, transportation, and service sectors. By the beginning of the 1960s, the Peruvian economy, though still quite underdeveloped, was clearly moving beyond a purely agro-extractive one. In addition, the period between the mid-1950s and the *golpe* in 1968 witnessed an increase in the number of political parties, labor unions, and peasant organizations.

In spite of this trend toward economic diversification and political pluralism, the process of policymaking and the content of policy changed little. Those who based their economic fortunes entirely, or primarily, on landholdings in the Sierra lost a good deal of political power by the 1960s. In contrast, the coastal landowners, especially the so-called "sugar aristocracy," extended their power either by direct involvement in financial and industrial pursuits or by allying—sometimes through marriage—with those active in the financial and industrial sectors (Bourricaud 1967:40).

Two other policy actors helped guarantee the elite's dominance of policy. One, and certainly the most important domestic ally, was the military. As an ally of the economic elite, the military provided the armed force to prevent any serious challenge to the system by disgruntled oligarchs, reformist political parties, or peasant uprisings. Whether the military stayed in the barracks or forced its way into the presidential palace, it consistently behaved to protect the interests of the elite. As we shall see, however, the military began to change its relationship to the elite in the early 1960s.

Following World War II, the elite picked up an unlikely ally, the American Popular Revolutionary Alliance (APRA). This group was founded in 1924 by Victor Raúl Haya de la Torre as a reformist, anti-imperialist party with a strong base among rural workers (Hilliker 1971:15–21). For years APRA competed in elections only to find victories denied by the elite and the military. By the late 1940s, however, Haya de la Torre, and others in APRA, seemed to move to the Right to reach an accommodation with the elite. By the mid-1950s this accommodation was made explicit. Though Haya de la Torre continued to be denied the presidency, APRA came to be the major party in the congress. But at this period APRA used its position to defend, rather than attack, elite-initiated policies (see, e.g., Bourricaud 1967:337–339).

As of the early 1960s, then, policymaking in Peru was dominated by a power elite composed of the sugar aristocracy, financiers, and industrialists, all linked rather closely, the military, a few U.S. corporations, and representatives of the U.S. government. On major political issues, especially those dealing with agrarian reform, industrial ownership, and mass participation, the elite usually shared a common set of values. Occasionally, and especially on less critical issues, intraelite conflict would erupt. For instance, several landowning families resented the power and "crass materialism" of foreign capitalists, and IPC in particular (Pinelo 1973:15–21, 53).

The first dissent to the dominance of the elite that signified a potentially serious alteration of policymaking occurred with the 1962 *golpe*. In that year the military intervened to deny APRA an electoral victory. The intervention was nothing new. What was new, however, was that in preventing APRA from taking control of the government, the military was stopping an ally of the elite, not a reformist party. Moreover, during its first few months in power, the military made it clear that it felt that economic modernization and social reform were overdue in Peru. In other words, "In 1962 the army was in power but not, for once, as an instrument of the oligarchy . . ." (Bourricaud 1967:315). The military remained in power for only a short time and returned power to civilians.

POLICYMAKING DURING THE VELASCO YEARS (1968-1975)

A large number of factors, including those of narrow, personal, and institutional interests, caused the military to intervene in October 1968 and grasp the reins of government. Among all the causes, military experience with peasant poverty, guerrilla uprisings, and the abuse of rural workers by the wealthy were critical in shaping military action from 1968 until about 1975. In the remainder of this section, we concentrate our attention on outlining the process of policymaking during those years.

The October *golpe* was an army coup, spearheaded by several generals and colonels and led by General Juan Velasco Alvarado. Once the army took control of the government it brought the navy and air force into the governing junta. From the beginning, the Peruvian military regime (1968-1975) differed from the Brazilian in that in Peru civilians played a more minor role. As the military consolidated its control during October and November, almost all key policymaking positions were given to uniformed officers (see Stepan 1978:312). (One notable exception was the civilian Carlos Delgado who came to be the regime's prime architect for participation policies.) In addition to the presidency, the military monopolized cabinet positions and administrative control of the territorial units, and dominated the body that had continuous and easy access to Velasco, the Presidential Advisory Committee (COAP). Of course, the Velasco government was never completely isolated from civilian support, nor did it—nor could it even if it wanted to—exclude civilians from important administrative positions. Throughout much of the period, the Velasco government also received support from the Communist Party and "leftist" unions.

Civilians staffed most positions in the bureaucracy and, therefore, were important in implementing policy. In addition, various left-of-center intellectuals and former party activists assisted in developing policy ideas and served as speech writers, propagandists, and ideologues for the regime. In spite of all this, the policy process was dominated by military officials, and civilians took a back seat. Peru, under Velasco, had no equivalent of Roberto Campos or Antônio Delfim Netto.

Even with such military dominance, the Peruvian policy process exhibited as much dissension and conflict as did the Brazilian—in fact, probably even more. As was true in Brazil, so in Peru we find a military college, the Center for Higher Military Studies (CAEM), helping to develop and disseminate the notion that internal security and international respect depended upon the military's assuming control of the government and promoting economic modernization. Though the CAEM seems to have been less important in Peru than was the ESG in Brazil, CAEM did help foster a consensus about military-led economic development. However, there was a good deal of dissension about the nature of the development program. Soon after the coup there emerged several conflicts about the direction and extensiveness of the reform effort.

Early in 1969 President Velasco dismissed a number of cabinet members and replaced them with officers whose views generally were closer to his own. This did not end the problem of reaching consensus within the policy elite, though by mid-1969 until about mid-1973 a broader consensus existed than had previously.

For much of his administration, Velasco successfully encouraged a centralized decisionmaking process. Two entities stood as the core of the process: Velasco himself and COAP. Initially, there were eight members of COAP; later this expanded to twelve. On the really critical issues, especially agrarian reform and industrial reorganization, policies were formulated primarily by Velasco and COAP with limited participation by the Council of Ministers and a few advisors. On "lesser" issues, the number of participants would increase but, generally, only to include a broader range of bureaucrats. On a few occasions, as in the development of some policies with respect to education or the urban shantytowns, individuals outside the government would play a role in helping to formulate policy. But this was rare.

One widely shared characteristic of the policy actors ought to be noted. When Velasco, or other uniformed bureaucrats turned to civilians for policy advice, or appointed civilians to government positions, they tended to go to *técnicos*. According to Cleaves and Scurrah, at the upper levels of the bureaucracy approximately 75 percent of the appointments went to *técnicos* (military and civilian) (1980:80).

Even though much of the policy-formulation phase occurred in a centralized and closed fashion—even secretive, as in the development of the 1970 Industrial Law—the implementation phase often generated a good deal of reaction and, therefore, a more "open" political process. This is very much like what Grindle describes in the Mexican policy process (see Chapter 5). In fact, this may be typical of all authoritarian regimes. In any event, policy implementation obviously cannot occur entirely in secret since this is the point at which representatives of the state come into direct contact with the public. Let us look briefly at an illustration. The case study in this book by McClintock provides a more detailed illustration of the point.

One of the more critical policies of the Velasco period was the Industrial Law, issued in September 1970. The Industrial Law was a very broad policy that sought, among other things, to reconstruct the industrial sector to allow for social and state, as well as private, ownership; to provide for worker participation in decisionmaking at the plant level; and to establish guidelines for state investment in industry (see Fitzgerald 1979:284–288). This policy was formulated entirely within the government. Conflict did occur among some ministers, but the more "radical" members of COAP seemed to have pretty well controlled the drafting. Once the law was publicly announced, there was a tremendous uproar from the business community. Eventually, several provisions were modified and the concept of worker participation greatly weakened (Philip 1978:124–125).

Three final points should be made about policymaking in Peru under General Velasco. On virtually all of the critical policies, both demand making and agenda setting were controlled by the military. For instance, although the 1969 Agrarian Reform Law was in part designed to help rural workers and the 1970 Industrial Law was partially designed to benefit urban workers, the policies were reactions to what Velasco and a few of his advisors wanted. Neither policy can be said to have resulted from demands by workers, except in the most indirect and implicit sense. The demands from people outside the government that were heeded were the type triggered by the announcement of a law or decree, i.e., demands in reaction to implementation.

The second concluding point to be made is that Velasco and the military seemed to have attempted a rational policymaking process. Like their Brazilian counterparts, so in Peru did the military leaders try to make policymaking an exercise in order, rationality, and technical expertise—once given the military elite's definition of the problems. This explains the hiring of so many *técnicos* and the great increase in the amount of resources devoted to planning. To a significant degree, agenda setting and formulation did occur rationally. But the process of implementation was another matter; in this area we find a more pluralistic and incremental reality.

Finally, we note that during the last two years of the Velasco administration the policy process tended to fragment and the original conflict between "conservatives" and "radicals" reemerged. Three principal reasons may be cited for this growing fragmentation and conflict. First, the Velasco government failed to establish much organized support for the regime. The government created an organization, the National System to Support Social Mobilization, popularly known by its acronym SINAMOS, designed to organize the people in a massive, corporatist structure. But this failed soon after its creation and nothing arose to replace it.

A second factor, and one which exacerbated the first, was the declining health of the economy during the last few Velasco years. Increasing costs of oil imports and a decline in revenue for sugar and fishmeal, along with increased inflation, forced the military to cut back on several reforms and led to criticism of the military. Actually, the combination of these two factors created a situation in which there was hardly any popular support for Velasco during his last year.

Lastly, in March 1973, Velasco became seriously ill. From that point on his control over public policy consistently declined. Conservatives in the army and, especially, the navy, took advantage of his weakened and depressed condition and moved to counter Velasco's "radicalism." This culminated in a coup in August 1975 in which Juan Velasco Alvarado was replaced by the more conservative General Francisco Morales Bermudez. General Morales continued in the presidency until July 1980 when the military, with a touch of historical irony, returned power to a civilian government headed by the very man they overthrew in 1968, Fernando Belaúnde Terry.

CASE STUDY

Social Welfare Programs in the Brazilian Amazon, 1970–1975

STEPHEN G. BUNKER

One issue central to analysis of present authoritarian regimes involves their ability to instigate and direct social and economic changes that tend toward "modernization" or development (O'Donnell 1978; Malloy 1977). Another issue for analysis of authoritarian regimes has been their power and autonomy vis-à-vis different sectors of society and their potential for stabilizing, institutionalizing, and legitimating control (see Portes 1979; Schwartzman 1977). Theories of the corporatist state and, especially, of the bureaucratic-authoritarian state have dealt with both of these issues, primarily in terms of the political and social processes accompanying accelerated industrialization. In this essay I argue that various theories of the authoritarian state may exaggerate both its developmental potential and its degree of autonomy from the dominant civil sectors. To substantiate this argument, I present evidence of distortions and failures in recent colonization and rural development programs in Pará, the easternmost state of the Brazilian Amazon.

In order to assess the state's developmental capacity and autonomy, I distinguish between two kinds of developmental programs and policies: those that are of interest not only to the state but also to dominant and civil sectors and those that are of interest only to the state and to portions of the politically excluded popular sectors. The latter are aimed primarily at stabilization and legitimacy. I make this distinction because the only way to analyze the state's autonomy and independent developmental capacity is to isolate cases in which the state's interests and the dominant sectors' interests diverge. The state's primary need for legitimacy is with the dominant sectors; it can achieve this through political and technical competence in promoting economic growth. Social welfare programs designed to legitimate the state may, however, diverge from dominant sector or class interests and create oppositions between these interests and those of the state.

Restraints on the Authoritarian State

Theories of the authoritarian state in Latin America assume that recent political developments represent the emergence of forms of government not adequately explained by previous theory. One of the most comprehensive treatments of this idea is Guillermo O'Donnell's (1975; 1977; 1978) theory of the bureaucratic-authoritarian state (henceforth, BA). Drawing primarily on data from Brazil, Chile, and Argentina, but including both Mexico and Uruguay as well, O'Donnell (1978:6) lists as defining characteristics of the BA:

1. Occupation of higher government positions by persons who come to them after successful careers in complex and highly bureaucratized organizations—the armed forces, the public bureaucracy, and private firms;
2. Political exclusion, through the closing of channels of political access to the popular sector and its allies both by repression and by the imposition of vertical controls on organizations such as trade unions;
3. Economic exclusion, by the reduction or indefinite postponement of the popular sector's economic participation;
4. Depolitization, by the pretension to reduce social and political issues to "technical" problems to be resolved by interaction between state-controlled organizations;
5. Correspondence to a stage of important transformations in the mechanisms of capital accumulation, which are part of a "deepening" process of a peripheral and dependent capitalism characterized by extensive industrialization.

Other features (O'Donnell 1975; 1977) include military predominance, the priority of security goals such as the elimination of subversion and of popular sector agitation, the attempt to create a politically and economically attractive environment for international capital investment, the progressive concentration of income in the upper classes, and a tendency toward bureaucratic expansion and technocratic decisionmaking.

Alejandro Portes (1979), in his study of public policies toward the urban slums (*favelas*) in Rio de Janeiro, examines the constraints that the need for legitimacy imposes on the BA together with the restrictions on its autonomy and efficiency that result from the organization of its own bureaucracy and from the penetration of dominant class interests in its legitimacy-seeking programs. Like the *favela* eradication programs, rural development can be defined as legitimacy seeking. The *favela* eradication programs, if successful in terms of their stated purposes, could be used by the BA to demonstrate that it is capable of improving living standards for the excluded urban poor. Similarly, if successful, the rural development programs, by turning landless peasants into middle-level capitalists, could be used to argue that the BA's imposed economic model is accessible to all classes and an apt vehicle for social as well as economic development.

The BA could use such an incorporation of rural poor into its economic model to demonstrate its capacity to solve one of Brazil's most dramatic and highly publicized social problems. The exploitation of the rural poor by both the rural propertied class and the commercial sector, especially in the drought-prone Northeast, has been a major target of criticism of Brazilian society. It has formed an important part of the national literary tradition, has received considerable attention in both the national and international press, and has been the focus of studies and projects of various international agencies, including the Food and Agriculture Organization (FAO), and the Organization of American States (OAS), as well as of aid missions from different countries. It can also be defined as a legacy of colonial traditions. Successful rural development programs would therefore be especially effective in the BA's search for legitimacy, as they could be used both as a response to national and international criticism and as an affirmation of the BA's superiority over previous governments.

The intended effect of *favela* eradication and of rural development programs is merely demonstration. The proportion of the rural and urban poor actually affected by either type of program, even if maximally successful, would be too small to change overall patterns of income distribution, and thus would pose no direct threat to the dominant sectors' privileged access to economic resources.

The BA's need for legitimacy requires that these programs succeed. Indeed, the publicity with which the BA inaugurates such programs makes their failure especially harmful to its attempt to legitimate itself. To the extent that the dominant sectors are able to penetrate these programs and profit from the infrastructure they create and from the funds they receive, the programs tend to be diverted from the BA's original purposes. In this sense, such programs represent a clear conflict between the BA's interests and those of the dominant private sectors.

Central Government Policy and Peripheral Land Tenure Institutions

Rural development programs in Pará, in addition to being marginal to dominant political and economic interests, are hampered by a set of institutions deriving from the Amazon's historically peripheral position in relation to the south-central region of Brazil. The 59 percent of national territory officially defined as *Amazonia* contains only about 8 percent of the national population and produces only about 4 percent of its income (INCRA 1972). Only within the last two decades has the Amazon had road connections to the rest of Brazil, and there are still large areas, including the capital of one of the territories, accessible only by water or by air.

The most recent national and regional development plans both clearly envision the Amazon's function in the national economy as helping to improve Brazil's balance of payments through large-scale lumber, mineral, and ranching enterprises oriented to the international market, contributing both renewable and nonrenewable natural resources to permit the continued rapid industrialization and economic growth, which is primarily centered in the south-central area (Brasil 1974; 1975). Though Pará is somewhat favored in relation to the rest of the region by including the major Amazon port as well as its major financial and administrative center, these effects are largely limited to the capital city, Belem, and to its immediate hinterland. The rest of Pará's 1,248,042 square kilometers are still sparsely settled, little developed, and very much subject to extraregional economic interests.

The peripheral position of the Amazon, and specifically of Pará, within the national context has two important effects. First, as a region, it is much more subordinate than determinant in terms of economic planning (Mahar 1979). Few of its major industries are locally based, and despite the existence of regional planning agencies, official development policy tends to originate in Brasilia. Second, the capitalist forms of production and exchange, together with their corresponding relations and institutions, while firmly established in large parts of the agricultural and industrial sectors of the south-central region, are still incipient or nonexistent in much of the Amazon, especially in the rural area (see Santos 1977; Sawyer 1977). The forms of mercantile capitalism that have flourished in the region, based largely on the commercialization of such extractive products as rubber and Brazil nuts, have favored the accumulation of capital in the urban centers at the cost of high rates of appropriation that help keep the actual extractive gatherers in debt servitude to long chains of monopolistic intermediaries. The major exceptions to this form of extractive economy have been sizable ranches with very low levels of capitalization. Like the extractive economy, traditional ranching is subject to systems of commercialization in which intermediaries control almost all the capital and appropriate most of the surplus generated.

Land tenure institutions in Pará have reflected the precapitalist modes of production general to the region. The national civil codes on property functioned only in those areas, primarily urban, in which capitalist development required institutional forms permitting and controlling the registered alienation of land and its use in credit transactions.

Land and control of it are important factors of wealth and power, so there were formal and informal institutions regulating its occupation and use. These included both state and *municipio* (township) deeds and authorizations to exclusive extraction rights over specified areas, as well as other rights of direct and indirect control, dating from the colonial period. Even in deeds certifying legal ownership, however, actual boundaries tended to be vague, though size might be specified.

Transfer of land rights through sale or inheritance were frequently not registered officially. The remoteness of the areas and the lack of commercial value of the land itself did not compensate the costs of journeys to administrative centers and of transactions with the seldom-present authorities. Informal institutions of land tenure based on occupation or use, and sometimes superior force, frequently superceded the neglected juridical forms of possession. Official processes were in some cases complicated by *municipio*, state, and national governments' having ceded the same land to different people at different times, even though previous rights to the land were still legally valid.

Central government decisions to connect the Amazon to the rest of Brazil with highways caused drastic changes in land use with which the existing institutions were not equipped to deal. The completion of the Belem-Brasilia highway in 1959, by providing access to unoccupied lands and guaranteeing their communications with markets, stimulated a massive migration to the newly opened areas. The first occupation was effected by dispossessed peasants from other regions, especially the Northeast.

An influx of highly capitalized ranching enterprises quickly followed. Using their greater political and economic power, and frequently violent force, the ranchers were able to take control of the land that the peasants had cleared, and exploit the labor reserve created by the expulsion of the peasants (see Velho 1976; Ianni 1977; Hebette and Acevedo 1977; Foweraker 1981).

The expansion of capitalist enterprise into these new lands disrupted the normal functioning of land tenure institutions that were not adapted to treat land as a valuable negotiable good on the scale that the sudden influx of capital required (see Mendonça 1977; Santos 1977). The state government sold vast tracts of land in a disorderly and frequently corrupt fashion. The *cartorios*, licensed land registry offices, were swamped both by legitimate requests to transfer properties flawed by previous, unregistered sales and inheritances and by demands to register and sell fraudulent titles.

The establishment of an authoritarian and centralist regime in 1964 created the conditions for further disruptions and changes in land tenure institutions. In 1968, the central government, acting through the SUDAM, Superintendency for the Development of the Amazon, extended its program of fiscal incentives to large, highly capitalized ranching enterprises in the Amazon. As the SUDAM was not obliged to consider the validity of titles for the land on which its enormous subsidies were to be applied, the immediate effect of the development program was to aggravate the already severe land tenure crisis. In 1970, the Médici government planned a system of roads through the Amazon to serve a double purpose: first, to secure the region for the nation by permitting its occupation and rapid military and commercial movement through it; second, to allow the settlement of thousands of landless and unemployed families from the drought-scourged Northeast. This plan was followed in 1971 by decree-law 1.164 by which the government imposed national control of all state lands in a 100-kilometer deep belt on each side of any federal highway already constructed, in construction, or planned in the entire Amazon region. In the case of Pará, this amounted to 30 percent of its total area.

The BA's expropriation of immense areas of the various states' public lands and the bureaucratic apparatus set up to manage and dispose of them reflect the authoritarian state's pretensions to regulate and arbitrate social and economic relations as described by Malloy and the predominance of military administrative control through bureaucratic and technocratic organization described by O'Donnell. INCRA, the National Institute of Colonization and Agrarian Reform, formed in 1970 by merging three lesser agencies, was given control over these newly acquired federal lands, with the responsibility of discriminating, surveying, selling or colonizing, and titling them. Its assigned goals were to impose an order which would control conflict between various segments of the rural population, and regularize the possession and use of land in ways conducive to economic growth within capitalist institutions of production and exchange. The INCRA, while legally an autarchy within the Ministry of Agriculture, was subordinated by decree-law 1.164 directly to the National Security Council for the determination of policy toward the administration and occupation of the federal lands in the Amazon.

An examination of the tensions among INCRA's multiple mandates illustrates the contradictions within the BA's own bureaucratic logic and its assumption that it can arrogate a position of supreme economic and social regulation and arbitration. Instead of reinforcing its capacity to carry out its assigned goals, INCRA's diverse functions subject it to unequal pressures from different sectors, pressures that tend to distort its own programs and, by extension, those of the BA.

INCRA's control over land in the Amazon is directed to six basic tasks: First, it examines claims to occupied or titled land, documenting those found to be legitimate in terms of the 1964 *Estatuto da Terra;* regularizing those whose divergence from its norms it considers to be soluble; expropriating wholly or in part those with insoluble divergences from its norms; and evaluating and paying for the improvements made on the land it expropriates. INCRA thus may validate or invalidate existing forms of occupation without recourse to legal procedures and solely in terms of its own norms. These measures most directly affect subsistence farmers or traditional ranching or extractive enterprises located in areas that INCRA has designated for other activities, such as colonization projects or large-scale capitalist ranching enterprises, or that the government has indicated for transfer to other ministries.

Second, it surveys and sells by public bidding specified areas of federal land in lots of 3,000 hectares (or more with national senate approval) for agricultural and ranching projects. Bids are subject to INCRA's approval of a five-year development plan for each lot. It retains the right to reappropriate the land if these projects are not executed within the specified time limit and guarantees the necessary financing from the *Banco do Brasil.* INCRA itself keeps all revenues from these sales. Successful bidders have generally been highly capitalized companies and individuals from the south-central region of Brazil.

INCRA's mandate to sell land directly, together with the importance of the revenues thus generated, directly links it to the interests of the national bourgeoisie. At the same time, its power to expropriate land and control its subsequent use represent the BA's interest in extending capitalist institutions and relations of production. The huge job of discriminating, surveying, selling, and titling land, once completed, would permit the full use of land as an alienable or negotiable good without the disruptive problems of prior and conflicting claims, sanctioned both by formal law and by regional custom based on use and occupation without formal title.

Third, it establishes and administers government colonization projects and supervises and regulates private colonization companies. The first ten kilometers on either side of the Transamazonic Highway were reserved for the settlement of small farmers on 100-hectare lots. INCRA was to coordinate the settlement of 100,000 families over more than 5,000 kilometers of still inaccessible jungle. From the outset, this scheme provoked criticism from the private sector and from regional development agencies in both the north and the northeast regions of Brazil. These groups feared the diversion of their own funds to pay for the huge expenses projected.

The plans for colonization responded to international and internal political pressures on the government to resolve the social and economic problems of an extremely uneven distribution of land, aggravated in the Northeast by recurrent droughts and in the south-central regions by the rapid advance of large-scale export-oriented agricultural businesses. While even the greatest numbers of colonists considered for settlement would not have taken care of more than a small proportion of the dispossessed rural population, the BA sought to legitimate itself by a massively publicized project that would both demonstrate its concern with the problem and validate its economic model by showing that it was accessible even to the traditionally poorest and least privileged sectors of Brazilian society.

Fourth, it carries out an agrarian reform as defined by the *Estatuto da Terra*, based on criteria of productivity and the "social function of land." It is charged with the resolution of conflicts over land and empowered to expropriate and redistribute land whose ownership or use is not productive or leads to social tensions. INCRA's evident reluctance to use these powers has provoked criticism that the government itself had no intention of implementing the *Estatuto da Terra*, which it created.

Fifth, it collects the national rural property tax and collects, analyzes, and publishes the necessary cadastral statistics for the whole of Brazil. INCRA keeps 20 percent of the revenues thus collected.

Sixth, it regulates all agricultural cooperatives and promotes them where they do not exist. As all government colonization projects can only be "emancipated" after the effective foundation of a cooperative to manage transport, storage, processing, and commercialization of crops, INCRA has been required to establish cooperatives along the Transamazon. Cooperative law, however, and INCRA's own bureaucratic procedures for dealing with cooperatives, are primarily geared to the large, autonomous, and highly complex cooperatives of the south-central regions rather than to the needs of small organizations whose commercial potential at the time of their foundation is usually inadequate to support the administrative costs that INCRA's own cooperative model involves.

INCRA's multiple mandates create tensions between the conflicting demands and needs of diverse sectors of the economy and society. Its partial dependence on its patrimonial revenues creates a direct pressure to favor the economically and politically more powerful sectors in its allocation of financial, administrative, and productive resources. Its capacity to respond to all of its mandates is further limited by its direct subordination to the military, which aims at assuring the maintenance of order and internal security on the BA's terms, while establishing the conditions prescribed by its model of economic and social development.

Multiple Demands on INCRA and the Failure of the Colonization Program

The problems in the BA's logic that led to INCRA's combination of diverse social, political, and economic functions with a vulnerable, patrimonial bureaucracy weigh most heavily on the programs whose clientele include the politically excluded classes, that is, colonization and agrarian reform. INCRA's patrimonial interests dictate a greater dedication to activities favoring the dominant sectors than to the expensive and difficult problems of colonization or to the politically sensitive tasks of land redistribution. Its multiple mandates have subjected it to political and economic pressures from capitalist groups interested in acquiring lands and to rapid changes in the central government's Amazon policies. The contradictions in INCRA's assigned tasks played an important part in the BA's failure to implement its own stated goals for colonization and rural development.

The BA's expressed goals for the occupation of the Amazon by small farmers represented a clear digression from the historically dominant development policy for the area, a policy that had concentrated on fiscal incentives and other supports for industry, large-scale ranching and agriculture, and mineral extraction. The SUDAM had managed all of these efforts, and the umbrella program for the colonization projects, the Program for National Integration (PIN), was to receive 30 percent of the income tax revenues for fiscal incentives from 1971 to 1974. The sudden emphasis on colonization posed an obvious threat to the SUDAM's predominant position in Amazon development programs and to the private-sector interests benefitted by these programs. The resulting competition between INCRA and the SUDAM generated several impasses between these two organs and between the various agencies that receive rural development funds from each of them.

The SUDAM programs all continued, though with reduced funding. The failures of colonization, however, provoked mounting dominant-sector criticism and opposition within the government itself. The BA's rapid retreat from the policies it proclaimed in its first (1972) Plan for the Development of the Amazon (PDA), which emphasized the settlement of small-holding farmers as the solution to social and economic problems, indicates that the BA is highly susceptible to pressures from the dominant sectors. A series of concessions to large-scale capitalist enterprise, including a new PDA in 1975 that emphasized the need to develop the Amazon through large-scale ranching and mining operations oriented to the export market, strengthens the impression that the

BA was not able or willing to resist dominant-sector demands, even where its own credibility and claims to legitimacy were at stake.

In coordination with a major national publicity campaign and the central government's political commitment to the PIN (INCRA 1972), the bulk of INCRA's activities and budget from 1970 to 1974 was dedicated to the ambitious *Projectos Integrados de Colonização* (PIC) along the Transamazonic Highway. Publicized as a program to give "land without men to men without lands," the declared purpose of these projects was to solve the problems of overpopulation in the Northeast and of *minifundios* (small landholdings) in the South. INCRA was charged with selecting the colonists who were to receive 100-hectare lots, surveying and documenting these lots, providing perpendicular access roads from the newly opened highway, housing, access to credit, transport, warehouses, health services, education, and technical assistance, both directly and in coordination with other federal agencies (Moran 1981; Smith 1982).

INCRA had enormous difficulties in coordinating all the various facets of these projects. Selection and transportation of colonists were complicated by political corruption and logistic snarls. Access roads were not built on time, and credit facilities were bogged down in bureaucratic procedures that rendered them uneconomical for most of the colonists. The geometric patterns in which the 100-hectare lots had been laid out and along which the various administrative and residential centers had been built had completely ignored problems of soil fertility, land relief, drainage, and availability of water. Seeds distributed to the colonists for their first rice crops had not been tested in the colonization areas and proved totally inadequate, causing almost total crop failure. Transport failures due to the delays in building access roads impeded the marketing of the few crops that were produced. Because of the failure of the rice crop and the losses occasioned by lack of access roads, many colonists were unable to pay back their loans and were thus prevented from using bank credit in subsequent years.

The problems encountered by INCRA and its own inadequacy in solving them reinforced both the private and the public sectors' criticisms of the colonization programs and heightened the pressure for other applications of government resources and alternative strategies for occupying the Amazon (Wood and Schmink 1978). At the same time, a number of important changes in the composition of forces within the BA itself and in its supporting alliance further undercut official support for the colonization projects. Cardoso (1975), Martins (1977), and Pereira (1977) have all described a major transition in the relations between the technocratic sector of government, or the "state bourgeoisie," the national "capitalist" bourgeoisie, and international capital. The technocratic sector had grown rapidly in size, strength, and autonomy during the years following the 1964 revolution. In the early 1970s, however, as the result of direct pressures on the BA from both national and international capital and of the penetration of key positions within the BA bureaucracy by capitalists, these sectors significantly increased their participation in determining development policy.

The colonization schemes and the policies restricting the size of landholdings in the Amazon were an immediate and relatively easy target. INCRA decided in 1972 to sell public lands in the Amazon to private interests. The minister of agriculture, Cirne Lima, resigned, protesting interference and restrictions on the colonization projects. In 1973, Moura Cavalcanti, who left the presidency of INCRA to replace Cirne Lima, stated that the Amazon occupation policy had to be changed to allow for more dynamic private initiative. Significantly, he had earlier taken a strong position against Reis Velloso, then minister of planning, and other high members of government who were urging publicly that the Amazon be occupied by large-scale private enterprise. The superintendent of the SUDAM at this time was advocating that economic integration of the Amazon could best be achieved by large ranching projects (Cardoso and Muller 1977:157–158).

Finally, in 1974, INCRA's president, Lourenço Tavares da Silva, formally acknowledged major policy changes. INCRA, he said, was opposed to *latifundios* (large estates), but not to large enterprise in itself, and the colonization projects would be oriented toward a joint composition with large and medium enterprises (cited in Cardoso and Muller 1977:181). By 1976, two presidential "expositions of motives," 005 and 006, authorized INCRA to regularize titles of up to 600,000 hectares and 3,000 hectares respectively for large and medium enterprises whose "paralyzation might hinder the economic development of the region" (cited in Santos 1977).

With the publication of the second PDA (Brasil 1975), the government explicitly abandoned the idea of developing the Amazon through the settlement of small farmers and emphasized instead the establishment of large, highly capitalized ranching and mining enterprises, which would supposedly be more effective in generating foreign revenues.

The BA's colonization policy was merely a brief digression from the historically prevalent policies that aim to develop the Amazon by offering fiscal incentives and tax relief to large-scale enterprise controlled by national and international capital. It formally endured less than five years. Informally, its duration had been even less. Well before the second PDA appeared, colonization budgets had been cut and the number of families to be settled had been drastically reduced from the originally projected 100,000 families.

In 1975, INCRA was instructed by DASP, the Administrative Department of the Public Sector, to reduce drastically the number of its functionaries in the colonization programs. INCRA has since increasingly left assistance programs to other, less powerful agencies, restricting its own activities in the colonization areas to surveying lots and expediting titles, though even in these tasks there continue to be lengthy delays. Many of the original colonists still do not have titles and cannot, therefore, obtain investment credit from banks. Many have left the area, selling rights in their lots to other colonists or to the ranchers who are buying land behind the colonization areas.

From the beginning, the colonization programs suffered both from the other demands on INCRA's resources and from direct criticisms and pressures from the dominant sectors. INCRA's difficulties in implementing the colonization programs, though, and its highly visible errors in planning and execution, made it especially vulnerable to these demands and pressures. These difficulties and errors, however, were in large part an inevitable consequence of the BA's administrative structure and of its political needs. In another article (Bunker 1982), I have shown how the BA's own organizational logic and its need to legitimate its economic and social policies by demonstrating that the policies accessible even to the dispossessed rural masses imposed a self-defeating model of colonization and rural development. This model forces INCRA and the other agencies with which it must collaborate to obey norms and to follow procedures that, because they presuppose institutions that do not yet exist, contribute directly to program failure. This institutional failure combines with and fortifies the dominant-sector demands for access to Amazonian resources.

Conclusion

Despite their expressed aims and despite the BA's need for legitimation, rural development programs in Pará became instruments for the expansion of capital through the concentration of the means of production. Small farmers were increasingly marginalized by the political pressures of larger, more highly capitalized individuals and enterprises. Mainly because of the interest stimulated by the publicity campaigns that were an essential part of the legitimacy-seeking process, present distortions and failures in the colonization and rural development projects are highly visible, thus augmenting the counterproductive effect on the BA's original purpose. In this sense these programs are as much a failure for the BA as they are for the small farmer. In view of the BA's need for legitimacy, it appears more adequate to interpret this failure and its subsequent advantages for the expansion of capital as an indication of limits on the BA's power than to its deliberate favoring of or preferential treatment of the national bourgeoisie or international capital. Its inability to implement these programs effectively left them vulnerable to interference from the dominant sectors. To imply that this interference is compatible with the BA's own real goals because it is necessary for the kinds of capital accumulation that the authoritarian state must promote to maintain desired levels of industrialization and economic growth would be a serious theoretical error. It must be remembered that, as with most legitimacy-seeking programs, only a miniscule part of the national population was actually affected. Enormous as costs per farmer were, they hardly affected the general patterns of accumulation and concentration of income on which the BA's development strategies are based. Thus, in terms of the BA's own interests and needs, the political advantages and the legitimacy to be gained by successful colonization and rural development far outweighed their economic costs. There is thus no plausible reason to impute deliberate government sabotage of its legitimacy-seeking programs.

The failure of the programs here considered can be attributed to the BA's inability to implant the institutions on which its administrative structure and procedures are based, on its lack of control over its own bureaucracy, and on its consequent vulnerability to interference from the dominant sectors. Thus, both the state capitalist model that is the basis of the BA's alliance with the national bourgeoisie and with international capital and the bureaucracy on which it relies to realize its developmentalist pretensions contribute to the limitations of its power to implement programs necessary to its own stability.

CASE STUDY

The Agrarian Reform Policy in Peru

CYNTHIA McCLINTOCK

The agrarian policy of Peru's military regime was unusual. It was an undeniably redistributive policy; by most criteria it was as sweeping, or more sweeping, than all previous Latin American agrarian reforms save the Cuban one. Yet, of these major agrarian reforms—including the Mexican, the Bolivian, the Venezuelan, and the Chilean—the Peruvian was the only one carried out by a military regime. And, as previous chapters have pointed out, Peru's military regime was *definitively* military; on the issues that officers considered most important, civilian input was small.

Why did Peru's military officers, unlike their counterparts elsewhere in Latin America, favor a radical agrarian reform? How did they successfully implement the reform? And, with the advantage of hindsight, how should we now judge the reform? This case study seeks to answer these questions.

Issue Formation

Land has been an explosive issue in Peru for centuries. Gradually, despite Indian protest, the Spanish and their descendants appropriated more and more of the land as haciendas. The Indian "peasant communities," as they are called, were confined primarily to rugged, infertile mountainous areas. As rural population grew and the land could not support everyone, the Indian peasants sought work on the haciendas, and by the mid-twentieth century permanent hacienda workers constituted a rural proletariat.

The quantity of land in Peru has always been extremely limited. At a mere one-fifth of a hectare per person in 1979, Peru's ratio of land to person is the lowest in Latin America save El Salvador's (Martínez and Tealdo 1982:39). By the 1960s, land was also extremely unequally owned. Approximately 1.4 percent of landowners—or 3,000 people—controlled over 62 percent of the productive land in 1961 (Astiz 1969:9–10). Among this elite, "forty families" were commonly identified as Peru's oligarchy (Malpica 1968). Peru's Gini index of land distribution in 1961 was the most unequal reported for fifty-four nations (Taylor and Hudson 1972:267).

After the Cuban Revolution in 1959, the possibility of rural revolution loomed much larger to both guerrillas and governments. Influenced in part by the example of the Cuban Revolution, a number of Peruvian guerrilla leaders tried to mobilize the peasantry, especially in the highland Cuzco area. At the same time, the U.S.-sponsored Alliance for Progress called for agrarian reform as an alternative to revolution, and political party leaders in many Latin American countries took up the call. Campaigning for the presidency in 1962 and 1963, Fernando Belaúnde Terry promised land reform to peasants throughout Peru.

The more the issue of land reform was discussed, the more large sectors of Peruvian society thought the time for reform had come. Certainly that was the attitude of the peasantry. Hoping to carry out a de facto reform, approximately 300,000 peasants from some 350 to 400 rural communities invaded hacienda lands between 1960 and 1965 (Handelman 1975:121). A much smaller number of peasants joined guerrilla groups.

After his election to the presidency in 1963, Belaúnde failed to keep his promise of agrarian reform. In part because of congressional opposition to a radical reform—opposition that was based primarily on partisan interests—only a very weak reform law was passed that benefited less than 2 percent of Peru's farm families by 1968 (Palmer 1973:191). Belaúnde's response to the peasants who invaded lands was repression. He called upon the military to oust "squatting" peasants from hacienda lands and to defeat the guerrillas. The military did so, at a cost of approximately five hundred lives.

The military's counterinsurgency experience of the early 1960s had far-reaching implications (see Stepan 1978:117–157; Villanueva 1982; Philip 1978). Officers believed that they had been used by the oligarchy one more time, and they were indignant. Especially in the view of the intelligence officers who were active in the counterinsurgency campaign, and knew the lot of the highlands peasantry, the military had done the oligarchy's "dirty work," without so much as a protest. It was the oligarchy that was responsible for the unrest and the killings—yet, the military was shouldering the blame. Officers were angry too at the civilian politicians, who had promised change without any capacity to deliver it.

Peruvian officers probably reacted more critically to the counterinsurgency campaign than their counterparts in other Latin American nations because of their own social class background. Peru's army is drawn from lower ranks of the middle classes than are most other Latin American armies. Many officers were not only sympathetic to the peasantry, but also concerned that friends or relatives would be killed in army actions. Officers were also sensitive to the restrictions on opportunity and mobility in Peru imposed by the oligarchical nature of Peruvian society. Officers wanted a transition from an "oligarchical" to a "populist" society (to use the terms of Guillermo O'Donnell) and they felt that they would be one of the middle-class groups to benefit from such a change.

Officers became committed to reform, especially agrarian reform, intellectually as well as emotionally. The poor economic performance of Peruvian agriculture in the four years just prior to the coup was one point in favor of change. (Agricultural production declined at an average annual rate of −1.3 percent between 1965 and 1968. See Cabieses and Otero 1978:210.) Probably more important, international and domestic political debate favored reform, as we have seen. In particular, reform was proposed as an alternative to revolution at the Military School, the CAEM. Despite the Peruvian military's relatively easy victory over the guerrillas in the early 1960s, officers were concerned about further unrest, and heeded the CAEM's counsel that "One property-owner more is one Communist less" as an ex-instructor at the CAEM put it. CAEM courses, as well as other new educational programs for the military, taught a widening array of topics in social and political development; soon, officers were confident that they could govern better than the clannish, unprincipled civilian politicians.

The Policymaking Process, 1968–1975

When the military seized power in October 1968, land reform was a top priority on its agenda. Yet, despite the relative consensus among officers on the need for agrarian reform, the military leaders had not worked out the specifics of their policy. While all officers apparently wanted to see *some* reform, there was a wide spectrum of opinion about exactly how much.

The controversy continued, virtually unabated, during the six-years-plus of Velasco's rule. Yet, despite the importance of the issue and its immediate significance to millions of Peruvians, by far the most important decisionmaker was one man: General Velasco. Unfortunately, especially as Velasco was a rather obscure general prior to 1968 and as he died soon after the 1975 palace coup, less information is available about his goals and strategies than for most leaders. However, it is clear that he was very concerned about social justice in Peru, and deeply critical and resentful of the Peruvian oligarchy and its traditional powers. These qualities were most evident in Velasco's leadership between 1968 and 1973, when he strongly supported what has been called the "progressive" tendency in the military ranks, against the "bourgeois liberal" tendency (see Pease Garcia 1977). It is also clear that Velasco was an anti-Communist who, around 1973, became worried that further reforms might help the Communist cause in Peru, and thus shifted away from the "progressive" tendency toward "La Mision" (an intensely anti-Communist group that yet favored a strong role for the Peruvian state).

Velasco led the Council of Ministers meetings, at which most key decisions were taken, and until 1973 he successfully cajoled and badgered ministers so that the actual agrarian reform was considerably more radical than most officers had originally contemplated. Velasco also enjoyed the full support of the four colonels who had helped him plan and execute the 1968 coup, and three of these colonels (Leonidas Rodríguez Figueroa, Jorge Maldonado, and Enrique Gallegos) were "progressives" who were gradually promoted to top positions in the government. The top decisionmakers were almost exclusively military officers—both in the Council of Ministers and the COAP.

In contrast to other Latin American military regimes, civilian input was small, as previously noted. It was not nonexistent, however. Despite the military's confidence in their own abilities in 1968, officers were not really that knowledgeable on many issues, and they turned to civilians who were, and who were sympathetic to their goals. Often, it was the civilians who, as members of commissions or as advisors to ministers, prepared laws that would then be put on the table for approval at a meeting of the Council of Ministers.

As Chapter 2 pointed out, interest groups have traditionally been weak in Peru, and they were relatively insignificant in agrarian policy formation, at least prior to 1973. However, they did have some impact on certain policy debates. Rural workers' strikes were one factor in the government's decision to prohibit land subdivision in 1971. Both ministry of agriculture officials and small and middle-sized farmers' organizations played a role in the 1973 decision to set a fifty-hectare maximum for coastal landholdings.

Policy Adoption, 1968–1973

Gradually, between 1968 and 1973, the agrarian reform program became more radical. At first, only a mild reform was expected, in part because the minister of agriculture, General José Benavides, was a "bourgeois liberal" with political clout: He was a wealthy landowner, a respected officer, and the son of a former president of Peru. Benavides did indeed draft a mild law, but it was sharply criticized by "progressives" at the Council of Ministers meeting, and in June 1969 Benavides's resignation was forced by Velasco.

A COAP commission, including various civilians, drafted a new law in twelve days' time. In a marathon meeting of the Council of Ministers, beginning at 3:00 P.M. on June 23 and ending at 6:00 A.M. on June 24, the law was approved. Civilians were not allowed at the meeting, but stood by in the presidential palace in case of questions or whatever—watching cowboy movies (Cleaves and Scurrah 1980:108, 109). The next day the huge sugar complexes on the northern coast, the agro-industrial base of the Peruvian oligarchical apex, were militarily occupied and expropriated.

Still, it was not clear that the reform would affect most haciendas. The new minister of agriculture, General Jorge Baradiarán Pagador, frequently emphasized that the reform's goals were moderate: to increase agricultural productivity, stimulate private industry, and enhance social peace. Medium-size landowners believed that, if they subdivided their estates among various "purchasers," usually their relatives or friends, each subdivision would fall below the legal landholding maximum, and they could maintain their haciendas more or less intact. *Hacendados* (landowners) in many Latin American nations, especially in neighboring Chile, successfully used this strategy to undermine agrarian reform programs. Subdivision became prevalent in Peru in 1969 and 1970.

In February 1971, Velasco issued one of the most important decrees of the agrarian reform: the retroactive annulment of the subdivision of the large coastal orange estate, Huando. Both hacienda workers and *hacendados* had been trying to pressure the government on their own behalf: the hacienda workers by a series of strikes, and the *hacendados* by a media campaign orchestrated through the National Agrarian Society, the landowners' interest association. It is doubtful that either lobbying effort greatly influenced Velasco, who was personally committed to the devastation of the Peruvian oligarchy, although he may have cited the workers' strikes as a point in favor of reform to other ministers.

Velasco's annulment of the Huando subdivision was the signal that the government would truly enforce the legal landholding limits (at the time, 150 hectares for coastal, irrigated land and some 30 to 70 hectares in the highlands, depending on the province and on irrigation facilities). Expropriations accelerated. Gradually, as it became more and more apparent that, under the official landholding limits, some haciendas would not be affected and a relatively small number of peasants would be benefited, other conditions for expropriation were applied. As these provisions had existed in previous laws but never had been applied, landowners were taken aback. Absentee ownership and illegal labor practices were the conditions most frequently cited.

In 1972 and 1973, Ministry of Agriculture officials became increasingly zealous in their application of these provisions. Certainly, equity required expropriation of farms under 150 hectares, and indeed under 50 hectares; average property size in Peru was well under 5 hectares (CIDA 1966). However, when farmers with fewer than 50 hectares became concerned about expropriation (their numbers were substantial, and they had friends in the top ranks of the armed forces) they began to lobby intensively, and the "progressives" at the Ministry of Agriculture were on the defensive for the first time. In August 1973, a new regulation was passed effectively prohibiting the expropriation of coastal property under 50 hectares, whatever the conditions (Cleaves and Scurrah 1980:122–127).

Ultimately, the 1973 expropriation provisions proved permanent. By the end of the military regime, most properties over 50 hectares on the coast, and over 30 hectares in the highlands and jungle, were expropriated. The hacienda was eliminated. Approximately 8.5 million hectares, that is, slightly more than 35 percent of all agricultural land, were expropriated and transferred to about 375,000 peasant families—roughly 25 percent of all farm families. If these figures, as well as other reform features, such as terms of compensation, are compared to other agrarian reforms in Latin America, the Peruvian reform emerges as more radical, or at least as radical, as any save the Cuban (McClintock 1981:60–63).

During the early 1970s, considerable controversy also erupted over the kind of enterprise that would replace the hacienda. Many officers were uncertain about the alternatives. Only gradually did some top officers become familiar with the proposals for cooperative enterprises developed by Peru's Christian Democratic Party or its Social Progressive Movement, and with the models implemented in Yugoslavia, Mexico, and Chile. The 1969 agrarian reform law established cooperatives out of the haciendas and devolved considerable power over important decisions in the cooperatives to the members.

After the enactment of the reform law, however, many officers apparently had second thoughts. Only about six months later, a new decree was passed, much more corporatist in nature, that gave more power to technicians and administrators and prohibited union activists from leadership posts.

Velasco probably did not favor the new decree, but he was not able to rescind it until March 1972, when most "bourgeois liberal" ministers had been ousted. In mid-1972, the original law on the political structure of the cooperatives, Supreme Decree 240-69-AP, was once again in force; entirely free, one member/one vote elections were held in the new cooperatives. The basic political framework established for the cooperatives by the original decree lasted through the military regime.

However, the decree was silent on many key issues; thus, conflict continued, especially among the various bureaucracies. The powers of technical managers in the cooperatives was the most controversial issue. Yet, after years of argument from both the Right and the Left, the 1972 resolution of the question endured. (The cooperatives were legally required to employ a technical manager, but they were also free to fire him: To choose a new manager, the cooperative's leaders would first nominate three candidates, and then the Ministry of Agriculture would select one of the three.)

Policy Struggles, 1973–1975

The contours of the Peruvian agrarian reform were thus set roughly by 1973. However, this fact was not clear at the time. The "progressive" tendency, which had been pushing the reform to the left since the first months of the military regime, continued to urge a more radical policy. This group had little success, however, after 1973, as it had lost the support of Velasco.

Although there were "progressives" in almost every agency, the tendency's institutional base was SINAMOS (National System for Social Mobilization). SINAMOS was a government agency established in mid-1971 and led until early 1974 by one of Peru's most radical generals, Leonidas Rodríguez Figueroa. The agency, which was assigned the lofty and abstract goal of building a "fully participatory social democracy" in Peru, was the military's answer to the question of political participation in the regime. To a much greater extent than most policies of the Velasco government, participation policy was influenced by a civilian: Carlos Delgado, a Cornell-trained social scientist.

Essentially, the "progressives" wanted to extend agrarian reform benefits to a larger percentage of the peasantry and to the more disadvantaged sectors of the peasantry in particular. They felt that if reform provisions remained as they were in 1973, reform benefits would be very disproportionate to human needs. The "progressives" were right.

As we have seen, Peru's economically active agricultural population comprises various types of workers and peasants. Roughly a third are small, private farmers; a third, peasant community members; one-fifth, landless temporary workers; and one-tenth, permanent estate workers (McClintock 1981:93). The incomes of the small farmers vary a great deal. Among the other groups, the estate workers are an elite. In the 1960s, before the reform, the average hacienda worker earned at least double the earnings of the average peasant-community member (see Webb 1974:2–34). The hacienda worker earned in the range of $200 a year, versus about $100 for a peasant-community member (Webb 1977:13–14).

Yet, reform benefits were heavily skewed in favor of the ex-hacienda workers. Almost all became members of new cooperative enterprises. The average value of the property transferred to each cooperative member was nearly $2,000.

Peasant-community members and landless temporary workers (together, a majority of Peru's economically active agricultural population) gained much less from the reform. Indeed, very few temporary workers and less than 25 percent of Peru's peasant-community members actually gained land (McClintock 1981:93). Moreover, that land averaged only $50 in value per beneficiary, much less than what an ex-hacienda worker received (Caballero and Alvarez 1980:63). Peasants gained some other benefits: the end to feudalistic obligations to *hacendados*, the resolution of boundary disputes, and greater social respect. Yet, in the 1970s their actual living standards declined (McClintock 1983c:Table II).

The "progressives" advocated various measures to help the disadvantaged peasantry, to no avail. They fought against the coastal landholding maximum of fifty hectares, passed in August 1973, hoping for a lower maximum. After this defeat, the primary "progressive" initiatives were unauthorized ones, by SINAMOS recruits in the field.

Two SINAMOS concerns were especially evident. First, in many regions SINAMOS sought to require cooperatives to admit more temporary workers as enterprise members—a measure that would have benefited a group that was gaining very little from the reform. Second, in highlands peasant communities, SINAMOS encouraged programs of land equalization and disqualification of village commercial elites. Both SINAMOS initiatives were interpreted as disruptive and naive at best and as an attempt at "Communist" control of cooperatives and communities at worst. These critiques weighed heavily on Velasco's thinking at the time, and were probably a factor in the removal of Rodríguez Figueroa as head of SINAMOS in early 1974.

Yet, the great bulk of SINAMOS officials remained, albeit under new leadership. Probably the agency's primary responsibility during 1973–1975 was to organize the National Agrarian Confederation (CNA). The organization, perhaps intended to be corporatist by some generals, included local, regional, and national tiers. By the conscious decision of SINAMOS officials, membership in the CNA was weighted heavily toward peasant communities and away from the cooperatives. At the 1974 inaugural congress and thereafter, the CNA, with the support of its "progressive" allies in SINAMOS, called for vigorous redistributive measures in Peru's countryside. For example, the CNA urged the radicalization of the agrarian reform; sharper price increases for peasant community products; the admission of temporary workers to cooperative membership; a new agricultural marketing plan; and other similar steps. The CNA's proposals were almost all rejected by the government. By the logic of corporatism, the CNA was supposed to move docilely to the right with the government, but it did not. The organization persisted in representing the concerns of the disadvantaged peasantry, and as a result the government severed its ties with the CNA in 1978.

Evaluating Velasco's Agrarian Reform

Evaluation of Velasco's reform is difficult for numerous reasons, many of which are briefly mentioned in other parts of this book. First, the goals of the reform were numerous, and their priority rankings were unclear. Second, the Velasco era was relatively brief, and the record might have been different if the general had been in power, with good health, longer. Third, data on various key questions are unavailable; the government was hastily making policy, not trying to evaluate it. Finally, and perhaps most important, the agrarian reform record cannot be isolated from other key issues, or (even now) a real end-date set. It is hard to separate what was from what might have been.

Yet, a balance sheet can be drawn up. Probably, for Velasco and his key allies, the top priority was undermining the oligarchy. The trajectory of land expropriations—the largest and most lucrative first, on down to small haciendas in remote areas—is a strong indication of the regime's priorities. (If quelling peasant unrest had been the most important goal, presumably much more attention would have been given to disadvantaged highlands peasant communities, the traditional source of peasant protest.) The Velasco government certainly achieved the goal of eclipsing the oligarchy.

The government also attained a secondary but important goal, the establishment of viable peasant cooperatives. Although the current regime has depreciated the cooperatives, they were a boon to their members. For the first time, a significant sector of the peasantry gained access to "middle-class" opportunities in Peru. As the military had hoped income was no longer so concentrated at the pinnacle of the distribution—among the top 5 percent; the next 20 percent, which included many cooperative members, gained handsomely, although the next six or seven deciles did not (Webb 1977:77–90). Materially and symbolically, the Velasco government was more supportive of the peasantry than any previous Peruvian government, and large numbers of peasants felt a new pride (McClintock 1981).

The cooperatives were not a major economic success, but they did not fail economically either. In the first decade of the reform, the cooperatives performed about as well economically as the haciendas, typically producing the same kinds of agricultural goods in similar, or slightly higher, quantities

(McClintock 1983:12–18). By 1980, the cooperatives seemed "institutional-ized," having resolved the social and political crises of their creation and ready, in many cases, to settle down and commit themselves to higher pro-duction standards.

In various other respects, however, the reform failed. Although alleviating the most wrenching poverty in the countryside and thereby diminishing peasant unrest was not the number-one goal of the Velasco government, it was an important concern of many officers. This goal was far from met. In the early 1980s, a new peasant movement emerged in the southern highlands, around Ayacucho, called *Sendero Luminoso*, that has been unprecedented in its size, scope, and commitment to violence and terror. As a result of the agrarian reform, beneficiaries—primarily coastal cooperative members—were unlikely recruits for *Sendero*, but by the early 1980s this fact was of limited significance. The southern highlands peasantry has been neglected by every recent Peruvian government, and the region is now a "Fourth World" in a "Third World" country (McClintock 1983b). The area could have been helped by various programs, especially those for small-scale irrigation and soil replenishment; but it was not, and it is now taking its brutal revenge.

Implicit in the rise of *Sendero Luminoso* is the failure of the Velasco gov-ernment's political organizations. The government's political ideals were always ambiguous. The regime claimed to be seeking a "fully participatory social democracy," but some officers seemed to harbor visions of corporatism. In any case, most of the government's political organizations did not endure. SINAMOS was defunct by the late 1970s and the CNA was transformed into a very different type of peasant confederation.

The failure of the regime's political plan is very significant. As Chapter 2 points out, Latin American nations are highly politicized, and many policies are tentative experiments. Most reforms can be reversed, and often have been. Without more effective peasant organization and articulation, the Peruvian agrarian reform is vulnerable to reversal. In the early 1980s, under the civilian Belaúnde regime, the reform came under heavy attack (McClintock 1983a). The Peruvian agrarian landscape is now changing once again.

[4]
Policymaking in Democratic Regimes

It is important at the outset to refresh our memories concerning the tentative and usually nonpermanent nature of what political scientists refer to as civilian democratic regimes—or any regime for that matter—in Latin American politics. At the most basic level, democracy implies popular participation, directly or indirectly, in political decisions. Minimally, when we refer to democratic regimes, we mean governments that adhere to free, competitive elections as a means of guaranteeing popular participation in the selection of decisionmaking officials. In the Latin American context, this would clearly eliminate regimes that have abolished elections entirely, such as Chile since 1973. Also, this criterion would eliminate regimes where the elections that are held are really not competitive. As shown in Chapters 3 and 5, some regimes, such as Brazil in the 1970s and 1980s, allow elections, but the electoral process and the ability of political parties to contest the elections have been thoroughly controlled and limited by the governing elites. Likewise, Mexico has used peaceful, seemingly democratic elections for the transference of power between administrations for more than fifty years. But the elections, by and large, are far from competitive. Instead, they serve more as legitimating devices for the elites to continue ruling as they please.

A second major criterion of a democratic regime is the relative freedom and autonomy allowed—if not outright encouraged—for mass participation in other phases of policymaking. The existence of fairly autonomous interest groups would be one clue to whether a regime was democratic. The extent to which such groups were permitted to play a role in demand making, agenda setting, policy formulation and, finally, policy implementation would give us some indication as to how democratic a regime is.

At one time or another, many Latin American governments could claim some semblance of democratic procedures in the way they went about making policy. Most of those claims are usually scoffed at by scholars and practitioners alike. Although there was much publicity about the "honest" elections held in the spring of 1982 in El Salvador, few seasoned observers of Latin American political life claim that those elections were the first in a linear process of democratization in that war-torn country. In the cases of contemporary Venezuela and Costa Rica, however, there are few raised eyebrows when someone uses the term democratic to describe the policy process of their respective regimes. It should be noted, however, that both countries entered the now-dwindling ranks of democratic Latin American regimes only a relatively short time ago: Costa Rica, in the late 1940s; Venezuela, in the late 1950s. Before that time, Venezuela's political history was replete with political violence and military coups, and Costa Rica "earned" its place in the democratic category only after a bloody civil war.

What we are suggesting here are two considerations: the tentativeness of regime classification and the "looseness" of the democratic category in particular. It would be a mistake if the student of Latin American politics were to expect policymaking in terms of procedures and outcomes within Venezuela and Costa Rica identical with what he or she is likely to find in the United States or Great Britain. Nonetheless, the student should expect to see some differences between the policy processes in Costa Rica and Venezuela, on the one hand, and those of Brazil and Cuba, on the other. This chapter will first describe briefly the policy process in Costa Rica and Venezuela and then present two detailed case studies of a particular policy issue in each country.

Costa Rica

THE PRE-1948 POLICY PROCESS

Costa Rica's political background is perhaps the least violent of any Latin American country—a propitious sign for the establishment of a democratic regime. Its independence from Spain was gained without a drop of blood being shed. And while there were a few extended dictatorships in the late nineteenth and early twentieth centuries, the normal operating procedure for political institutions was an elite-controlled "democratic process complete with executive, legislative and judicial branches" (Denton 1979:379). The coffee-growing families were the key political elite of that period, and they generally elected one of their own to political office. The modern period of Costa Rica began in 1940, when issues and actors other than coffee and coffee elites began to emerge. During the presidential administration of Rafael Calderón Guardia (1940–1944), the first labor code was enacted into law and the only labor organization then in existence, which was Communist-organized, was permitted to function legally. The first stages of social security legislation were also initiated during Calderón Guardia's administration, making his a decidedly reformist regime. The following presidential election was bitterly contested, resulting in Calderón Guardia's handpicked successor, lawyer and friend Teodoro Picado, winning under the *Calderonista* banner of social reform. Increasingly, however, the *Calderonistas* alienated many of the elite sectors of the society and, consequently, found themselves relying more heavily on the support of communist organizer Manuel Mora and his labor group, *Vanguardia Popular.*

POLICYMAKING SINCE 1948

This relatively peaceful, though tense, political process gave way rather abruptly in 1948, when it became apparent that the major opposition candidate had defeated Calderón Guardia in his bid for reelection. The national legislature, controlled by the *Calderonistas,* nullified the results and declared Calderón the winner. José "Don Pepe" Figueres Ferrer, a key opposition leader, led an armed rebellion in response to this electoral fraud. After several months of fighting, the Figueres-led National Liberation Movement emerged victorious and, in a move unprecedented in Latin America—and as yet unrepeated— Figueres disbanded the military forces. Shortly thereafter, a new constitution was written and was subsequently ratified on November 7, 1949. This constitution, with several amendments, remains the primary source of legitimate political authority today. It is worthwhile for us to discuss briefly the constitutionally prescribed decisionmaking process, because it has had both intended consequences—such as limiting the power of the chief executive vis-à-vis the legislature—as well as ramifications unforeseen and largely unplanned. (Much of the following discussion relies on Denton 1971 and 1979 and Mijeski 1977.)

   Under the constitution of 1949, the president was specifically assigned only four independent functions: first, the appointment and removal of ministers without legislative participation and, second, serving as commander-in-chief of the *Guardia Civil,* which is what remains of Costa Rica's disbanded army. Although the first of these powers could easily imply significant presidential control over the policy-implementing bureaucracy, we shall see that this has not been the case. And to be in charge of a severely limited quasi-military establishment does not provide the president with an overwhelming power base. Moreover, the remaining two independent powers are essentially lacking any real policymaking clout: representing the nation at official ceremonies and presenting a state-of-the-union address before the legislature.

   Even the president's powers that are "shared" with the legislature were further limited by the new constitution. Previously, and like the contemporary situation throughout most of Latin America, the Costa Rican president had a broad-ranging authority to issue *decretos con fuerza de ley* (decrees with the force of law). Essentially, this power—frequently used, for example, by presidents Eduardo Frei Montalva (1966–1970) and Salvador Allende Gossens

(1970–1973) of Chile—enables the president to "make laws" unilaterally without going through the legislature. The 1949 constitution stripped the chief executive of this power. The president does have the power of the veto over the legislature, though he lacks an item veto, and he is even prohibited from exercising his blanket veto without the concurrence of at least one of his ministers. Finally, the budget bills can only be initiated by the president, though the legislature is able to modify any or all parts of the budget bill and retains the definitive authority to approve or disapprove the final calculation of the budget.

Clearly, the Costa Rican constitution places significant limits on the president's policymaking role, even though presidential effectiveness probably varies for other than constitutional factors (Mijeski 1977:64–68). Indeed, as we argued in Chapter 2, Costa Rica probably has the weakest executive vis-à-vis the legislature of the six countries focused upon in this book. We suggested that there was a rough equality regarding the policymaking ability of these two branches. Might we readily conclude that the executive and legislative branches are the most important governmental actors in the Costa Rican policy process? On the contrary, some observers have argued just the opposite. That is, neither branch is particularly effective in policymaking. Along these lines, Charles F. Denton's position is that:

> Despite its apparent powers the National Assembly is as limited as is the president in its ability to carry out its functions. The fact that the deputies cannot seek reelection until a four-year term intervenes tends to limit the continuity of the body and discourages specialization in particular policy-making areas. The committee system, with its revolving membership, assures that most issues will be acted upon in a piecemeal fashion and on the basis of limited information (1971:38).

This policymaking balance or trade-off between the legislature and executive branches may well be an unforeseen consequence of a constitution that was designed to decentralize governmental power to prevent the executive hegemony so commonly found in Latin America. The bureaucracy itself has further added to the dilution of executive and legislative control of the policy process, particularly regarding the proliferation of autonomous and semi-autonomous agencies in the post-1948 era. As historian James W. Wilkie (1974b) has documented, of the nearly 130 public decentralized agencies in Costa Rica by the late 1960s, all but 9 were created since 1948. In addition to the autonomy of their day-to-day operations, presidential appointment of directors to these agencies is staggered and overlaps presidential administrations, thereby inhibiting both a spoils system—by design—and executive oversight of the institutions' practices. As we shall see in Chapter 5, this practice is in stark contrast to the Mexican president's ability to control numerous bureaucratic appointments and, therefore, bureaucratic loyalty. And

TABLE 4.1

Legislative Representation in Costa Rica's Legislative Assembly,
1978-1982

Parties/Coalitions	Number of Seats
Pueblo Unido[a]	3
Liberación Nacional	25
Unidad[b]	27
Frente Popular Costarricense	1
Unión Agrícola Cartaginesa	1
TOTAL	57

Source: del Aguila, 1982: p. 363.

[a]Coalition of Vanguardia Popular, Socialista Costarricense y de los Trabajadores.
[b]Coalition of Renovación Democrática, Republicano Calderonista, Union Popular,
Demócrata Cristiano.

although the legislature itself was the creator of these agencies, legislative oversight of bureaucratic policy practices is equally inhibited by similarly staggered directorial appointments, the constitutional prohibition against legislators succeeding themselves, and, in some cases, the raising of revenues for administrative budgets independently. Even major national policy decisions are made by autonomous agencies beyond the purview of the legislature. For example, during the summer of 1981 the Board of Directors of the Autonomous Central Bank contracted foreign credits in order to finance government projects without the knowledge or consent of the legislative assembly (del Aguila 1982:359).

In the 1970s, efforts were made to return some control over these agencies to the executive branch (Mijeski 1977:63). These efforts were undertaken when the party of the president in power—in this case the National Liberation Party (PLN) founded by Figueres—also controlled the National Assembly. Since the PLN continues to be the major, though not the only, party in the National Assembly, and since interparty struggles have been the norm in recent political life, only successive PLN victories in the presidency make this effort at controlling the bureaucracy worthwhile. Thus far, there has been but one such instance of two PLN presidents in succession: Figueres in his second term (beginning in 1970), followed by his protégé, Daniel Oduber, in 1974. In short, the PLN, in contrast to the Mexican PRI, has never been able to gain one-party domination of the executive branch, thus further inhibiting either presidential or legislative control over any particular bureaucratic agency.

In fact, as Juan del Aguila points out, and as Table 4.1 demonstrates, the fundamental polarization in Costa Rican politics is between Liberación Nacional and a plethora of opposition parties (1982:363). Not only has the PLN failed to muster sufficient public support to gain long-term control of the majority of the legislative seats, it has also suffered severe internal splits that resulted in its presidential defeat in 1958 and a near defeat in 1970—probably rescued only by the popularity and prestige of Figueres. Recently, the PLN has made a comeback, winning the 1982 presidential elections by temporarily neutralizing its own vocal left wing with a solid centrist position. It also gained control of the National Assembly, with the largest PLN majority since 1970 (1982:364). In general, the PLN will likely continue to face what it has faced for the last three decades: opposition from shifting, ad hoc coalitions of essentially pragmatic, vaguely anti-PLN "parties," many of which will not endure beyond one election. Apparently, the constitutional structure and the evolving party system have resulted in a struggle between the legislative and executive branches where neither emerges as clearly dominant in the policy process, and where the increasing numbers of autonomous bureaucratic agencies further detract from the decisionmaking capabilities of both branches.

There is also evidence that the dispersion of decisionmaking responsibility has been increasing throughout the political system, thus inhibiting any systematic efforts at national policymaking. For example, the programming function for various national development efforts is spread over OFIPLAN (the National Planning Office), the presidency, ministry planning departments, and the planning sections of dozens of semiautonomous agencies. Moreover, George Guess argues that policy coordination mandates from the staffs of most agencies are unaccompanied by the authority to issue binding orders. For example, in the area of agricultural development, many commissions, councils, and other such agencies exist, but, since they lack policymaking authority, turn into mere debating societies (1980:273, 274).

Is there an answer, then, to the question of who does decide public policy in democratic Costa Rica? Given the apparent "mutual deterrence" that the governmental institutions provide each other, does this allow for behind-the-scenes control of the policy process by certain key interests in Costa Rican society? Here, the evidence is sketchy and controversial. The standard textbook answer, to which we alluded in Chapter 2, is that although no power elite is clearly identifiable in Costa Rica, the nation's policy process is probably weighted in favor of important agricultural and landowning interests represented by groups such as the Chamber of Coffee Growers, the Chamber of Banana Growers, and the Cattlemen's Association. Rodrigo Facio, one of Costa Rica's leading policy thinkers, argues that public policy is dictated by foreign and domestic capitalists through a civil oligarchy. As evidence he cites the 1938 contract between the United Fruit Company and the Costa Rican government. This contract, he claims, favored the company, its domestic clients, and well-placed public officials at the nation's expense (Guess 1980:275). Giving at least indirect support to Facio's argument, Mitchell A. Seligson points out that the coffee industry was both regulated and taxed beginning in the twentieth century, but the banana industry, controlled by the U.S.-based United Fruit Company, escaped similar attempts to regulate its affairs. In 1930 a law was passed setting up a regulatory board to arbitrate conflicts between the local Costa Rican banana growers and United Fruit. There is no record, according to Seligson, of this board's ever having been utilized. Moreover, he argues, it was not until the 1960s, with the establishment of new companies, that the government attempted again to regulate the banana industry, still with questionable success (Seligson 1977:223). In a similar vein, Samuel Stone argues that even after the introduction of a modern welfare-state apparatus, Costa Rica continued to pursue monocultural agriculture-export politics because a tradition-oriented agricultural elite had maintained hegemony in agricultural policy (Guess 1980:277).

Facio's, Stone's, and Seligson's accounts give the impression of agricultural policy being virtually controlled by an identifiable and powerful elite. In contrast, Mark B. Rosenberg's analysis of social security policy, included in this chapter, paints a picture of anything but vested interest dominance in a smooth, carefully planned fashion. As Rosenberg has summarized elsewhere, the history of social security policymaking between 1925 and 1961 was often ad hoc, accidental, and serendipitous (1979). In fact, he points out, in 1941 the Social Insurance Act was passed in secret, with no public debate or public pressure, and without any real interest group activity (1979:121–122). While it is premature to draw any general conclusions concerning the role of various interests in the Costa Rican policy process, Rosenberg's case study can nonetheless provide us with a deeper understanding of the process in one key policy area.

Venezuela

THE PRE-1959 POLICY PROCESS

Venezuela's political history—full of caudillos, tyrants, dictatorships, and coups d'état—stands in marked contrast to the comparatively peaceful history of Costa Rica. While colonial political arrangements were not necessarily fair, just, and incorruptible, they nevertheless provided a complex bureaucratic framework to resolve disputes. After independence, political power came out of the barrel of a gun or through the point of a saber. The militarization of political authority—rooted in Spanish colonialism—became complete after the wars of independence. Civil strife dominated the scene. Landowners, coffee growers, and other elites of the Creole class skirmished among themselves for political and economic control. One observer has argued that foreign interests were powerful enough to shape much of the political and economic realignment in the late nineteenth and early twentieth centuries (Lombardi 1977:12–16). Almost the first third of the twentieth century in Venezuela was characterized by a tremendous concentration of personalistic power under the dictatorship of the famed "Tyrant of the Andes," General Juan Vicente Gómez. It was under Gómez that a major key—oil—to understanding politics and economics in modern Venezuela emerged. In his efforts to centralize power, Gómez granted several concessions to foreign oil prospectors. Oil eventually transformed the country and influenced contemporary Venezuela in several ways. For example, oil exploration solidified the power of foreign corporations (and often their respective governments) in Venezuelan policymaking. Moreover, the post-Gómez years—both peaceful and nonpeaceful—were marked by various groups struggling over the kinds of politics the state should formulate to deal with the question of oil exploration, production, and distribution of profits. Gómez's death in 1935, rather than signaling the final power resolution of Venezuelan politics, was the beginning of three decades of turmoil, which included three military coups and four national constitutions. According to political scientist David Blank, much of the political struggle following Gómez's death involved the efforts by nascent, urban-based political movements to expand their power base through mass political mobilization. These movements contained the seeds of the contemporary political party system that has been heralded as one of the most democratic systems in today's Latin America (Blank 1973:18–27). One of the great ironies of Venezuelan democracy is that its birth (1945) and its "rebirth" (1958) were achieved through military overthrows of the established governments.

The period from 1936 to 1958 saw the emergence of fledgling democratic movements, which began to recruit supporters from the previously disenfranchised segments of the population. The primary group involved in this effort was Acción-Democrática (AD), the Democratic Action Party, which, as we shall see, has come to play a major role in contemporary Venezuelan political life. AD joined forces with a group of young military officers, the Patriotic Military Union, to overthrow the government of General Osaías Medina Angarita in 1945. The period of 1945 to 1948, commonly called the *trienio*, was characterized by the efforts of AD to create a mass-mobilization democracy and, consequently, involved the politicalization of peasants. To some extent, this resulted in a shift of power away from the traditionally powerful large landowners—*latifundistas*—to peasant union leaders. However, some observers would argue that the shift in political power was really to the urban-based, middle-class politicos who "used" the peasants for their own ends. As Domingo Alberto Rangel put it, the AD under Rómulo Betancourt merely "created a clientele with which to guarantee AD's electoral predominance." Moreover, there is evidence that the agrarian reform law enacted during the *trienio* was neither a reflection of peasants' political demands nor a policy that affected their interests in any significant way (Blank 1974:22).

The *trienio* was important for other reasons. The AD-military junta created the state-run Venezuelan Development Corporation (CVF), which was to act as a major source of entrepreneurial activity. The junta also made inroads into the foreign-owned petroleum companies by obtaining an arrangement guaranteeing for the state at least 50 percent of the industry's profits. In addition, other political parties that have remained important in contemporary politics—the Social Christian Party (COPEI) and the Republican Democratic Union (URD)—were created during this period. COPEI in particular, with stronger roots among Venezuelan Catholics than AD, began its largely unchanged role as major partisan opponent to AD. This opposition, coupled with the increasing concern in the military that AD was threatening its power base, led to the bloodless coup that ended the *trienio* in 1948 and subsequently exiled the AD stalwart, Rómulo Betancourt.

The ensuing military junta and dictatorship under Colonel Marcos Pérez Jiménez alienated many of the social and economic elites. These elites became increasingly convinced that the key to Venezuela's future lay in some semblance of stable, middle-class democracy that would allow for the free action of groups such as those in the increasingly wealthy business community, both domestic and foreign.

POLICYMAKING SINCE 1959

The "final" democratic resolution—as reflected in the legitimating constitution of 1961—was based on an agreement between political leaders bent on creating a middle-class-directed democracy and social and economic elites (business, agricultural, commercial). As David Blank put it:

> The keystone of the understanding reached between the middle-class political leaders and the social and economic establishment was the latter's expressed willingness to support the return of a mass-based democracy and middle-class political rule via free, competitive elections. In return the elected political elite would undertake a program of moderate, broad-based reforms, avoiding excessively divisive issues and direct challenges to the prerogatives of such power contenders as the church, the military, and the business community (1973:27–28).

Since 1961, Venezuela has been able to maintain a multiparty, democratically elected system of government. Though there were various plots and attempts at coups in the early 1960s, the integrity of the system has not given way to the common pattern of civilian-military coups. This success may have been partly due to Castro's revolution in Cuba in 1959, which helped to coalesce sometimes disparate factions into a common commitment to avoid political radicalism, particularly from the left.

An examination of the policymaking powers granted by the 1961 constitution should provide us a useful beginning to assess the institutional decisionmaking process and to compare it with that of Costa Rica. In contrast to the constitutionally constrained powers of the Costa Rican presidency, the Venezuelan presidency is constitutionally powerful, reflective of the tendency toward executive hegemony found in most of Latin America. (See Martz 1977a:98–100, for a brief, yet relatively detailed, enumeration of constitutional presidential authority.) Among the powers granted to the president are the right to name and replace cabinet ministers, state governors, and all boards of autonomous institutes and state corporations. The president also has the right to create autonomous agencies. In addition, under his other decree powers, he can declare a state of emergency and suspend constitutional guarantees for as long as ninety days, and at his discretion, issue extraordinary economic and financial measures. Although such decrees necessitate the approval of the cabinet, the president's power to appoint and remove cabinet members at will vitiates that particular "restraint" on executive power.

The constitution of 1961, not unlike constitutions of many Western presidential systems, provides checks on presidential authority via the legislature, which is, in the case of Venezuela, a bicameral institution. For example, budget proposals by the executive branch require congressional approval, and the congress is aided in this respect, as is the one-chambered National Assembly of Costa Rica, by the functioning of an independent comptroller general. This official, selected by each new congress, submits annual reports to the legislature on the fiscal performance of government agencies. Other constitutional provisions give to the congress the right to censure a cabinet minister. If a motion of censure passes by a two-thirds vote, the president is required to remove the minister. The congress also has the authority to limit any supplemental budgetary decrees.

How do the legislative and executive branches rank in terms of their respective policymaking authority? The answer to this question from the constitution's standpoint would seem to be that, legislative powers notwithstanding, the presidency is clearly the more dominant institution. Moreover, R. Lynn Kelley has argued, neither chamber of congress has strong, well-staffed committees, thereby inhibiting the legislature's efforts to act as an effective policymaking body. But Kelley modifies this overly broad conclusion by suggesting that, even though the Venezuelan legislature has not been a particularly effective policy initiator, it has served from time to time as a "vetoing agency" vis-à-vis the presidency (1977:40). In short, congress has been neither the dominant policy initiator nor the president's rubber stamp. To understand more completely the decisionmaking dynamics between the presidency and the congress we must leave the constitution and turn our attention to the aspect of Venezuelan democracy that has received significant attention and has been at least partially credited with the adoption and persistence of civilian constitutional rule since 1958—political parties. Venezuela has the most vigorous and competitive multiparty system in all of Latin America and, as one scholar has observed, this multiparty basis of Venezuelan politics both enhances and limits presidential authority (Kelley 1977). In particular, the congress, poorly staffed as it is, is not the executive's rubber stamp mainly because of the development of strong, well-disciplined legislative parties. Only two parties have elected presidents since 1958— Democratic Action (AD) and the Social Christian Party (COPEI)—and each president, with the exception of AD's Carlos Andres Pérez (1974–1979), faced either an opposition-controlled congress or a congress whose opposition members often boycotted controversial presidential legislation. In addition, given the existence of smaller but durable congressional parties, such as the Republican Democratic Union (URD) and the Communist Party (PVC), most Venezuelan presidents before Pérez have had to put together and try to head, often with limited success, multiparty coalitions (see Martz 1977a and Kelley 1977). These factors have allowed political parties to strengthen congress relative to the presidency and have necessitated that presidents from 1958 onward adopt a deferential stance toward the legislature.

The presidency of Pérez (AD) was mentioned as an exception. His has been the only administration that has enjoyed an absolute majority in both houses of congress, thus giving the president at least a short-term enjoyment of decisionmaking hegemony. It was during Pérez's administration, for example, that the AD-controlled legislature passed a law granting him extensive decree authority over the important areas of finance and economics. This elimination of the need for a president to politic and bargain with the congress gave rise to a concern that Venezuela might be headed for a test of its constitutional system (Kelley 1977:41, 45).

But it led also to the (successful) charges in 1978 by COPEI presidential candidate Luis Herrera Campins that AD, in total control of an oil-rich state in the boom years of OPEC's cartel, had been inept. As a result, Herrera argued, AD reigned over declining agricultural production, mushrooming bureaucratic "employment," and high unemployment (Needler 1983:96). In a final field of ten candidates, Herrera Campins won by 47 percent of the vote in an election where approximately 88 percent of the electorate cast their ballots (Fitzgibbon and Fernandez 1981:149). If the 1978 campaign to "kick the rascals out" is a valid indicator of constitutional survival, then we are likely to see a continuation of the sharing of decisionmaking power between the executive and the legislature as mediated by political parties.

Like Costa Rica, Venezuela has witnessed a sizable increase in the number of bureaucratic agencies since 1958. And, also as in Costa Rica, there is some evidence that bureaucratic policymaking and implementation is less than efficient or effectual because of an array of agencies with overlapping, and sometimes contradictory, responsibilities. In the area of agricultural policy, which, along with oil policy, continues to be a key concern of the Venezuelan regime, the National Agrarian Institute (IAN) is the main agrarian reform agency. Yet in specific efforts at agricultural reform, policy decisions may include not only the IAN but also the Agricultural and Livestock Bank (BAP), the state-owned Corporation of Agricultural Marketing, the Bank of Agricultural Development, the Council of Rural Welfare, and even various state agencies for particular crops (Martz 1980:38). This plethora of agricultural-related state agencies both confuses the implementation process and leaves that process open to influence by various organized interests.

As we have argued in Chapter 2, interest group activity in the policy process is quite pluralistic in Venezuela, with most groups more autonomous and less "corporatized" than, for example, those of Brazil and Mexico. Nevertheless, there does not appear to be a consensus as to just how pluralistic the system really is. In her study of population policy, Ieda Siqueira Wiarda suggests that Venezuelan society and politics "to a considerable extent is organized in a corporate and elitist manner, with certain key groups in the society playing a decisive role in policymaking and implementation . . ." (1974:345). Daniel Levine, focusing on the church elites in Venezuela, concluded, in general, that "the articulation of demands in Venezuela is, for all practical purposes, monopolized by the political parties that penetrate and control other demand-making institutions such as trade unions and professional associations" (1979:56). Still another perspective is provided by José Antonio Gil, who pointed out that all contemporary governments have had to bargain and deal with organized, autonomous business interests, particularly the powerful peak association, the Federation of Chambers of Commerce and Production (FEDE-CAMARAS). Moreover, Gil argued, any arrangements made by the major political parties (AD and COPEI) with these business interests have always been tentative and provisional, necessitating skillful political maneuvering and bargaining (Gil 1977).

For example, the delicate maneuvering that laid the groundwork for the entry of Venezuela into the Andean Pact included President Rafael Caldera's politically astute appointment of Dr. Julio Sosa Rodríguez as plenipotentiary minister to negotiate the entry. Sosa Rodríguez, a leader of one of the smaller business groups, also enjoyed personal friendships with many FEDECAMARAS directors who, before Dr. Sosa's arrival on the scene, had lobbied against Venezuela's joining the Andean Pact (Gil 1977:150). Moreover, before oil was nationalized in 1976, FEDECAMARAS, rather than being monopolized by one or another political party, served as the locus for the massive propaganda campaigns of private oil companies (Tugwell 1975:161).

Similarly, William P. Avery argues that FEDECAMARAS is probably the most powerful private interest group in Venezuela. Avery points out that FEDECAMARAS, in alliance with the Venezuelan Exporters Association and the Caracas Chamber of Industrialists, was the source of private opposition to Venezuela's proposed entry into the Latin American Free Trade Area (LAFTA). President Leoni ultimately pushed LAFTA through congress with a few compromises, but private opposition spearheaded by FEDECAMARAS delayed Venezuela's entry for six years (Avery 1976:544–545). In addition, it is quite possible that the private-sector opposition to LAFTA triumphed ultimately in the implementation of that policy since Venezuela's participation in LAFTA has been half-hearted at best. It is reasonable to conclude that the organized private business sector, while not always cohesive, makes the public sector actors (president, congress, ministries) reluctant to force on it unfavorable policies.

Earlier in this chapter we alluded to the role allegedly played by foreign concerns in the policy process. A recent and enlightening study by Fernando Coronil and Julie Skurski describes the impact of foreign-based transnational automobile companies on the implementation stage of policymaking (Coronil and Skurski 1982). As part of the regional economic cooperation with the Andean Pact alliance, Venezuela was to make efforts to become an auto and truck producer. President Pérez, using his constitutional decree powers, enacted the so-called Auto Policy Law in May 1975. By the time the policy got to the implementation stages—which necessitated bargaining with major foreign-owned companies—the power of these transnational corporations was sufficient to derail the Auto Policy Law. As Pérez himself said in an interview in 1980: "The auto transnationals appear to struggle but in reality there are underlying accords. When we attempted to implement the automobile policy we noticed how the transnationals divided up markets and fields of action and influence in order to obstruct our plan" (Coronil and Skurski 1982:88).

As we have said previously, oil policy has been a preeminent concern of Venezuelan policymakers since the 1920s. It is in this policy area also that powerful foreign interests have seemingly had their greatest impact on the Venezuelan policy process. Yet there was a perceptible, though incremental, movement on the part of Venezuelan political elites that caused the shift of power from the oil multinationals to the Venezuelan state, ultimately resulting in the 1976 oil nationalization law. Much of the research on this process, in contrast to the above-mentioned study on the Auto Policy Law, emphasizes the relatively open, ambiguous, nonoligarchic nature of policymaking (see Tugwell 1975, 1977; Martz 1977b). In the concluding section of his book on the politics of oil in Venezuela, Franklin Tugwell wrote that "as far as Venezuela is concerned it would seem that many common generalizations about corporate power and the ability of foreign investors to manipulate the domestic affairs of dependent countries are wide of the mark, not so much because the influence is not there, but because of the problems involved in wielding it under conditions of uncertainty and rapid political and social change" (1975:159). Part of this context of rapid change included the flexing of their respective muscles by the two major political parties, COPEI and AD, who used the oil issue as a political football, resulting in a diffraction of the power of initiative between the executive and legislative branches. This fragmented party system gave way propitiously in 1973 when AD president Pérez had a majority control in both houses for the first and, thus far, only time in modern political history. This fact allowed AD to have enough control to push the nationalization bill through strident party opposition (Martz 1977b:499).

In a more cautious vein, however, Tugwell suggested that at least part of the reason for the seeming demise of the foreign oil companies vis-à-vis the power of the state was simply a matter of luck: namely, the huge increases in state oil revenues that preceded and, for awhile, followed the nationalization decision (1977:251–252). Tugwell claimed that, to some extent, the very success of Venezuela's democratic experiment thus far has been due to the relative wealth provided by oil-filled state coffers:

> Put succinctly, [political leaders] were able to move ahead with state-directed expansion of the economy, increasing the income and political administrative power of the middle class, but without directly threatening the interest of established elites. Generous import substitution protection, favorable fiscal and monetary policies (especially the absence of significant income taxation), and extreme caution in foreign economic policy . . . all have made life relatively comfortable for the domestic private sector.

Tugwell's comments give one the uneasy feeling that the bargain struck between middle-class politicians and domestic elites in 1958 might not have been kept were it not for Venezuela's wealth. And Venezuela's version of democracy, remarkable as it is in the context of Latin America, needs even more careful nurturing in the 1980s as the "OPEC Connection" seems to be, at least temporarily, drying up. For the time being, public policymaking in Venezuela appears to be relatively pluralistic and relatively open. Its bias, if it exists, seems to be toward certain business groups over others and toward business and other commercial elites at the expense of the less well-to-do Venezuelans. Agrarian reform policies (as John Martz will discuss along with oil policy in this chapter), putatively made in the interests of the peasantry, often neither reflect peasants' demands nor satisfy peasants' needs (Martz 1980).

CASE STUDY

The Frailties
of Venezuelan Policymaking

JOHN D. MARTZ

Introduction: Pluralism and Policymaking

In the literature of Latin American politics the concern with regime types and systemic characteristics has persisted for years. The elaboration of case studies of policymaking in the Latin American context, however, has received somewhat peripheral attention until recently. Yet the politics of policymaking merit both theoretical formulations and detailed case studies.

Three prevailing ideologies—the Social Christian, Social Democratic, and the Marxist—have helped to set public policy objectives in pluralistic Venezuela. Despite significant differences, the three have generally concurred with one another over four policy objectives: nationalism, statism, populism, and developmentalism (Gil 1981:173). Furthermore, there has been a general willingness to follow what Hughes and Mijeski in Chapter 6 term a "middle path" between the model of economic growth (Mexico and Brazil) and that of basic social redistribution (Cuba). For petroleum policy, this middle path is reflected in the gradualistic approach toward nationalization, accompanied by the willingness to draw upon foreign, and even "imperialist," sources of expertise. Nationalism and populism were enhanced by the takeover of the nation's major economic resources, while the role of the state was stressed, and developmental measures were adopted. With agriculture, there emerged an early emphasis on the populist social concerns of agrarian reform and peasant welfare, to be followed by economic growth, agricultural technification, and the continuing involvement of the state.

The analysis of policy patterns in Venezuela can be illuminated by such typologies as that of Theodore Lowi categorizing policy instruments in terms of redistribution, regulation, and distribution (Lowi 1964:690–691, 713). The first takes from one sector for the benefit of others, resulting in cleavages between entrepreneurs and the government. The regulative type sets conditions in a situation of limited opportunities, calling for alternating coalitions among private and public sectors. Lastly, the distributive type presumably occurs in response to diverse interests, wherein opportunity is extensive. As applied to petroleum and to agriculture, both instruments and objectives can be defined. With petroleum, the nationalization itself met objectives of statism and nationalism while employing redistributive instruments. The postnationalization era placed its concern on maintaining and then expanding industry, recognizing its enduring centrality to the Venezuelan economy. In the area of agriculture, the 1960 Agrarian Reform reified the objectives of nationalism and populism. The instrumentality of the Agrarian Reform Institute was avowedly dedicated to redistributive goals. With the passing of years, there was a shift toward developmentalism, an implicit result of which was a strengthening of regulative instruments at the expense of the redistributive. In both instances, the politicization of the policy arena was perceptible.

The choice of two cases—petroleum and agriculture—derives from our broader concerns over the role and impact of actors in the policy process, the characteristics of public policymaking, and the blend of strengths and weaknesses in a pluralistic polity. What emerges will be a pair of policy arenas that, although they differ, are equally crucial to Venezuelan development and modernization. Both exist at the "macro" level and are integral parts of the Venezuelan democracy. Petroleum, only recently nationalized and therefore more fully under the control of the state, has provided the wherewithal for socioeconomic progress for several decades. Agriculture, basic to the feeding of a populace, has been converted into an instrument for social justice and political mobilization as well as income production. Its effectiveness in each of these categories has been mixed at best.

The pronounced politicization of the Venezuelan system is reflected in the record of both petroleum and agriculture. The form that pluralistic democracy has assumed in Venezuela—quite properly a source of pride for Venezuelans and envy for millions of Latin Americans elsewhere—at the same time incorporates problematic elements. Even a superficial overview of the petroleum industry suggests that the societal consensus that led to nationalization in 1976 has more recently been endangered by government fiscal chaos and bureaucratic incompetence in the handling of the economy. For agriculture, the alleged objectives of social justice as embodied in the 1960 legislation were ultimately subordinated to the needs of production and economic growth at the macro level.

The Politics of Petroleum

The near-mythic Los Barrosos strike of 1922, a blowout of a million barrels daily for nine days, marked the initiation of Venezuela's petroleum-based economy and society. Its historical evolution has been traced in detail by numerous scholars, including this writer (Martz 1984; Tugwell 1975; Lieuwen 1954; Vallenilla 1975; Rabe 1982). Through the years prior to 1958, large earnings had infused the economy and society. Income was of such a magnitude as to produce a powerful symbiotic relationship of oil with national politics. The British authority George Philip provides a summation.

> During this time, massive income had found its way to the Venezuelan Treasury and Venezuelan society. The high profits which the companies earned for many years, the massive corruption of certain of Venezuela's rulers and even the relative weakening of the country's market position after about 1957 were not sufficient to check the impact of oil wealth. With its oil income, the country's political order had been consolidated by successive Venezuelan presidents. . . . Acción Democrática governments [from 1959 to 1969] subsequently spread the wealth among unionised workers (especially the oil workers) and among a provincial, even rural, electorate in order to oil the party's efficient electoral machine. By the 1970s, practically the whole of Venezuela had benefitted to some degree from the oil industry and none showed any eagerness to damage this source of fabulous wealth (1982:293).

The initial years of the democratic experience were dominated by the AD and its *técnicos*. Party founder and leader Rómulo Betancourt, the 1959–1964 constitutional president, had long relied upon and worked closely with Juan Pablo Pérez Alfonzo in petroleum matters. The latter, who became his minister of mines and hydrocarbons in 1959, had indicated the basic outlook in a June 1954 memorandum written while in exile.

> Venezuela has a great resource in its petroleum, but it is also faced with great responsibility. It must not impede use of this resource to satisfy the needs of other peoples but, in protecting its own national interest, it must never let the industry become dilapidated.
>
> Petroleum is the principal of all indispensable fuels in modern life. . . . Venezuela needs to maintain and even to increase the income it receives from petroleum (Pérez Alfonzo 1961:83–84).

Such a view ran parallel to that of other party leaders and to existing AD party doctrinal theses (see Acción Democrática 1958a:24–25). It also largely coincided with views of other democratic party leaders in Venezuela, for a basic national consensus had emerged over petroleum objectives and strategies. As synthesized by Blank, these latter were (1) achievement of a "just" share of oil profits; (2) the "sowing" of oil profits to gain integrated national development; (3) conservation of proven reserves; and (4) encouragement of global conditions to assure stable markets (Blank 1984).

When the *adeco* (AD) hegemony was shattered by the 1968 electoral victory of Rafael Caldera and COPEI, Venezuela entered "perhaps the most crucial [administration] of the whole democratic period with regard to the oil industry" (Philip 1982:301). Its experience under Caldera led to the virtual disappearance of the conservative view, which sought long-term accommodation with the multinational corporations. The role of congress and of all the non-Marxist political parties proved central to the convergence of opinion regarding nationalization. The Hydrocarbons Reversion Law, adopted on July 30, 1971, directed that annual deposits from foreign corporations assure the good condition of installations when turned over to the nation after the forty-year concessions (most of which would be due by 1983). Although the *copeyano* (COPEI) president initially seemed to waver between his own accommodationist inclinations and opposition attacks on the oil industry, he eventually moved vigorously in questioning the multinationals and their intentions (Tugwell 1975:158). Although the AD and the People's Electoral Movement (MEP) had provided early initiatives in the reversion discussions, ultimately the COPEI concluded that it would be "firmly in the nationalist camp, calling for greater Venezuelan control over the country's resources" (Herman 1980:157).

By the close of the Caldera administration it was undeniable that there was "an almost irresistible combination of factors leading to a 'nationalization situation'" (Sigmund 1980:364). Two sets of concerns could be extrapolated from the debate of the day: the political and the technocratic. In relation to the former, the 1973 campaign had stressed the idea that partisan elements should be minimized. As the victorious AD candidate had insisted, "*no voy a petrolizar las elecciones*" (loosely, "I'm not going to 'petroleumize' the elections"). Early in his new administration Carlos Andrés Pérez set up a commission to study the process of nationalization; a major purpose of the commission was to channel or mitigate possible political conflict. The 1974 nationalization of iron ore was also undertaken as a training ground for petroleum. The government hoped ultimately to carry through the nationalization without partisan controversy, but it was not to be.

The reliance on a variety of public, private, congressional, and party-based mechanisms and forums was an attempt to show national concord. But for one crucial provision of the nationalization law, the objective would have been realizable. Article 5, which empowered the state to sign "agreements of association" with foreign companies subject to congressional authorization, provided the basis for political dissensus. According to the initial draft,

In special cases and when it suits the public interest, the National Executive . . . may, in the exercise of such activities, enter into agreements of association with private entities, but with participation such as will guarantee State control, and for a limited duration. Such agreements will require prior authorization of Congress meeting in joint session to fix conditions of the contract after having been duly informed by the National Executive as to all pertinent circumstances (República de Venezuela 1975:unpaginated).

The opposition, particularly in congress, raised a host of objections, all of which focussed basically on the question of national control over the industry. As the leading opposition party of the moment, COPEI could have been expected to find some basis for sharp disagreement with Acción Democrática, although there was genuine nationalistic concern inside the party over the implications of Article 5. The Marxist Left was inevitably outspoken in its sensitivity to any possible concession to international economic interests. Moreover, there was the widespread practical concern for opposition parties that the nationalization—inevitably and justifiably an historic event for Venezuela—would be credited exclusively to Pérez and the AD. Through mid-1975 the administration continued to seek a compromise, but this proved impossible. Granted its majority in both houses of congress, the *adeco* government had the votes to enact the legislation, and in the end exercised its control. On August 29, 1975 the Petroleum Industry Nationalization Law was signed by Carlos Andrés Pérez. Pledging not to undertake any of the controversial joint service ventures during his term, he ignored partisan differences and spoke of unanimity of opinion. He vowed "our irrevocable purpose of showing that a just society is possible only through respect for human freedom. We are committed . . . to a grandiose work of taking the initial steps for the economic liberation of Venezuela, and I invite my countrymen to achieve the task that is ours. *Manos a la Obra!*" (Pérez 1976:15).

The actual act of nationalization, dramatic though it was, nonetheless represented a form of incrementalism that had evolved over a period of decades. The relationship between the government and multinational corporations, the progressive technification of the industry, the rise of nationalistic sentiment, and the character of international economic forces all contributed to the movement toward nationalization. Despite differences of outlook on certain details, the fundamental choices had gained the approval of all political forces. As these helped to mobilize public opinion, the very existence of a pluralistic democracy assured popular enthusiasm for the measure. Having enacted the nationalization, attention turned more directly toward technical and professional rather than political factors.

History amply confirms in Latin America, as I contended elsewhere (Martz 1984), that the transferral of nationalized industries to state control is difficult. Among the perils are declines in productivity, inefficiency, mismanagement, and a reduction in profitability. For Venezuela, the undeniable pride in nationalization was accompanied by apprehension over its ability to manage the industry effectively. Even before the enabling legislation, veteran AD leader Manuel Pérez Guerrero had expressed his concern over "management capacity" (*NYT*, 12/2/1974). The minister of mines, Valentín Hernández Acosta, had observed that had Venezuela nationalized "heroically," it would not have allowed the nationalized industry "to continue to bring in the income which the country requires for its development plans" (*Resumen*, 12/21/1975). As events would prove, the nationalization was unusual in the degree of continuing cooperation with foreign companies. The transition to national ownership was also smooth. Thus, "in the first two years of operation, the nationalized oil industry . . . avoided most of the pitfalls . . . associated with nationalization of foreign mineral investments" (Sigmund 1980:247).

As nationalization took effect, with twenty-two concessionary companies reorganized as fourteen entities under the holding company structure of Petroleum of Venezuela (PDVSA), the petroleum industry gave the appearance of aging. Nearly two-thirds of the daily output came from a half-dozen fields which, with one exception, had been opened in the 1920s and 1930s. In the absence of new discoveries, more sophisticated recovery techniques would be required. Production had also been gradually declining. As a consequence the industry undertook substantial investment and development programs. From a cautious investment in 1976 of $323.5 million, expansion had reached $2.27 billion by 1980.

The Venezuelan Petroleum Company (PETROVEN) had also been actively engaged in expanding refinery facilities at Amuay and El Palito, along with modernization of the Cardon catalytic cracker. In addition, the national petrochemical industry's Venezuelan Petrochemical Institute (IVP), notorious for years of unparalleled squandering and mishandling of funds, was placed under PETROVEN control in March 1978. The IVP was renamed Pequivén; it was drastically reorganized, foreign technical help was introduced, and by 1981 the corner toward profitability had been turned.

These and other accomplishments of PETROVEN were the result of two major elements: the administrative structures that were adopted, and the systemic commitment to the "democratic management of the industry" (Blank 1984), a maximum of administrative discretion and economic self-sufficiency as assured by Venezuela's political elites. There had been careful and thoughtful consideration of both the structures and the operating principles. The first was best exemplified by naming as head of PETROVEN retired General Rafael Alfonzo Ravard, who enjoyed an exceptional record of technical and managerial skill as head of the Venezuelan Guayana Corporation (CVG). He easily secured the pledge from Carlos Andrés Pérez that PETROVEN would be isolated from political forces. It would operate as a commercial company affiliated with the state. This was a position neither easily nor automatically won nor was it to endure indefinitely.

Administrative and structural cleavages initially arose less from partisan sources than from bureaucratic conflict within the executive branch. President Pérez's minister of mines, Hernández Acosta, from the outset, was displeased with PETROVEN's independence, which he saw as diminishing the ministry's role. "We have to be as careful with Petróleos de Venezuela with respect to the technical matters and the development of the industry as we have been with the concessionary companies. . . . We cannot let Petróleos de Venezuela treat the subject from the purely commercial point of view, without taking into account national policy on prices as well as the commitments Venezuela has accepted in international organizations like OPEC" (*Resumen*, 3/28/1976). The corporation's understandable desire to control its own technical, bureaucratic, and financial fate was, equally predictably, a source of ministerial disapproval.

At the same time, there was substantial support for General Ravard's insistence that PDVSA be free of external interference. As he told a leading Venezuelan news weekly in early 1977, "financial autonomy is an indispensable condition for guaranteeing the operational efficiency and expansion of the industry" (*Resumen*, 1/16/1977). This was connected to the effort to retain the basic prenationalization structure. In time, the operating companies were reduced to four: Lagoven (essentially Exxon's former Creole subsidiary), Maraven (derived from Shell of Venezuela), Meneven (based on the Mene Grande subsidiary of Gulf Oil), and Corpoven (an amalgamation of several smaller companies, including Mobil). For PDVSA and its director, then, the early years of nationalization were characterized in large part by a decentralized structure designed to protect the professional *técnicos* from political interference.

The effect of technical planning during the first years of PDVSA could be seen in the apolitical character of industry activities. As Venezuela slipped into a fiscal and economic morass by the turn of the decade, however, both substantive and organizational problems became public and resulted in increased political attention from both the government and opposition. Among the issues that bore meaning for both the process and the implementation of policy was that of basic organizational structure. This was best exemplified in the conflicts, both potential and real, between PDVSA and the Ministry of Energy and Mines. The concern of Valentín Hernández at the outset of nationalization is recalled. Moreover, other critics saw his emphasis on international oil policy in 1976–1978 as permitting undue independence to PDVSA. When Herrera took office, his newly appointed minister, Humberto Calderón Berti, emphasized that "there are not two oil industries, just a single one which is governed by the Ministry of Energy and Mines, the entity that guides and formulates the policy that Petróleos de Venezuela and the operating companies must execute" (*Business Venezuela*, 1979). This suggested not only the possibility of personal clashes between personnel of the two respective bodies, but also an organizational distinction between centralization and decentralization.

During the Pérez administration, PDVSA had successfully pushed for the latter. This was seen as a means of "protecting the position of the professional technician and keeping him in the industry despite the great international opportunities for qualified men of this kind" (Philip 1982:479). It became increasingly questioned after the Pérez years, however. In addition to tensions between PDVSA and the Ministry, there was growing concern emanating from the opposition. By early 1981 Acción Democrática was issuing public statements criticizing alleged extravagances of the PDVSA investment program. Party president Gonzalo Barrios and former Interior Minister Octavio Lepage both expressed the desire for greater PDVSA accountability to congress (*SIC*, 1981:231). Such partisan pressures encouraged the Herrera administration to seek greater control. The minister of energy and mines began chairing meetings of PDVSA stockholders.

In the meantime, the autonomy of the industry was being questioned by a series of policy decisions with which it disagreed. A prime example centered on PDVSA control of its own fiscal reserves, estimated by early 1982 at some $9 billion to $19 billion. The planning minister conceded his interest in drawing on PDVSA funds to help service the foreign debt. Meanwhile, the president of the Venezuelan Central Bank (BCV), Leopoldo Díaz Bruzual, bluntly charged the industry with producing more new employees than new wells. Arguing that the industry's reserves were part of the national patrimony, Díaz Bruzual— "El Bufalo" in Venezuelan political argot—ultimately persuaded the government to place $4.51 billion of PDVSA reserves under Central Bank control.

The interplay of economics and the petroleum industry became ever more pronounced. In February 1983 Alfonzo Ravard conceded that PDVSA was considering foreign financing for its investment programs. The industry itself could not sustain the $4.4 billion projected for 1983. By May it was evident that the industry was retrenching on a massive scale. Projects of more than $10 billion were cancelled.

As the Herrera administration drew to a conclusion, the once-sacrosanct petroleum industry found itself seriously exposed to partisan intervention, its vaunted technical competence challenged, and its resources for investment growth greatly diminished. With the inauguration of the new government in January 1984, it remained to be seen whether the earlier benefits of systemic pluralism would once again provide the public support and administrative insulation from the bureaucratic mismanagement present in other policy arenas. One of the most handsomely funded sectors—agriculture—sadly testified to the frailties of Venezuelan policymaking.

The Agonies of Agriculture Policy

Agriculture policy in Venezuela presents a different dimension from that of petroleum. While the earnings of the latter are necessary to finance development and modernization, the output of agriculture reaches the citizenry directly. If agricultural production is low, prices inadequate, land poorly divided, and foodstuffs poorly marketed and distributed to the public, benefits from petroleum wealth are also dissipated. For Venezuelans to speak of "sowing the oil" is to mean, in part, channelling of funds to strengthen the agricultural sector and better feed the people. Agrarian reform, to serve especially the undernourished marginal masses, has been a major social and economic policy objective under the post-1958 democratic system. After a full quarter-century, it can only be concluded that the results have been of limited benefit to most Venezuelans. One Venezuelan scholar wrote that despite "enormous investments allocated to this program by democratic administrations, neither agricultural production nor the peasants' living conditions have changed enough to justify such investments" (Gil 1981:27). There are other, less harsh, assessments, but few deny the failure to attain many of the original goals.

The multiparty coalition government installed in March 1959 was dominated by President Betancourt and his Acción Democrática. The party commitment to agrarian reform was longstanding, with three major objectives: (1) expropriation and redistribution of lands; (2) utilization of uncultivated land; and (3) protection of private enterprise where modern technology assured efficient production (Acción Democrática 1958b). For some, there were inherent contradictions. In 1969 the then-director of the National Agrarian Institute (IAN) spoke of "antagonistic concepts" and "contradictory provisions" in the 1960 Agrarian Reform Law. He saw a conflict between promised "transformation" of the agrarian structure and the preservation of large landholdings "which performed a social function" (Alegrett 1971:75). At the same time, however, Venezuela was avoiding the pitfalls of many Third World countries that redistributed ownership without considering patterns of productivity and efficiency. In any event, as Betancourt pledged upon signing the measure on March 5, 1960, the rule of law would be followed, while his administration would invest some $550 million. He saw the strategic objective as that of creating other peasants; "the agrarian reform program was designed to mold some 300,000 subsistence farm families into a productive sector of the national economy" (Powell 1971:109).

The availability of petroleum wealth greatly enhanced the prospects for implementation of the program. As John Lombardi put it:

The Venezuelan land reform proceeded on the basis of compensated expropriations, distribution of publicly held land, and provisional titling of beneficiaries. . . . By compensating owners of expropriated land at market prices, the government avoided the worst consequences of an outraged landowning class and reinforced its moderate, responsible international reputation. By awarding provisional titles to peasants who lived on or had invaded agricultural properties, the governments of the 1960s managed to deliver land to a relatively large number of households without resolving the many difficulties involved in awarding final, legal title to the land. . . . Under the provisions of the 1960 land reform law, moreover, landholdings may be of any size;

hence large estates, if judged to serve a useful social purpose, could be left intact (1982: 235–236).

As adopted in 1960 and put into action, the program endured through the Betancourt government and that of his AD compatriot Raúl Leoni as well.

Various Betancourt goals were not met, e.g., the redistribution of land to 350,000 landless families. However, there were notable achievements, including the strengthening of political consensus behind the program, expansion of government credits and funding sources, and improvement of productivity for several basic foodstuffs. Under President Leoni a similar reformist strategy was maintained, although some diminution in momentum was perceptible. Greater attention was directed to the productivity and efficiency of private holdings, larger areas of uncultivated government land were made available to redistribution, and higher priority was accorded to the consolidation of earlier *asentamientos* (settlements).

After a decade of *adeco* government the Social Christians came to power with Rafael Caldera, whose party was less intimately involved in agricultural policy than was Acción Democrática. However, changes under Caldera were incremental rather than basic. The new government did not alter credit policies, continued to diversify methods, and allowed a further burgeoning of the bureaucracy responsible for agriculture. By the early 1970s there was a myriad of agencies dealing with agriculture, including the Ministry itself, the National Agrarian Institute, the Agricultural and Livestock Bank, the Agricultural Marketing Corporation, Agricultural Development Bank, Council of Rural Welfare, Unified Program of Agricultural Development (PRIDA), and others (Soto 1973:73).

Although the Caldera administration did not reverse the reformist–social justice approach, it introduced at least two major structural entities. PRIDA, presented during COPEI's first year in office, was described by its partisans as changing the social process of land redistribution to an economic process; the main goal was "incorporation of the farmer into the economic, social, and political life of the country via a series of projects destined to consolidate the process of the ten-year-old agrarian reform program" (Herman 1980:162). PRIDA identified four geographic zones in which to promote development, with $190 million invested by the administration. It served as a focus for partisan competition between COPEI and the AD for rural political support. At the least, it reinforced the commitment of Venezuela's political elite to agrarian reform. Beyond this, the Caldera government also promulgated the Law of Agricultural Marketing on August 21, 1970, which created the Corporation for Agricultural Marketing (CORPOMERCADEO). It was charged with overseeing food marketing, setting minimum prices, defining limits on basic commodities, fixing government subsidies, and so forth. Typical of its activities was the payment of a $4 million annual subsidy to wheat importers to maintain the price of bread at its forty-year level.

By the close of the Caldera government, Venezuela had experienced fifteen years of social reformism in the *campo* (countryside). With the electoral campaign of 1973, earlier assumptions linking agrarian reform with agricultural productivity and modernization were increasingly questioned (Martz and Baloyra 1976:140,150–51). It was evident that the peasant had not been converted from sharecropper to modern agricultural producer. Neither peasants' improved living conditions nor greater national productivity appeared to have been enough to balance massive state investments. There were still some 250,000 landless rural families, while subsidization both drained the national treasury and, in supporting modest market prices, failed to offer incentive for more efficient production. It was time for a different approach.

Both major candidates saw the situation in similar terms. While COPEI's Lorenzo Fernández could scarcely criticize his old friend and colleague Rafael Caldera, it was possible for the 1973 platform to stress change. The watchwords were "accelerated agricultural growth," "efficient, modern and integral agrarian reform," and "conservation and promotion of renewable natural resources" (Fernández 1973:7). Carlos Andrés Pérez could decry an agricultural crisis without attacking his own party ex-presidents. "The government over which I will preside pledges to the country priority attention to the needs of Venezuelan agriculture as the essential motor of economic development, as the generator of employment for the most numerous sector of our economically active population; as a primordial base for the nourishment of our growing population; and as the indispensable source of primary products" (Pérez 1973:31). Having first praised the early *trienio* policies, Pérez reiterated the view that agrarian reform per se was "one of the fundamental government objectives in all countries in the process of development in the contemporary world" (1973:38). At the same time, he appeared more concerned with modernization and development than with landownership.

Having won an impressive victory, the new president soon announced a five-year program of irrigation and water resources; construction of dams and other projects creating 120,000 jobs. Public works abounded, and in April 1975 President Pérez boasted that an agricultural miracle was at hand. Available data seriously questioned such assessments, but the administration proceeded with efforts that seemed to favor agribusiness and organized economic interests. Debt cancellation benefited large farmers rather than small producers. The rise in corruption and inefficiency, encouraged by the flood of "petrobolívars" produced in the post-1973 financial markets, reached the agriculture ministry as well as such agencies as the Agricultural Development Fund (FDA).

The Pérez commitment to agricultural development was undeniable, and massive funds were provided. However, structural weakness in agriculture had become increasingly evident. Data were damning. For instance, in 1971 Venezuela had imported 46 percent of its basic foodstuffs; by the close of the Pérez years it was approaching 70 percent. Three-fourths of fats and oils, 36 percent of chickens, 27 percent of eggs, 43 percent of sugar and—most disturbing of all—70 percent of the *caraota negra*, Venezuela's staple black bean, had to be imported (*Financial Times*, 1978).

With the coming of a new electoral campaign, there were the inevitable promises of greater efficiency and more fruitful policymaking. There was an implicit agreement that agricultural technification was more appropriate than the agrarian reform of earlier years. The Venezuelan political elites in effect were prepared to accept emphases on economic growth, while promising more effective administration. In the case of Acción Democrática, party candidate Luis Piñerúa Ordaz faced the inevitable problem of eschewing criticism of fellow *adeco* Pérez. He supported technological modernization, capitalist expansion, and a strengthening of ties between the party and the business sector. From the Social Christians, and their candidate Luis Herrera Campins, there was predictable opposition criticism of Pérez but relatively little was constructive.

Luis Herrera Campins, the victor, was convinced that the overheated economy required a heavy dose of austerity and restabilization and brought into office a number of Venezuelan "Chicago boys." Chief among these was Finance Minister Luis Ugueto, who remained a major architect of economic policy until December 1982. As Ugueto saw it, there were four major economic concerns: (1) control of spending and reduction of public-sector expenditures; (2) a diminished pace of expansion for imports and liquidity; (3) removal of price controls to encourage domestic production; and (4) a diminution of import tariffs to promote manufacturing competition and efficiency. Tight credit policies would combat inflation, restore economic growth, and stimulate domestic production. Agriculture was seen as a vitally important sector, one therefore to be subject to this basic approach. State controls were to be reduced gradually, with free enterprise responding in kind.

During his first year in office the new president began by removing price controls from approximately 175 consumer items, exempting only a few products defined as "essential." Domestic production would grow, it was argued, as tariff exemptions were withdrawn from both raw materials and capital goods. The business sector applauded this reversal of previous policy, and the administration expected that agriculture would be prodded toward greater output. However, the anticipated price rise and growing inflationary pressures inevitably drove the AD-dominated Venezuelan Workers Confederation (CTV) to demand compensatory salary increases. When prices rose 9.4 percent between August and October 1979 (compared to 7.2 percent for all of 1978), the administration agreed to legislation calling for salary increases.

In November, raises of from 25 to 30 percent were extended to low-paid workers.

The removal of subsidies on many other imported foodstuffs in January 1980, though consistent with administration policy, added further to inflation. Price controls had held the annual inflation rate in Venezuela to an average 3 percent from 1930 to 1970—then growing to some 8 percent under Pérez—the figure now leapt toward 20 percent. The cost-of-living index for metropolitan Caracas, which rose 7.1 percent in 1978, spurted an additional 11.6 percent the following year.

Agriculture soon reflected the growing malaise, which gripped the national economy as stagnation set in. Despite increased income from oil imports during the early Herrera years, the growth of the domestic product in 1980 fell to 1.5 percent. Inflation that year registered 21.6 percent, while the underestimated official unemployment rate was over 10 percent. The administration, convinced that economic austerity was unavoidable, conceded that stimulation of the private sector had not been totally successful. In March 1981 President Herrera told the Congress, "Our decision to free prices has been a healthy and patriotic economic objective, but it cannot be left to the market to impose efficiency. The state will continue to stimulate competition, but can never renounce its regulatory function" (*LAWR*, 3/27/1981).

By the close of 1981 the administration's resolve appeared to be wavering. Higher subsidies and support prices were gradually reintroduced and new financing provided low-interest ten-year loans to farmers. Overall, agricultural output grew by a mere 2.8 percent.

In the meantime, food imports were setting new record highs. By mid-1983 over two-thirds of Venezuela's food was being imported from abroad. Official explanations of the faltering record were multiple, including a rainy season of unusual ferocity. At the same time—as had been customary with the previous administration—small producers received limited attention while agribusiness was sympathetically treated. Bureaucratic shortcomings inevitably worsened existing problems. For example, in early 1983 there was decision-making paralysis for weeks while the administration debated the details for implementation of new foreign exchange policies. The president of the local branch of the Inter-American Council of Commerce and Production explained the resultant difficulty for agriculture. "When this began, we had seven weeks' worth of food inside our borders, but we have taken three weeks arguing over the economic measures, and in this time the country has been paralyzed—the bureaucrats haven't known what to import and at what price, and we are eating commercial inventories and prime materials. If you consider that we import up to 70 percent of what we eat, that means we have only four more weeks of food left" (*NYT*, 3/21/1983).

The bureaucratic obstacles include the overlapping authority and responsibility of the plethora of existing agencies, as already noted. While a few operated with a degree of efficiency, the majority have become notorious for their shortcomings. Perhaps the prime example by the early 1980s was COR-POMERCADEO, the agricultural marketing and distribution agency. Frequently a focus for partisan exchanges between the AD and COPEI, it had become an agency whose inefficiency is matched only by its corruption. In part, the CORPOMERCADEO record mirrored the broader national problems of agricultural policymaking. For despite a quarter-century's infusion of vast funds through an ever-expanding array of state agencies, the actual operating infrastructure remained sadly lacking. A task force that studied the situation in late 1982 upon the request of President Herrera placed particular emphasis on shortcomings in marketing and storage. Inevitably, the task force also saw the past flow of petrobolívars as having encouraged either faulty or sloppy execution of programs. Speaking as foreigners, the members couched their findings in diplomatic language. In a masterpiece of understatement, they remarked that "the Government of Venezuela has implemented numerous programs designed to improve and expand agriculture, but the results have been disappointing" (NYT, 3/27/1983).

The coming of 1983 brought the next electoral campaign. Former president Rafael Caldera, eligible to run for another term, carried the COPEI banner against the AD's Jaime Lusinchi. The financial and exchange crisis that hit Venezuela with a vengeance in early 1983 dominated the substance of campaign rhetoric, and agriculture received little meaningful attention.

At the same time, national political elites were by no means cavalier about problems endemic to agriculture. It was no secret that the 6.2 percent of GNP provided by agriculture was the lowest of any Latin American country. The enormous investments since 1959 had not greatly increased productivity, nor had they improved significantly the quality of life in the countryside. The migration from a rural to urban setting during this period also showed a profound alteration of demographic patterns. Accompanying such conditions were the implications and priorities for broad strategic approaches, especially given the vigorously competitive pluralism of contemporary Venezuela. It cannot be forgotten that initial demands for reform had come less from quiescent campesinos than from rising middle-class activists seeking a democratization of the entire system. The creators of Acción Democrática were the first to articulate such concerns.

Contrary to early doctrinal claims, the AD program was eminently capitalist in its assumptions and objectives. As in other Third World countries, the forms of latifundia agriculture were "entirely consistent with, indeed rested upon, capitalist relations of production" (Redclift 1978:4). The AD combined its interest in economic modernization and agricultural productivity with a preoccupation over the quality of life in the countryside. The trienio experience demonstrated the concern with rural social justice, and this was consistent with the underlying rationale of government policy during the Betancourt-

Leoni decade. Much of the agenda was clearly political, given the initial emphasis on state leadership to transform the traditional peasant into a modern agricultural producer—all the while supporting the prevailing political system and national power structure. Policies produced positive effects in the 1960s, strengthening peasant ties to democratic parties and severely crippling would-be guerrilla movements in the countryside. Moreover, the social justice–reformism strategy did indeed see the redistribution of land—to some 150,000 peasants in twenty years—and theoretically extended technical assistance, credit, and the like (granted that in practice this was often missing).

Political as well as demographic and agricultural conditions inevitably shifted. The rural vote, now greatly diminished, is nonetheless significant in a close election, and can no longer be easily delivered. Even in 1983, the Lusinchi campaign team had yet been unable to reorient its strategies toward a predominantly urban population, although it should have been doing so for a decade. COPEI, never strong in rural areas outside the Andes, was forced to rely primarily on candidate personality. The Left, weak in urban areas, was even weaker in the farming districts. The fiscal and monetary crises of 1983 seemed to assure that issues of economic growth and agricultural technification would, at last implicitly, receive heavier emphasis in coming years.

The growing emphasis on economic growth and agricultural technification, which some advocates of meaningful social justice programs have criticized, has struck other observers as inadequate. For one such student, all the democratic administrations have pursued agrarian policies that favored the peasants while neglecting small- and medium-sized rural entrepreneurs. In his words,

> Despite the difficulties and risks of agriculture and cattle raising, small and medium-sized entrepreneurs are regarded as capitalists and so do not seem to qualify for public assistance. Recent and sporadic loans are just exceptions. And they have not yet fulfilled their objective, because so many years of negligence have hindered the development and technical capacity of recipients. Therefore these loans have been used with less efficiency than might have been expected. . . . As a result, the country has not adequately improved its cattle-raising or agricultural industry, and suffers from rural exodus, marginality, and political strains. It seems that the political sector prefers to see the masses living marginally in urban areas rather than employed in rural ones. (Gil 1981:28)

Such an assessment is harsh, and one with which I cannot agree. Moreover, the pattern of policymaking for agriculture has been rather different since 1974, as already noted. Today, critics focus more on what is viewed as exclusion of even medium-sized entrepreneurs, maintaining that the huge agribusiness corporations are those to receive sympathetic treatment from Caracas. Granted that there are ideological, political, and technical grounds for disparate approaches to agriculture, it must be kept in mind that the broader context of national patterns and bureaucratic behavior also pertains to agriculture. Professionalism, dedication, and technical skill are blended in Venezuela with opportunism, dishonesty, mediocrity, and an occasional shrug of the shoulders, if not outright irrationality. Yet the process is by no means bereft of reason. What it does demonstrate, however, is the existence of a policymaking arena in which the best of approaches will meet a mixture of failures and successes. For a polity as open and competitive as Venezuela, the political element is also writ large.

Conclusion: The Problematica of Policymaking in Democratic Venezuela

At the national level, several aspects of policymaking in contemporary Venezuela are self-evident. Owing partly to the lessons taught by the disruptive 1945–1948 *trienio* and the deadly repression of the decade which followed, party elites have deliberately pursued a moderate and incrementalist path as a means of facilitating a strengthened democratic system. The hegemonic domination exercised by COPEI and Acción Democrática over the past decade has further buttressed the stress on self-interested moderation.

As again illustrated recently, the *copeyano-adeco* collaboration in defense of the present system remains alert to possible threats. When, in early 1983, the Herrera government was toying with the notion of a moratorium on the foreign debt, military rumblings suggested that this presumed loss of face internationally might well provoke intervention by the armed forces. Partisan electoral debate was abruptly interrupted, with AD and COPEI leaders forcing a night meeting at Miraflores Palace. The result was to suspend official consideration of a moratorium—at least at that juncture—and to mollify the military. Only after the crisis had passed did the party leaders return to electoral controversy.

The character of Venezuelan state capitalism would seem to assure exaggerated bureaucratic infighting. The petroleum industry, for years untouched by partisan dispute, is now subject to a wide array of interacting influences. There are personal and organizational differences between the PDVSA president and the minister of mines and energy; between their respective staffs; the president of the Central Bank, planning minister, and finance minister are also involved; and relevant party figures are also concerned about policy questions. In agriculture, the proliferation of agencies and entities is even more extreme.

The broadest overview of our two cases suggests, in conjunction with other studies of the Venezuelan polity, that the patterns of policymaking in agriculture—as well as the disappointing results—are typical. Petroleum has been an exception in terms of technical expertise, professionalism, and freedom from external partisanship. This latter condition has now been eroded—perhaps less a result of party aspirations than the economic crisis now being felt. In a study of Venezuelan public administration, William Stewart has written that "mass-based democracy resting upon the patron-client relationship and a consequent particularistic focus is in many ways inconsistent with universalistic conceptions of justice. The gap between the real and the ideal has always been large in Venezuela, however, with the bureaucracy caught in the middle. In a time of intense and basic change, the present political system is consistent with both Venezuelan culture and democratic ideals" (Stewart 1977:233–234). In the final analysis, the vitality of Venezuelan pluralism suggests that the comparative immunity of the petroleum industry cannot, nor should not, be continued indefinitely. At the same time, the lamentably familiar failings suggested in agriculture are disquieting to the nation.

CASE STUDY

Bureaucratic Politics and Social Policy: The Emergence of Costa Rica's Welfare State

MARK B. ROSENBERG

In Costa Rica, public policy has been consistently utilized by political elites to shape the socioeconomic environment. Nowhere is this better illustrated than in the area of social security. Since 1961, political elites have made a serious commitment to the expansion of social security coverage to include almost all of the country's citizens. The result has been a higher standard of living for those citizens and one of the healthiest populations in Latin America (Rosenberg 1979).

Social security in the United States is almost exclusively limited to pension and income maintenance and some health care programs for the aged; however, in Costa Rica, as throughout Latin America, social security programs provide not only old-age pensions but also health care for individuals and the families of those who are actively engaged in the work force (Mesa-Lago 1978; Malloy

1979). This latter area has become a crucial public service, especially in those Latin American countries where the cost of private physicians and specialized medicine makes ongoing medical care prohibitively expensive.

The expansion of the Costa Rican social security system since 1941 has roughly paralleled the consolidation of democracy in that country, particularly after the Civil War of 1948. Since then, Costa Rican political life has been dominated by the competition of two political forces. The National Liberation Party (PLN) has tended to follow a reformist, state capitalist model of development. Its most important political leader has been the charismatic José Figueres Ferrer, a hero of the 1948 conflict (Vega Carballo 1972). Like most parties in Latin America, the PLN is not monolithic; it has managed to hold together a congeries of social democratic tendencies (Cerdas Cruz 1972). Pitted against the PLN has been a coalition of political groups whose only basis for agreement has been opposition to the PLN and its policies. Contrary to the political sentiments of the PLN, this anti-PLN coalition has generally favored a more conservative policy agenda, particularly on the issue of state involvement in socioeconomic problem solving. Leadership of the anti-PLN forces has ranged from the founder of the Costa Rican social security system and president of the country (1940–1944), Dr. Rafael Angel Calderón Guardia, to an ex-PLN leader and president (1978–1982), Rodrigo Carazo. Dr. Calderón's son now leads the anti-PLN political forces and will probably be a presidential candidate in 1986.

Despite the fact that the PLN has willingly embraced the mantle of reform in Costa Rica, the anti-PLN forces could not be classified as antireformist. The two political groups do clash on the issue of leadership style and the role of the state, particularly on issues of ownership and development policy. Most remarkable is the fact that both dominant political forces have tended to agree on the need for a responsive social welfare system and both have supported, aggressively at times, public policy initiatives designed to broaden and strengthen the social security system. It is unique by Central American standards to find two contending political forces in agreement in such a critical issue area. This general consensus on social security is critical for understanding the success of the program. This agreement has augured well for the average Costa Rican citizen whose daily concerns focus on the more mundane issues related to health and well being. What accounts for this consensus on social security issues in Costa Rica?

Consensus on social security issues in Costa Rica has a forty-year legacy beginning with the presidency of Dr. Rafael Angel Calderón Guardia, who as noted above, quietly introduced the social policy initiative in 1941. Calderón implemented social security because he felt that it was a necessary program long overdue in the country (Calderón Guardia 1942). Even though he represented (at the time) conservative interests that eschewed state intervention in social matters, and even though there was little direct political pressure on him by potential clientele groups, Calderón almost single-mindedly took the initiative to push the program (Rojas Bolanos 1980). Hence, when he and his handpicked successor were followed by the reform-minded PLN in the post–civil war era, the PLN was presented with a critical social program that was already in place and functioning. Since then, both political forces have competed to see who could provide the most support for the program. This competition and interest began to accelerate particularly after 1961, as we will see below.

Moreover, a critical and related aspect of this consensus has been the commitment of Costa Rica's political leadership to the enhancement of social security. This commitment can be found in both political tendencies. Even one of the most conservative of the country's presidents, Mario Echandi (1958–1962), made every effort toward program expansion (see below).

Because elite commitment is a major aspect of public policy in any country, the nature of this commitment in Costa Rica deserves scrutiny. First, Costa Rican social relations have been characterized historically by a deep respect for civility, order, and individual dignity. The relative isolation of the country as a colony, the lack of an easily exploitable indigenous population, the late nineteenth century incorporation into the world economy, the lack of extreme forms of income inequality, and the unique absence of a professional, organized armed force have contributed to this Costa Rican sociability (Stone 1975; Gudmundson 1983).

Second, Costa Ricans tend to have a positivist attitude toward both their environment and their government. The country's political culture is oriented toward problem solving and enhanced human well-being. In contrast to many countries where the state is regarded as a public trough and corruption is an accepted component of public officeholding, in Costa Rica the state is seen as an important and legitimate mediator, if not problem solver, in society. Although this often leads to paternalism and centralization (Stone 1975:307–337), it nonetheless gives the state and public officials a greater degree of receptivity and confidence among the masses. This receptivity and confidence is critical in those issue areas where private resources must be directly transferred to public institutions. In most Central American countries the private sector has resisted social security expansion; in Costa Rica, however, the country's business interests have generally supported social security program expansion because they have confidence in both the political leaders and institutions of the country.

Thus, while there have been exceptions in Costa Rica since the 1948 Civil War, political elites have generally tended to be concerned with mass welfare issues and have relied upon public policy instruments to effect changes. Just as important, mass expectations about state responsiveness as a whole and public understanding about how to realize constructively these expectations have allowed for a mutually complementary logic favoring public policy.

Another factor accounting for consensus on social security issues in Costa Rica can be found at the level of public bureaucracy, particularly among the administrative elites charged with running the social security system. Since the 1960s, a well-trained cadre of experts, or *técnicos*, has emerged to manage the expansion of social security. As will be illustrated below, this group has been very good at translating high-level executive and legislative interests in the program into measurable policy initiatives. Likewise, it has been extremely competent in defining its own needs and problems and communicating these problems to relevant actors throughout the political system. Moreover, social security administrative elites have aggressively carved out their respective domains. Thus, within the government few agencies or programs have been able to challenge or even reduce the program's momentum; and although users often criticize the wait necessary to get an appointment from a medical specialist, there have been few or no instances where users have called for an abandonment of the program.

In addition, social security administrative elites have taken care to ensure that their program maintains a high degree of public legitimacy. Corruption within the system has not been tolerated, and high service and health-care standards have been consistently encouraged. Competence at all levels is generally rewarded, and the system is relatively free of the political patronage and cronyism that has often crippled bureaucratic performance in other countries. Unlike the case in many issue areas where the specific policy to be implemented has several competing host agencies, Costa Rican social security has one agency, the Costa Rican Social Security Institute, and a well-trained custodian, the group of managers who implement and administer policy. During the past two decades, they have zealously pursued their institutional and clientele's interests. The forthright manner in which they have done this has only added to the general consensus on social security issues in Costa Rica.

A final factor accounting for consensus on social security issues can be broadly classified as environmental. In contrast to many issue areas, where the policy agendas are vague and diffuse as a result of radically divergent interests and views, social security and social welfare in general have been the subject of prolonged international discussion and debate since the 1920s. This discussion and debate has helped to structure a broadly agreed upon policy agenda that can be applied in specific countries according to local needs and interests. This policy agenda sets broad guidelines about health-care access and income-maintenance levels. So broad and general are the guidelines that it would be virtually inhuman to oppose them. However, they set an international standard by which all countries can and do measure themselves (Wolfe 1968; Mallet 1970). Costa Rican politicians love to boast about their health-care success in international meetings where countries traditionally market their reputations; and Costa Rican social security administrators use the same guidelines for both local political as well as resource-allocation decisions. Generally, the more professional and committed the administrator, the more seriously considered will be the externally derived guidelines.

Despite the general consensus on social security issues in Costa Rica, the system's development has not taken place without a number of serious public policy initiatives, particularly since 1961. These policy initiatives are the subject of the following sections.

General Patterns and Problems of Social Security Evolution

During the twenty-year period from 1941–1961, social security in Costa Rica evolved in much the same fashion as it had in other Latin American countries. Urban groups, rather than rural ones, tended to receive coverage, and those with employers were more likely to benefit than those who were self-employed. Throughout this period the major social security problem was not strictly political but rather financial: how to provide the necessary resources to support a complex people-oriented delivery system that was under constant pressure to offer more and better services. Costa Rica's rapidly expanding population (which had doubled in number every twenty years since 1927) and its accelerating urbanization placed the public sector and particularly the social security system under acute pressure (Araya Pochet 1983).

Thus, while elite political commitment is always a critical element to successful policy implementation, the necessary material resources must also be forthcoming or the policy will remain at the level of rhetoric only. Social security programs are complex in this regard. They traditionally have been financed by a coalition of state, employer, and worker groups who each bear a percentage of the total program cost. Additional financial resources to run social security programs may come from indirect taxes on consumption, through interest income generated by loans from available capital, or by outside loans from international agencies. However, the key to social security success ultimately depends on the tripartite system of taxes paid by the state, the employer, and the worker. This method of program financing is fraught with problems; historically in Latin America, the state has been delinquent in its financial obligations, particularly when it is also an employer. Workers have resisted taxes in general, regardless of the fact that these funds directly support programs of personal benefit. This problem is compounded by the severe problems of tax collection from workers who are self-employed. Adding to the complicated nature of social security financing is the fact that employers often evade their social security obligations in one of two ways. Either they simply delay making payments to the system, hoping that the subsequent sanctions, if there are any, are negotiable; or employers underreport the number of employees and their salary levels, thereby reducing their total social security financial obligation.

In Costa Rica, the basic consensus over social security issues as described above has reduced significant policy debates on the program to those related to financing and administrative questions. Thus, often the major policy question in Costa Rica, as elsewhere, is not how a program gets initiated, but how it can be kept going and at higher levels of capacity and accomplishment. This has been the basic policy dilemma concerning Costa Rican social security, as we will see below.

By 1961 the Costa Rican social security system faced serious financial problems. Middle age had set in; the program was not keeping pace in coverage with the country's rapidly expanding population. Something had to be done to correct this.

Two significant policy initiatives were formulated in response to the problem. In 1961, a policy was set calling explicitly for the extension of social security to all Costa Rican citizens in a ten-year period. By 1971, when it became clear that the policy was not being implemented, a new policy was established, giving the 1961 initiative the financial apparatus that it needed to be successful. We shall examine both of these policies by describing the process and the actors critical to their articulation. In each case, however, the critical actors were political and administrative elites directly involved in the decisionmaking process for social security in Costa Rica. Despite the country's status as a democracy and the well-accepted tradition of popular participation in decisionmaking, such participation was virtually absent in both decisions except at a few isolated points in the policymaking process (Rosenberg 1979; Malloy 1979).

In Chapter 1 of this volume it is suggested that policy can best be understood within the context of its "stages" of evolution. For analytical purposes, policy must be differentiated so as to make its complexities understandable. However, as will be abundantly clear, it is often impossible to neatly separate one stage from another. (The following discussion relies on Rosenberg 1976; Rosenberg 1979; Rosenberg 1980.)

The Universalization of Costa Rican Social Security in 1961

In 1961, an amendment to the constitution of Costa Rica was passed, stipulating that the social insurance institute should "universalize" its services within a ten-year period. In practical terms, this meant that all of Costa Rica's citizens would receive social security coverage by 1971. The universalization amendment established the strongest possible legal and political mandate for the expansion of social security. And it provided a time limit for the achievement of such coverage.

PROBLEM FORMATION

The need for the expansion of social security coverage can be linked to two sources. Internationally, the Cuban Revolution of 1959 and the U.S.-sponsored Alliance for Progress provided a broader climate of support for reform efforts throughout Latin America. The response in Costa Rica was certain; conservative president Mario Echandi initiated a land reform program and took Costa Rica into the Central American Common Market. Moreover, an important legislative commission was designated to examine the social security system. Its report stated that over 66 percent of all eligible workers and over 89 percent of all eligible families had not yet received any form of coverage. The report recognized that "the benefits of social security only cover a minority, remaining for the future an immense public task oriented in the direction of protecting against social risks the largest part of the Costa Rican population, especially low income groups" (*Acta* 1959).

This situation caused growing concern among social security administrators as well. By early 1960, they were actively campaigning for financial reforms to the program that would allow program expansion. The coincidence of the urgency provoked by Cuba's revolution and the U.S. response added an important sense of legitimacy to concerns about social security.

GOVERNMENT AGENDA

By early 1960, there seemed to be a broad government consensus about the need for social security policy reform. Headed by President Echandi, the executive branch indicated its general willingness to effect social security reforms. The legislature, controlled by rival PLN politicians, also moved forcefully to promote a policy designed to help social security. Finding themselves in the middle, social security administrators did not want to get caught in a political fight with either interest, and indicated that a nonpartisan solution was the most desirable from the administrative viewpoint. In essence, the competition between the rival political interests allowed the social security issue to be raised to the highest level of concern where it would remain until resolved.

POLICY FORMULATION

During this stage, the most important decisions were made regarding the universalization of coverage. In early 1961, a high-level meeting took place between members of the PLN (acting in their capacity as members of the unicameral legislature) and representatives of the social security program. The purpose of the meeting was to discuss the actual disposition of new funds that were to be forthcoming through modifications of the social security law. One of the legislators suggested that the modifications would finally give the program the necessary financial support to extend coverage. However, he asked, what guarantees were there that the extensions would actually be made? No guarantees could be provided by the social security officials. One of the legislators thereupon suggested that a special constitutional amendment call for the universalization of services in a period not to exceed ten years. Representatives of the social security agency immediately rejected this idea. First, any decision about the rate and timing of social security expansion was expressly an internal matter and beyond legislative purview. Second, the ten-year designation was arbitrary and had no scientific or technical rationale. According to the social security representatives, universalization within a ten-year period was simply impossible.

But the legislators were adamant. It was these terms or nothing, and they made it clear that there would be no needed financial reforms without an agreement on the universalization mandate. The social security representatives reluctantly agreed to this bargain and the legislators then promised to effect the needed financial reforms. Thus, legislators played a critical role in helping to formulate the basic outlines of policy. While they had no accurate information on which to base their decision, they nonetheless moved ahead against the advice of the social security experts.

POLICY ADOPTION AND EXECUTION

The actual universalization amendment was unanimously approved by the Costa Rican congress in May 1961. It was easily one of the most important pieces of social security legislation in the twenty years following the Civil War of 1948. However, while the reforms promised everything, they actually gave nothing concrete and immediate. It is true that new social security financing methods accompanied the policy, but they were not effectively implemented. In October 1961, social security administrators found themselves back in the congress calling upon that group to provide the financial resources that had been promised by the state. However, the legislators could hardly aid the program, for the government budget was far overextended as a result of the country's general economic difficulties.

In the years following the 1961 mandate, dramatic progress was made in extending coverage despite the lingering financial problems of the program. In fact, only 178,000 people received social security health-care coverage in 1959; this number had jumped to 780,000 by 1969, a significant 500 percent increase in coverage. By the end of the 1960s, over 46 percent of the total population had health-care coverage, while ten years earlier, only 15 percent were so covered.

The significant increase in social security coverage during the 1960s was clearly a function of the universalization mandate. It stimulated more decisive and self-confident bureaucratic leadership, which took the mandate seriously. And it ushered in a vigorous period of infrastructural development, which culminated in 1968 with the inauguration in Costa Rica of Central America's largest health-care facility, the Mexico Hospital.

EVALUATION

The renewed vigor of the social security program took place against a backdrop of continuing financial weakness. Despite the 1961 legislative assurances that the state's social security debt would be paid, it was not. Confidential internal studies conducted by the social security institute in both 1965 and 1967 pointed with alarm to the growing social security deficits. The studies were also critical of the manner in which financial reserves were transferred from the old-age pension fund to cover the ongoing and more immediate expenses of the health-care programs. Moreover, the social security expansions were impressive, but they plainly had their limits. By the late 1960s, large sectors of the urban and rural poor were still left without any coverage at all. The growing sophistication of health care and the increased life expectancy of the insured had raised per capita health-care costs precipitously in Costa Rica during the 1960s. Both studies therefore continued to share a certain gloom even about meeting the 1971 mandate. Thus, the policy evaluations emanating from the 1961 legislation were clearly not just casual estimates. They were serious and systematic, thereby laying the groundwork for the significant social security policy initiatives of the early 1970s.

Universalization and Finance in 1971: To the Heart of the Matter

In 1971 the Social Security Institute, with bipartisan legislative support, passed a reform calling for the elimination of limits to social security coverage based on salary. Prior to 1971, income groups with salaries above a designated monthly figure were exempt from either paying into or enrolling in the social security system. This new policy was crucial to an effective universalization, for it would provide the new financial wherewithal to extend services into the countryside. Moreover, it had the effect of forcing this previously privileged group to pay a proportionate amount of its income to support the social security program. Since the payment scale was a progressive one, it provided, for the first time, an element of cross-class redistribution through the social security system.

PROBLEM FORMATION

As suggested above, the basic outlines of the social security problem were known in the late 1950s. Without adequate financing, expansions in coverage could not occur. Financial reforms accompanying the 1961 universalization mandate were seen as immediate solutions to the problem, but their benefits were ephemeral. Concerns within the social security bureaucracy were well-articulated in both 1965 and 1967. Without financing reforms, the universalization could not take place.

This general problem recognition at the policy level coincided with an important political occurrence at the national level. In 1968, a group of PLN dissidents unhappy with the party's José Figueres issued a stunning critique of his leadership. The PLN was criticized for being conservative. It was challenged to be more daring in social and economic policy, thereby benefiting all Costa Ricans. Although the critique was officially ignored by the party hierarchy, it undoubtedly forced the PLN leadership to consider what it would do upon returning to power in 1970. Social security then emerged as an important priority area because it was here that the PLN knew it could effect policy.

GOVERNMENT AGENDA

Concern for realizing the universalization by 1971 began to grow in the late 1960s, particularly among social security bureaucrats and members of the congress. Finally, in late 1969, a PLN congressman, probably in close consultation with social security *técnicos*, presented a reform bill calling for the elimination of salary limits as the basis for coverage. As stated earlier, these salary limits were detrimental to the program's financial base because they excluded the higher-income salaried workers from obligatory social security. Following a careful examination of the reform proposal by the Social Security Institute, the proposal finally entered formal deliberations in the congress in mid-1970. At about the same time, a new PLN government led by President José Figueres was taking office.

POLICY FORMULATION

During the 1961 universalization efforts, the most important aspects of policy formulation took place among legislators and social security bureaucrats in closed meetings. Once these two groups were in agreement, the congress merely ratified the accord. Such was not the case in 1970. In fact, the congress played a critical role in policy formulation by structuring an open debate on the issue of eliminating the salary limits and, therefore, providing the new income and resources necessary for social security universalization.

Indeed, spirited public debate on the issue occurred in both the legislature and the country's main newspapers. Middle-class banking employees were the most vociferous in their campaign against the proposed policy. If the salary limits were eliminated they would be forced to join the social security program. They preferred their own health-care mutuality, which they argued was better and cheaper. Medical doctors also were critical of the proposed reform. Through their prestigious Board of Doctors and Surgeons, they suggested that the universalization ought to be postponed because of the shortage of trained medical personnel and supplies in the country.

Crucial to the entire policy formulation stage was the government's minister of labor, who put the executive branch squarely behind the suggested policies. Testifying before the congress on July 13, 1970, the minister chose to focus the issues at the highest political level possible. First, he asserted that the question of universalizing social insurance was a constitutional mandate to which the government was committed. He defused the physicians' argument by saying that "these and other preoccupations should not be a brake to prevent the realization of a hope for social justice." In the strongest possible terms, he then criticized the idea to delay universalization:

> The great changes that have been made in Costa Rica in the areas of education, health, and social security were not achieved by waiting for optimal situations. Never have social transformations been carried out which were based in studies which guaranteed that all of the necessary elements existed for such a change. It has been the expression of the popular will, of political direction and the outlining of an objective which has led governments to realize transformations in benefit of the majority of the people (Acta 1970:74).

For the minister, the issue boiled down to one in which the question was whether or not "we want to establish a just society in Costa Rica" (Acta 1970:79).

The strong political position did not deter other public criticisms. Two of the country's most important interest groups, the Catholic Church and the National Association of Economic Development (ANFE) also came out against the reform. The former was opposed because of the increased financial demands on the newly insured. ANFE was opposed because it wanted to see poorer workers receive coverage before those with higher incomes. This opposition was offset somewhat by publicly voiced support for the measure from labor organizations in both San José and a regional port city.

A more serious critique was presented by the country's Chamber of Commerce. Arguing that an immediate and total elimination of the salary limit would be harmful to the national economy, the chamber wanted the salary limit raised, but not eliminated. This was unacceptable to the minister. A compromise was subsequently arranged between the minister, the Social Security Institute, and the congress to implement the lifting of the salary limits incrementally, in accordance with the health facilities available.

Once the chamber was pacified, there was little to stop the proposal's legislative approval. It was overwhelmingly approved by the congress in late March 1971. The struggle that had begun in the 1940s to eliminate the salary limitations determining social security eligibility was finally over.

POLICY ADOPTION AND EXECUTION

The new policy allowing for a gradual elimination of the salary limits was immediately implemented by the social security program. Plans were developed to utilize new finances to underwrite the expansion of social security into regions of the country still lacking coverage. But something unexpected occurred. In October 1971 a momentous dispute erupted between the Social Security Institute's management and medical professionals. What did the latter group want? The struggle ostensibly was over higher wages and better working conditions, but in real terms what their demands amounted to was an estimated 31 percent of the newly acquired income from the salary limit elevation reform. The medical professionals (including doctors, nurses, and lab technicians) were in an excellent intrainstitutional bargaining position: no money, no work. Indeed, they went on strike for eleven days until their demands were met. The strike set a dangerous new precedent in Costa Rica. For the first time since before the Civil War of 1948, public employees had withheld their vital services in exchange for their demands.

What was the impact of the strike? It was claimed that the pace of social security expansion was slowed, but other claims point to the improved quality of health-care delivery as a result of improved staff morale.

The 1971 policy also led to a number of other significant social security policies that helped to raise the level of coverage to well over 90 percent of the economically active population by the early 1980s. In fact, the Social Security Institute's programs were so successful that all nonsocial security public hospitals were turned over to it in late 1974. And, in terms of staffing, it has grown to be one of the country's largest agencies.

EVALUATION

The policy initiatives to increase social security financing during the 1970s had long been contemplated and therefore were welcomed by social security officials and politicians alike. However, they were based on a larger assumption about the Costa Rican economy—that it would continue to grow at a moderate annual pace and that the productive base of the economy would gradually expand. But, when the Costa Rican economy virtually collapsed in 1981, the Social Security Institute, like all other agencies in the country, was left bankrupt. The agreements, bargains, and arrangements delicately forged during the 1960s and 1970s would need to be revised in accordance with the new economic reality.

Conclusion

This case study has examined social security policymaking in Costa Rica, one of Latin America's few stable democracies. Emphasis has been placed on the larger context of policymaking in Costa Rica and on the emergence of a basic elite consensus about the importance and role of social security.

Several conclusions are suggested by this study. First, there has been little popular participation in social security policymaking. Indeed, most major social security policy-level decisions have been made in isolation from the masses. These decisions, as the two case studies have illustrated, were made by political and bureaucratic elites within the context of a complex process of bargaining. Even when the issues involved mass welfare benefits, there was more open opposition than open support. Democracies often encourage particularistic interest group behavior in defense of privilege. This could be seen by the active, but ultimately ineffectual, opposition to social security financing reforms in 1971.

Second, this analysis illustrates that both political and administrative elites played a critical role in social security policymaking. Administrative elites consistently played the major role in the problem formation stage, but it was political elites from both the executive and legislative branches who emerged as critical actors in the policy formulation stage. Indeed, in both cases it was decisive political leadership that made the difference in the policy process. Bureaucrats tended to be more cautious than did their political counterparts.

Finally, this case study suggests how and why Costa Rican democracy has functioned so well. Although the policymaking process that we have studied

could be classified as "elitist" or "paternalistic," decisions have directly benefited the masses in measurable ways. Public policy has been utilized as an
instrument to respond to mass needs and bring the government closer to its
people. It would be difficult to make this same assertion for most of the other
countries in Latin America.

[5]
Policymaking in Postrevolutionary Regimes

Mexico and Cuba stand alone in Latin America (though some scholars would also include Bolivia) as two countries that have experienced significant, profound, and enduring revolutionary changes in their respective social, political, and economic systems. Mexico, after decades of postindependence violence and anarchy, underwent a harsh period of enforced stability and political centralization under the often brutal dictatorship of Porfirio Diaz, only to be convulsed again—this time with more profound effect—in a bloody revolutionary-civil war, which lasted from 1910 until 1917. What emerged from this seven-year conflagration of Mexican against Mexican was a political arrangement that, with the exception of some particularly stressful times, has proven to be the most stable in all of Latin America. Likewise, Cuba, whose independence from Spain was the last that occurred in Latin America—and only as a by-product of the U.S. war with Spain at the end of the nineteenth century—passed through years of corruption under dictators and popularly elected presidents alike. Ultimately, in a revolutionary effort more bizarre, much less bloody, and of considerably shorter duration than that of Mexico, Fidel Castro and a ragtag band of rural guerrillas (with considerable help in the urban areas from now-forgotten compatriots) eliminated the increasingly decaying rule of Fulgencio Batista. Like Mexico, Cuba since 1959 has experienced the longest period of political stability in its less-than-century-old independent history.

We should take a short pause here to discuss briefly our notion of postrevolutionary regimes and to point out why we do not include Nicaragua in that category. First, the early phases of a revolutionary movement are generally violent; however, the degree and duration of such violence is quite varied, as in the cases of Mexico and Cuba. Second, this turmoil culminates in a political process that transforms previously accepted political and economic relationships by essentially eliminating one or more previously powerful policymakers.

131

The Cuban revolution eliminated an array of former political elites, such as the U.S. government, foreign-owned economic interests, and a substantial portion of the middle- and upper-middle-class professional interests. Likewise, the Mexican revolution eliminated the whole class of *técnicos* who, along with their foreign allies, wielded power during the reign of dictator Porfirio Diaz. Large private landholders also lost out, replaced, at least in part, by sizable communal arrangements known as *ejidos*. Third, the new revolutionary forms of political and economic arrangements eventually gain legitimacy, and politics returns to a new level of normalcy and stability that appears to be relatively enduring. Although it took Mexico some fifteen years after the onset of the revolutionary struggle in 1910 to achieve some degree of normalcy, the basic pattern remains the same in the 1980s. Cuba also survived both internal and external threats to its revolution in the years after Castro's 1959 victory march from Santiago to Havana.

Recently, Nicaragua under the banner of the Sandinistas—who took their name from the near-legendary Augusto César Sandino, a nationalist hero who opposed U.S. involvement and who was assassinated during the first Somoza regime—went through what many observers, and the Sandinistas themselves, have characterized as a genuine revolution. We agree that what seems to be occurring in Nicaragua is a fairly massive restructuring of political and economic structures, but we also suggest that it is premature to characterize Nicaragua as a postrevolutionary regime. There are significant pressures being brought to bear against the Sandinistas, both internally and externally, in an effort to forestall further revolutionary restructuring. John Booth's assessment of the still tentative condition of the Sandinista-led regime, in contrast to the relative entrenchment of the Mexican and Cuban revolutions, supports our decision to exclude Nicaragua as a postrevolutionary regime. Booth argued that

> the political, economic, and foreign policy programs of the Nicaraguan revolution all appeared to be at critical junctures, capable of redefinition should any of a variety of relatively probable events occur—escalated aggression against the revolution by exiles or by another nation, continued difficulty in achieving economic recovery, an increase of internal opposition from the remaining center or right, or increased labor unrest. The Sandinistas . . . brought an end to the Somoza dynasty and . . . established the beginning of a new Nicaraguan society, but their path was still littered—perhaps increasingly so—with obstacles that might confront them with critical choices about the future of the revolution (1982:227).

To put it another way, the revolutionary movements in both Mexico and Cuba have been successful in their efforts to effect a major overhaul of political life in their respective countries. In short, they are postrevolutionary regimes.

The Sandinista-led revolutionary movement in Nicaragua may also become a postrevolutionary "success" story. Then again, it may not.

Although there is essentially a consensus as to the revolutionary status of post-1917 Mexico and post-1959 Cuba, there is definitely something short of consensus among observers concerning the particular nature or quality of the process and substance of policymaking in either of the two countries. Moreover, Cuba's regime is unique in that it is the only one in the Western Hemisphere that claims Marxism-Leninism as an ideological foundation. In contrast, most observers of Mexican politics have argued that, rather than being ideologically pure, the postrevolutionary regime in Mexico tends toward the chameleon variety of ideology—always changing colors.

Our task here is clearly not easy. The student should be alerted to the possibility of a commonly shared postrevolutionary style and substance of policymaking in Cuba and Mexico, but he or she should also be aware of the differences that exist between the two regimes, as well as the differences among scholarly analyses of the same regime. In this chapter we shall attempt a brief description and analysis of Mexico and Cuba with the aim of helping the student navigate a course between the Scylla of careless generalizations and the Charybdis of irrelevant particulars. Finally, the case studies by Merilee Grindle and Juan del Aguila should provide the student with a firmer grounding in specific policy processes in the two countries.

Mexico

POLICYMAKING BEFORE THE REVOLUTION

Prior to the late 1870s, when Porfirio Diaz came to power by force of arms, Mexico's independent political history fluctuated between periods of abortive efforts at centralized control and utter anarchy. Divisive groups, including foreign ones, struggled for power after independence from Spain in 1821. As recently as the 1860s, during the presidency of Benito Juarez, Mexico found itself invaded by foreign troops that had established alliances with some of the domestic power contenders. Loyalist forces under Juarez succeeded in expelling France in her abortive attempt to install a puppet emperor in Mexico. One of the Mexican loyalists was General Porfirio Diaz, who emerged as a great national hero after the French defeat. Five years after Juarez's death in 1872, Diaz, the hero, in typical caudillo fashion, parlayed his mass appeal and his control of the military into a harsh, centralized government, which prevailed until the violent uprisings that began in 1910.

The nearly forty years of Diaz's rule witnessed the major beginnings of industrialization and economic modernization along with repressive, author-itarian control of the great masses of Mexican peasantry. Diaz welcomed foreign investment—largely British and U.S.—which resulted in extensive increases in mining, manufacturing, and transportation facilities. Railroads were built; beer, steel, and textiles were manufactured; and, after the turn of the century, oil became an increasingly rich line of production. The same laws that broke up large church landholdings in the 1860s were used to dismantle traditional community lands (*ejidos*) held by the Indian peasants. Political and economic power became concentrated as never before in the period of independence. Repression of the masses by the elites was justified on the grounds of economic modernization and a crude vulgarization of positivism and Social Darwinism. The increasing wretchedness of the vast majority of the rural populace (about 75 percent of Mexico's entire population) and the more vocal opposition posed by segments of the urban intelligentsia, who were quite critical of the Diaz regime's tactics as well as results, became the seeds of the revolutionary movement.

Diaz's system of governing combined three elements: (1) ignoring those social groups—like the Indian masses—that lacked the capacity for effective political action; (2) coopting, through patronage positions and other forms of bribery, all politically effective groups that he could; and (3) eliminating those groups that refused to be bought off (Hansen 1971:146–147). Loyalties were based on social and economic advancement at the public expense. Disloyalty was frequently dealt with through the barrel of a gun wielded by coopted rural hooligans passing as "law enforcement" officials. These techniques of control were summarized by Diaz's own slogan, *pan o palo* (bread or stick): "If they will cooperate, feed them from the public treasury; if not, exterminate them" (Tannebaum 1966:145).

By 1910, the sticks were wielded by aged and decrepit rulers, and the bread supply began to falter seriously. The mestizo-led revolt of Francisco Madero was able to force Diaz into exile within a year. Reportedly, Diaz remarked at his departure for France: "Madero has unleashed a tiger; let us see if he can control him" (Hansen 1971:156). As it turned out, neither Madero nor most of his successors were capable of controlling the tiger that the revolution was to become. The tiger was not tamed, in fact, until the creation of the official revolutionary party some twenty years later.

POLICYMAKING SINCE THE REVOLUTION

The revolutionary process itself was essentially a return to the anarchy and regional *caudillismo* of the time before Diaz, with army fighting army and revolutionary leader assassinating revolutionary leader. Beginning in 1929 under the politically astute leadership of outgoing President Plutarco Calles (a poor schoolteacher who became a revolutionary general and managed to escape assassination by his colleagues), what was to become the most encompassing, and most successful, political party in all of Latin America was pieced together. From behind the scenes, Calles dominated party matters until 1935, gradually strengthening the central party bureaucracy at the expense of the provincial bases of personal power originally included in the arrangement. After 1936, President Lázaro Cárdenas completed the sectoral structure of what was then officially named the Institutional Revolutionary Party (PRI) by incorporating two previously omitted interests: organized labor and peasants. In addition, Cárdenas was instrumental in bringing to the presidency a degree of popularity and legitimacy previously unheard of. In fact, the presidency from Cárdenas to the present has become the vital nerve center of both the PRI and Mexican political life. Finally, the Cárdenas years marked the beginning of a gradual demilitarization of politics, giving way by the late 1940s to a continuing succession of presidents who spent their adult lives as civilians working within the ranks of government.

It is clear that in the aftermath of the revolutionary violence, the carefully forged political apparatus of the PRI and its virtually all-encompassing sectoral organization has brought to Mexican politics a stability of process. The pistols and rifles of the various generals and their armies were either stored away or transformed into modern tools used only at the direction of civilian decisionmakers. Elections, the overwhelming majority of which are won by various PRI candidates, have become the legitimate source of authority for a period of time unmatched in duration in Latin America.

There have developed two broad schools of thought regarding the process of politics and policymaking in Mexico. One school, an older one, suggests that Mexico's revolution and the economic and political modernization that took place thereafter paved the way for the development of a democratic political system, however imperfect that system appeared to be (Scott 1964; Vernon 1963). The other school argues strongly that, if anything, contemporary Mexican politics is a more modern (and, thus far, more durable) version of the authoritarian rule of Porfirio Díaz (Brandenburg 1964; Hansen 1971; Reyna and Weinert 1977; Stevens 1974; Purcell and Purcell 1977; González Casanova 1970). While there may not be consensus yet, the latter of the two schools of thought has definitely become the more prominent. Indeed, the brief glimpses into the various actors in the Mexican policy process provided in Chapter 2 of this book clearly emphasize the authoritarian and corporate nature of the Mexican policymaking game.

A useful definition of an authoritarian political system has been provided by Susan Kaufman Purcell and John F. H. Purcell (Purcell 1973; Purcell and Purcell 1977). The basic elements of authoritarian politics are (1) centralization of power, (2) elite consensus, (3) limited pluralism, (4) low levels of political mobilization and participation, and (5) a patrimonial style of rulership.

Regarding the first characteristic, the Mexican government centralizes power in the presidency, particularly in the office of the president himself. Other political institutions, such as the courts and the legislature, are virtually powerless as policymakers. Regarding the second characteristic, the Purcells argue that there is a discernible consensus among decisional elites about the necessity to maintain political control, the importance of nationalistic economic development, and the concern for at least paying lip service to the revolutionary ethos of social justice (by implication, the *substantive* concern for social justice is often overlooked).

The Mexican system, although recognizing some interest group activity as legitimate, severely circumscribes both the activity itself and its impact on public policy. Interests that coincide with the policymaking elite's goals will, therefore, be more successful in making demands for government activities than interests that conflict with elite objectives. What this usually means is that business interests have more of an impact. Complementary to the limited autonomy of interest group organizations is the overall low level of political participation in Mexico. Usually, citizens are supposed to remain passive, waiting for the government to act upon them rather than with them. Finally, the patrimonial nature of leadership includes the marked tendency to be personalistic and hierarchical, with the government acting as a patron who is to be "petitioned" rather than pressured by clients (citizens with their interests). The following discussion should serve to illustrate at some length this basically authoritarian political system.

Historian Frank Brandenburg has suggested that Mexican policymaking is controlled by a "Revolutionary Family" with the president of the republic as its head (1964). Similarly, Roger Hansen refers to the existence of a "Revolutionary Coalition," which uses the PRI not as an institution that represents and articulates the demands of the people but as a control mechanism that coopts and coerces allegiance and obligation to the government's decisions. Hansen argues that the economic development strategy followed by all Mexican governments since the revolution clearly does not represent the demands and interests of organized labor and *campesinos*. Labor and peasant groups, he argues, have neither played a significant role in the formulation of that strategy nor reaped its benefits (Hansen 1971:107–120).

Basically, most citizens of Mexico see themselves and are treated as "subjects" rather than active, interest-pursuing political participants (Almond and Verba 1965). What evolved from the ashes and dead bodies of the revolution was not a democratic framework but a consensus among elites concerning the operation of the system. This consensus, carried down to the present, included an understanding that policymaking would flow from the top (the president) down, with the legislature being nothing more than a rubber stamp and the official "revolutionary" party being a cooptive and control device for facilitating obedience to and acquiescence in government decisions. The president, in a real sense, becomes the national *patrón* with the entire country as his *hacienda*. Moreover, given the particularly intense nature of personal friendship and kinship in Mexico—and the equally intense distrust of those who are not close friends or relatives—the political arrangements and processes forged after the revolution depend heavily on whom one knows. Consequently, political officials in Mexico depend for their success on "knowing" the right people (Stevens 1974).

The regime has a distrust for what the people want; however, it does not rely simply on repression but rather on systematic discouragement of popular participation. Although the Constitution of 1917 is unique in its embodiment of notions of social and economic justice, agrarian reform, and the rights of organized labor, the difference between constitutional mandate and political practice is profound. Article 27, for instance, provides for extensive redistribution of land to the peasantry. But when the decisional elites determine otherwise, those provisions of the article are ignored, and peasant protests of such actions are often summarily repressed. At other times, officials meet peasant complaints about illegal large landholdings with *tortuguismo*—foot dragging at a turtle's pace. Roger Hansen relates such an incident in the state of Puebla when, after twenty years of denials to protesting peasant organizations, the agrarian department of the state admitted that there were dozens of illegal holdings in Puebla and that action would be taken "in the near future" (Hansen 1971:119). Clearly, repression and delay are tactics designed to discourage "improper" political participation by nonelite elements of the society.

Furthermore, even when the government creates policies presumably designed to benefit a certain sector of the population, the policy process itself is a relatively closed one, with the "beneficiaries" being essentially told what will be done for or to them. Susan Kaufman Purcell describes such closed policymaking in the case of a proposed profit-sharing amendment to Article 123 of the Constitution. Article 123 is concerned with organized labor and already included a provision requiring profit sharing by private corporations with their employees. The amendment, proposed by President Adolfo López Mateos in 1961, would simply have removed the implementation responsibility of the provision from the municipal government and placed it in the hands of the federal government. As Purcell pointed out, with the exception of the large Mexican Workers Confederation (CTM), most leaders of the labor movement were, if anything, opposed to the amendment. Yet, given the essentially subservient nature of labor that was coopted into the PRI organization years ago, the amendment was rubber-stamped by the legislature (Purcell 1973:28–54). Additionally, Purcell's study sheds light on the decisional role of other actors in the Mexican policy process.

The president, as head of the so-called Revolutionary Family or Revolutionary Coalition, is the key decisionmaker, setting the tone and controlling the staffing of the bureaucracy so as to support his policies. His key advisors and top-echelon people in the various ministries constitute a second layer of the Revolutionary Coalition. Unlike the staffing model in the U.S. bureaucracy where the president directly controls only a rather small number of appointments, the president of Mexico appoints a large number of top bureaucrats who are loyal to him and who, in turn, appoint literally thousands of lower-level administrators all the way down to the state levels. In essence, there is a long chain of patron-client relationships with the president being the only patron who is not someone else's client, and all the appointees owe their positions to him. This structure gives the president the ability to control the decisional apparatus since bureaucrats at all levels jockey for position to gain their respective patron's favor. As one official reported: "The president's power to gain compliance with his policies from the various agencies of the government resides in the very instruments available to him through the political system. That is, they comply because of the possibility of upward political mobility within the system or because of fear of falling in political disfavor" (Grindle 1977b:527).

The beginning of each six-year presidential term (sexenio) brings with it not only a change in personnel, but also a desire on the part of the new president to put his own peculiar "stamp" on the content of public policies. Hence, the first year or so of the sexenio is characterized by the new staff of loyalists busily analyzing the previous administration's policies and coming up with new ones to suit the priorities and penchants of the new president. The clear expectation is that whatever was done during the previous sexenio will not be done in the same way or in the same order of policy priorities (Grindle 1977a).

Purcell (1973) noted the contrast between the influence of the top echelon of the bureaucracy in the policy process and the ambivalent and usually ignored role of the PRI leadership in the profit-sharing decision of President López Mateos. Similarly, Grindle found that an insignificant role was played by both the PRI and the national legislature in important agricultural policies during the Echeverría administration in the early 1970s. "As is generally the case," Grindle observed, "neither the legislature nor officials of the PRI, even at high levels, were directly involved or consulted in the formulation of the policy" (Grindle 1977b:548).

In short, in terms of demand making, agenda setting, and policy formulation, the most recent evidence points convincingly toward a closed decisionmaking system with the president and important bureaucratic heads as the key actors. In the implementation stages, it appears that the process, while still relatively closed and corporatized, is more open to bargaining and "lobbying" by groups who have an interest in the policy. (See Grindle's case study in this chapter.) On the whole, however, Hansen argues that the interests most successful in implementation bargaining are the large business groups, which are not even officially represented by the PRI, such as the Confederation of Mexican Chambers of Industry (CONCAMIN) and the National Federation of Chambers of Commerce (CONCANACO). Moreover, business interests seem more capable of eluding or changing the intent of government policymaking than either campesino or labor organizations. For example, shortly after President López Mateos assumed office in 1958, he began to speak of the need to govern "on the extreme left within the Constitution." In a matter of days, about a quarter of a million dollars of private-sector money fled the country, forcing the president to soften his rhetoric as well as his actions (Hansen 1971:169).

The bureaucracy, while being a powerful instrument of presidential control, may also serve as a limitation on the president's and his advisers' policy initiatives, particularly in the implementation stage. Generally speaking, bureaucratic infighting and territorialism has resulted in uncoordinated and ill-planned policy implementation. As one government technocrat has noted concerning agricultural policy:

> There's no real coordination of effort in agriculture. There's a dilution of responsibility. The Secretariat of Agriculture operates in the rainfall areas, the Ministry of Hydraulic Resources operates in the irrigation districts, the official bank gives credit, CONASUPO buys crops, the Secretariat of Agrarian Reform takes land, and Gravos y Fertilizantes (the government fertilizer company) makes fertilizer. No one wants to give up his slice of the pie (Purcell and Purcell 1977:219–220).

We have emphasized the importance of the PRI as a legitimating and coopting institution—if not a key policy actor—but we have not yet discussed the existence and policy role of other political parties. In a postrevolutionary, authoritarian political system where the PRI is tantamount to being *the* political party, it is quite easy to forget that there are other parties that seem to vie for decisional leverage. However, as Scott pointed out twenty years ago, "One can as correctly say that today Mexico has a single-party system as say that the United States has a two-party system. In both countries, the success of the major party or parties overshadows the very existence of minor parties . . . "(1964:145).

Even the oldest, generally most respected, and largest minor party, the National Action Party (PAN), offers no serious challenge to the hegemony of the PRI. The PAN, which shares many of the philosophical and ideological assumptions of Christian Democratic parties found elsewhere in Latin America (such as the COPEI in Venezuela), has been successful in electing several members to the national legislature, but its impact on policy has been negligible. Evelyn Stevens goes so far as to say that the PAN's failure has been the key to its "success":

Paradoxically, PAN's continued existence has always depended on the fact that it does not present a threat to the PRI. Its arrested development is a result of its failure to present a clear-cut alternative to the electorate, as well as its inability to employ the techniques of mass mobilization. But these deficiencies have made it acceptable to the elite, whereas a party that would propose real structural changes would surely have been repressed within a short time after its founding (Stevens 1977:246).

Stevens likewise claims that the other most prominent minor parties—the Authentic Party of the Mexican Revolution (PARM) and the Popular Socialist Party (PPS)—are simply "tame," personalistic, and coopted organizations, which serve as mere window dressing and help to tickle "the political vanity of many citizens to be able to assure themselves and to tell foreign observers . . . that Mexico is a multiparty state" (1977:246).

We have similarly avoided any systematic discussion of the structure and function of the bicameral national legislature and the state governments in Mexico's putatively federal system. Our discussion, however, has explicitly suggested that the national legislature is no more than a rubber stamp to policy initiatives undertaken by the dominant executive. Similarly, the vast majority of state governors and state legislators are members of the PRI and, as such, ultimately beholden to the president and his key advisers for their "nomination" to those offices. As the PRI exercises virtual hegemony in all political institutions and as the PRI is best seen by decisional elites as a tool to achieve compliance with their policy initiatives, one can quickly conclude that the national legislature, state legislatures, and state governorships are actors playing bit parts in a play starring top decisionmakers. Roger Hansen's assessment of national legislative and state level political offices bears quoting:

In summary, the president stands at the apex of Mexico's political pyramid. He designates some elected officials who in turn designate literally all the rest. Office holders owe their selection not to interest groups which support them with their votes, but to those few within the political elite who have co-opted them into the political hierarchy . . . And given the federal government's constitutional and fiscal dominance over Mexico's state governments, the governor cannot successfully retain either his position or his influence unless he has the approval of Mexico's president (Hansen 1971:113).

In her case study in this chapter, Merilee Grindle provides us with some substantive insight into the peculiar style of Mexican authoritarian policy-making in the agricultural area during two recent presidential administrations.

Cuba

POLICYMAKING BEFORE THE REVOLUTION

While Cuba is, like Mexico, a postrevolutionary society, it differs from Mexico in two important respects. The first key difference between them lies in the preponderant role played by the United States in Cuba's affairs before 1959. In fact, while the United States has played a significant policy role in many countries of Latin America, it is safe to say the the U.S.-Cuban relationship was especially intimate for a period of over fifty years, particularly until the 1930s.

Cuba certainly has its version of George Washington in the form of the Great Liberator, Jose Martí. Yet Cuba's successful rebellion against Spain came late—at the end of the nineteenth century—and Martí's glory had to be shared with Teddy Roosevelt's Rough Riders and their famous charge up San Juan Hill. History books in the United States compound the insult by calling the 1898 events the Spanish-American War, with Cuba's name not even mentioned. In short, Cuba was essentially a creation of the U.S. government and, for more than half of its life after the demise of Spanish colonialism, it was intensely dependent upon the United States, both politically and economically. In practice, Cuba was a U.S. protectorate with little, if any, autonomy. From 1898 to 1902 the United States ruled Cuba directly with military governors. In 1901, the new Cuban constitution included the so-called Platt Amendment, which was wholly designed by the U.S. government and which gave the United States the unilateral right to intervene in Cuban affairs. The amendment also circumscribed Cuba's autonomy in its foreign policy with countries other than the United States. The U.S. naval station at Guantánamo is the last remnant of that 1901 constitution, and today it remains a thorn in the side of the otherwise thoroughly transformed Cuban polity and society.

Until 1933, U.S. imperialism in Cuba was in full swing, with U.S. troops moving in and out and with U.S. ambassadors often exercising considerably more clout than Cuban presidents. In recognition of the predominant policy role played by the United States, competing power contenders in Cuba would make efforts to woo the U.S. ambassador to their respective sides. A major consequence of U.S. intrusion via the Platt Amendment was the inability of the regime to gain legitimacy on its own merit. The constitution, tainted by the amendment, failed in this respect. Charismatic would-be leaders such as Martí and Antonio Maceo—potentially legitimate rulers—were killed during the battle against Spain. As fiscal and monetary policies were controlled by the United States, Cuban decisionmakers were clearly powerless in this respect. Government in Cuba was perceived as illegitimate and irrelevant by many sectors of the population. Though not unique in this regard, the major purpose of government in Cuba, as Jorge Domínguez points out, was to advance the interests of the individual office holders (Domínguez 1978:35). Government certainly grew in the first three decades after independence, but it did not govern in an autonomous, decisive manner.

President Franklin Roosevelt's Good Neighbor Policy presided over the U.S.-Cuban abrogation of the Platt Amendment in 1934. After this point, U.S. involvement as a policymaker in Cuban affairs became somewhat less intrusive. U.S. Marines were no longer shipped in, and the U.S. government became less concerned with the details of Cuban politics and more concerned with the overall stability of the Cuban system. Domínguez characterizes the change as a move from U.S. imperialism to U.S. hegemony. The Cuban sugar industry—then, as now, a key feature of Cuban political economics—formerly owned largely by U.S. businesspeople, began slowly to pass into Cuban hands.

Another event—much less peaceful—occurred in 1933: the so-called revolution of 1933, which deposed the president-cum-dictator Gerardo Machado. There is no evidence that U.S. Ambassador Sumner Welles was behind the coup, but Domínguez argues that by "negotiating publicly with the opposition and withdrawing visible support from the Machado government, the Ambassador set the conditions for the President's removal. The revolution of 1933 was born in the United States Embassy" (Domínguez 1978:58).

The revolution of 1933 also was the stage for the national political debut of Sergeant-Stenographer Fulgencio Batista, who led the coup that overthrew the interim government after Machado's resignation. After installing university professor Ramón Grau San Martín as president, Batista reversed himself and ousted Grau in January 1934. From then until 1940, Batista became the power behind the throne. In 1940, Batista was elected president. After an electoral defeat in 1944, he voluntarily left the country, only to return in 1952 after a bloodless coup, ruling more or less effectively, though quite corruptly, until his demise in 1959. A major lesson to be learned from the post-1934 period, increasingly in the turbulent 1940s, was that "successful" politics came from violence or the threat of its use. Political democracy was widely—and accurately—seen as a facade. The promise of democratic reform, heralded by the highly touted Constitution of 1940, was drowned in a sea of corruption and violence. The political institutions themselves never achieved legitimacy.

POLICYMAKING SINCE THE REVOLUTION

Fidel Castro, a young university student in the 1940s, cut his political teeth on the "gang" politics of that time, in the university itself and elsewhere. Rival police gangs fought one another; other gangs fought over control of patronage in the Ministry of Education, and rightist gangs openly claimed responsibility for the assassinations of Communist labor leaders. Fidel himself was, in 1947, a member of a group that planned to invade the Dominican

Republic and overthrow dictator Rafael Trujillo. This plan was never carried out. The following year, Fidel was in Bogotá, Colombia, during the severe riots that began ten years of *La Violencia* in that country (Wiarda and Kline 1979:445). Finally, Castro was a member of one of the largest groups, the Revolutionary Insurrectionist Union (UIR), when he was accused of assassinating the president of the University Students' Federation, a charge that was never proved (Domínguez 1978:112). This violent context, within which Fidel Castro was clearly enmeshed, is not sufficient for understanding the eventual demise of Batista's regime in 1959. Although there is continued debate over the causes of the eventual downfall of the government, Jorge Domínguez's appraisal offers us a good working understanding of those times: "While the Cuban revolution did not have to happen, neither was it surprising that it did happen in a country such as Cuba. Modernization without modernity, weak political institutions and an economic depression in a context of political illegitimacy are the basic ingredients for the classic revolution" (1978:133). The serious student must certainly consult other sources for a broader comprehension of the Castro insurrection. Our primary purpose here is not to detail those insurrectionary activities, but to begin a more careful analysis of the processes of policymaking that have developed since 1959 in what is still the Western Hemisphere's only Marxist-Leninist regime.

The second of the two key differences between Mexico and Cuba lies in the fact that Cuba experienced a socialist revolution. Unlike Mexico's revolution, which has evolved into an authoritarian regime with a state-capitalist twist, Cuba under Castro's tutelage has become a thoroughly socialist state, which places heavy emphasis on egalitarian social justice through the redistribution of goods and services. Market competition was rapidly replaced by centralized planning; land was thoroughly transformed by two successive agrarian reform laws that strongly favored communal tenure and production; and properties and other assets held by well-to-do urbanites were confiscated outright. Large Havana hotels, which had catered predominantly to the foreign (i.e., U.S.) tourist trade, were closed, later to be used as housing for the sizable number of urban poor.

In 1968, almost a decade after the revolution, this move toward the socialization of the economy was vigorously revived with the announcement of a new "revolutionary offensive." In March of that year the National Association of Small Peasants (ANAP) decided to sell all private agricultural production to the state. In addition, the revolutionary government decreed the confiscation and nationalization of 55,636 small businesses that still operated in Cuba (Mesa-Lago 1978a:93–99).

Not only was the Cuban economy transformed from a capitalist to a socialist organizational mode but also the political structures, such as they were in 1959, were totally dismantled and replaced by the charismatic leadership of Fidel Castro. Decisionmaking, previously pluralistic, was centralized and concentrated in Fidel's hands. The citizens were to be led and enlightened by the revolutionary elite, whose duty it was to make "good" decisions in the people's true interests. Of course, the people themselves, it was argued, who were often incapable of knowing their interests, must be educated accordingly. As Fidel said: "The leaders in a revolutionary process are not infallible receptacles of what people think. . . . One cannot conceive of the leader as simple carrier of ideas, a simple collector of opinions and impressions. He has to be also a creator of opinions, a creator of points of view; he has to *influence* the masses" (Lockwood 1969:150). Jorge Domínguez characterized the first ten years of Castro's rule in Cuba as a mobilizational system of policymaking, with hierarchical authority (ultimately, Fidel himself) stifling criticism of the state's goals and policies. Another characteristic of this policymaking system is the perception of urgency and planning in a crisis atmosphere where loyalty to proclaimed policies is crucial and where policy change often results in abandoning entire programs rather than modifying them (1978:383–387). A good illustration of this style is the early decision in 1960 to choose industrialization over agriculture as the preferred road to development. Even when the disastrous consequences of this policy became apparent, no serious recommendations were made to increase sugar production while industrialization was being pursued. Fidel (the prime minister of the new regime) even chastised his brother Ramón on national television for suggesting that the sugar industry was being allowed to decay (Domínguez 1978:383). When policy change did come, it came swiftly, completely, and straight from the top. After the worst sugar harvest since World War II, Fidel announced in June 1963 that agriculture was the development policy of choice.

Fidel Castro's centrality in the decisionmaking process is pervasive and crosses all substantive policy areas. An excellent example of this centrality can be illustrated in the 1969 debate over dairy cows. Fidel had decided, apparently on his own, that crossbreeding imported Holstein bulls with native zebu cows would result in an efficient milk-producing cow. The program, therefore, was begun. Afterwards, two Englishmen, Dr. Thomas Preston and Dr. Malcolm Willis, who headed Cuba's new Institute for Research and Animal Husbandry, presented a paper that demonstrated the lack of wisdom in Castro's decision. Notwithstanding their credentials in this field and their empirical findings, Castro publicly denounced their work, since it was not in agreement with his own judgment (see Reckord 1971:153–161; see also Dumont 1970:40–57).

This mobilizational policymaking system continued through 1970, with repression of criticism becoming most strident after the purge of the so-called microfaction within the Cuban Communist Party (PCC) in 1968. The microfaction was not charged with attempting to overthrow the system, but simply with dissenting over specific leaders and policy choices. The purge had a chilling effect on even the mildest form of dissent and served to reinforce

Fidel Castro's position as the *líder maximo* (maximum leader) in Cuban political life.

In the first decade of revolutionary rule, the staffing of key policymaking institutions was carried out on the basis of loyalty to Fidel, defined primarily in terms of whether or not one had been a guerrilla fighter with him in the Sierra Maestra mountains. Expertise in policy areas seemed not to weigh heavily in these appointments. René Dumont (1970:50) relates how Ernesto "Che" Guevara got his job in 1960 as director of the National Bank. At a meeting of the Council of Ministers, the story goes, Fidel asked whether anyone present was an economist. Che, who was dozing off, thought that Fidel asked if there was anyone present who was communist. Che then raised his hand before anyone else and got the job! Even today, key guerrilla leaders and members of their families continue to play an inordinate role in national political institutions. For example, Vilma Espín, Raúl Castro's wife, has been the head of the Cuban Women's Federation (FMC) since its founding. One consequence of this pattern of staffing by a loyalty criterion was ineffectiveness in policy formulation and policy implementation. Though much of the poor Cuban economic performance of the 1960s and 1970s can be blamed on bad weather (hurricanes, droughts, floods, etc.) and, especially at first, the effects of the U.S. embargo on Cuban trade, the Castro-led regime must bear much of the responsibility. Fidel and his loyalists from the 26th of July Movement (named for the date of the ill-fated 1956 attack on the Moncada Army Barracks) centralized and closely controlled policy decisions. And, as the "dairy cattle debate" illustrates, this group was extremely reluctant even to accept or recognize information that was incompatible with its own preconceived goals.

Domínguez argues that the mobilizational policymaking style began to give way to a more incremental style by the late 1970s, but he also claims that Castro's policy role is still decisive in all areas of decisionmaking (1978:391, 405–507). Even the much heralded Constitution of 1976 (ratified by popular referendum on February 24, 1976), which creates a more decentralized institutional apparatus, still emphasizes the centralist part of the democratic centralism claimed by the regime. For example, the constitution provides for the same person to preside over the powerful Council of State and the Council of Ministers. Not surprisingly, the newly created National Assembly (one of the Organizations of People's Power) elected Fidel to be this person. As one observer concluded: "Even though the OPP [Organizations of People's Power] has brought about considerable decentralization of the central government by placing administrative agencies under its control, these agencies are still subordinated to the central government as well" (Azicri 1980:332). In addition, constitutional practice since 1976 has included the provision that decree-laws issued by the Council of State have equal standing with laws passed by the popularly elected National Assembly. In January of 1980, this decree-law provision proved not only equal, but superior, to Assembly laws. A decree-law was issued that created a major overhaul of the central administrative agencies, modifying the system passed by the National Assembly four years previously (Azicri 1980:337).

Is there a ruling elite that includes more than Fidel Castro? And does such an elite govern autonomously, gaining automatic compliance from a docile, intimidated (or satisfied) citizenry? Jorge Domínguez claims that there are four key institutions that govern Cuba and there are eighteen people who belong to two or more of them, who are the country's most important decisionmakers (1978:307). Two of the institutions are within the Communist party: its Political Bureau and its Secretariat. A third is the executive committee of the Council of Ministers and the fourth (since the 1976 Constitution) is the Council of State of the National Assembly. Can this ruling elite get people to do what it wants them to do? The short answer is a muted yes, but only imperfectly so. A longer answer would include a statement that citizen organizations, although not effective at all in directly challenging government policies, occasionally manage to resist policy initiatives from the central government.

One example of the first answer illustrates citizens' avoidance of policy by creating an alternative (an unofficial one). Such was the case in the 1960s when Castro ruled by whim and created bureaucratic and economic anarchy. The citizens' response was to create a black market where *sociolismo* (the buddy system) replaced *socialismo* (socialism). This unofficial (and illegal) black market continued to operate through the 1970s. As an illustration of the second answer we offer the continued intransigence of the peasantry to various versions of official land tenure and production policies, even when ANAP, the official organization, increasingly became a tool to extend the central government's control over the peasantry rather than an organ to represent them (Domínguez 1978:450–460). Peasant intransigence has been such that it has resulted in the government modifying some of its efforts to dictate and shape agricultural policy.

Some general comments concerning popular participation in the policy process might help us round out this discussion of elite-mass relationships. Domínguez concluded that the masses and lower echelon officials are typically consulted only about the details of policy implementation at the local level. Policy identification, initiative, and formulation are done in a centralized, elite-controlled fashion (1978:421). Mass organizations such as the Committees for the Defense of the Revolution (CDR), the FMC, the Cuban Labor Federation (CTC), and the ANAP never directly and publicly challenge overall national policy. As in Mexico, these organizations are essentially corporatized and serve regime-legitimation functions. However, there is some evidence that such groups and others have occasionally taken issue with some aspect of government and sometimes even "won" (Domínguez 1978:422). These mass efforts are usually in the form of complaints, such as the Cuban National

Rifle Association's complaints about certain government restrictions on hunting. Government responses to these citizen complaints vary from apparent sincere concern to no response at all (1978:409).

A final object of interest in our introduction to policymaking in Cuba must be the role of the Soviet Union. Has the USSR simply replaced the United States and become a new imperial power behind Castro? Is the Cuban regime a puppet, one manipulated from Moscow? There is no simple answer to these questions. The best way to begin answering them is to point out that the questions themselves are overly simple. The history of Cuban-Soviet relationships since 1959 has been both sweet and sour (see Mesa-Lago 1978a:1–29). Relations were of the honeymoon variety until 1962 when the U.S.-USSR confrontation over the latter's missiles in Cuba was solved with a nice sugar-purchase deal offered by the Soviets along with other long-term economic and trade agreements. Cuban-Soviet relations reached their lowest ebb when Fidel denounced the Russians' decision to decrease their supplies of oil to Cuba and when Castro purged the microfaction of pro-Soviet members of the PCC in 1968. This breach was repaired when Castro, experiencing severe economic difficulties at home and the symbolically important death of Che Guevara in the mountains of Bolivia, supported openly the Soviet invasion of Czechoslovakia later that same year.

Since mid-1970, Soviet influence seems to have increased significantly. Partly, this has occurred through the Soviets' urging the creation of a more rational bureaucratic system that would be more compatible with the Eastern European countries. Also, Soviet technical training of Cuban managers increased substantially since 1970, along with a trend toward establishing long-term economic plans such as the New Economic Plan of 1976–1980. Former Prime Minister Brezhnev himself visited Cuba in January 1974 and heard Castro promise in his welcoming speech at a mass rally that "we will never be disloyal or ungrateful to the U.S.S.R." (Mesa-Lago 1978:24). As we noted in Chapter 2, however, there is no consensus among scholars regarding the degree of policy control exercised by the Soviet Union. Mesa-Lago argued that there *is* a consensus, however, concerning an increase in Soviet influence throughout the 1970s (1978a:10). Jorge Domínguez suggested that although the closeness of a Cuban decisionmaker to power sources in the Soviet Union is one of the main sources of power in Cuban policymaking, it is also the least dependable, being outweighed even in the 1970s by closeness to Fidel Castro (1978:382). Moreover, Domínguez argued, it is likely that Soviet influence (and interest) varies across substantive policy areas. He suggests, for example, that "direct Soviet influence may also be consistently greater in science than in other aspects of intellectual life" (1978a:407). On a level of influence that goes beyond particular policy areas, there seems to be growing evidence that the formalization of institutional structures, particularly in the second half of the 1970s, has come about under pressure from the U.S.S.R. (Mesa-Lago

1978a; Azicri 1980). Recently, Susan Eckstein has argued that increasing dependence on the Soviet Union has restricted Cuba's efforts at diversifying and improving its already fragile agricultural economy for several reasons: (1) Because the Soviets tend to pay above the market price for sugar, they induce Cuba to continue to produce it at the expense of other crops. (2) The Soviets, notoriously inefficient at farming, are ill-equipped to help Cuba diversify. (3) Because Soviet technology is not competitive on the international market, Cuba's industry can only expand within the context of a sheltered domestic market. (4) The bartering between the two countries seriously limits Cuba's ability to generate foreign exchange earnings with which to purchase goods in capitalist markets (Eckstein 1981:188). While Eckstein's arguments do not demonstrate direct policy control by the Soviet Union, they nonetheless depict the limits of the decisional context within which Cuban elites have autonomy to affect major economic policies.

The study of Cuban policy toward Nicaragua by Juan del Aguila (later in this chapter) will provide us additional insight into the directions and policy consequences of the institutionalization process still going on in Cuba in the 1980s.

CASE STUDY

Rural Underdevelopment and Public Policy in Mexico

MERILEE S. GRINDLE

Mexico has a postrevolutionary regime. Its regime is also authoritarian (Purcell 1973; Reyna and Weinert 1977). These two characteristics profoundly influence the content of public policy and the way it is made and implemented in that country. As a postrevolutionary regime, the political system must maintain important symbolic commitments to the workers and peasants in whose name the Revolution of 1910 was fought (Brandenburg 1964). As an authoritarian regime, the system has a highly centralized policy formulation apparatus. These characteristics of Mexico's regime affect the pursuit of policies that address the poverty and underdevelopment in rural areas. In 1970, a new administration assumed office, and the highly centralized nature of decision-making made it possible for the president to go beyond rhetoric and to reorient the direction of public policy so that the needs and productivity of the rural poor were considered more fully. The succeeding administration also attempted to increase the flow of public resources to poor rural areas. Ultimately, however, centralization and authoritarian control limited the ability of the country's rural poor to participate effectively in the policies and programs pursued by the government, to make effective demands on the political system, or to counter the political influence of those with greater economic resources. As a result, rural underdevelopment was even more pronounced in the mid-1980s than it had been in 1970. In the rest of this chapter, the case of policymaking for rural development in the 1970s and 1980s will be explored. First, however, it is important to understand the scope and origin of poverty and underdevelopment in Mexico's rural areas.

The Problem of Rural Underdevelopment

Mexico appears to be a wealthy, industrialized, and well-developed country when compared to most other countries in the Third World, particularly many of those in Africa, Central America, and parts of Asia. But such an impression masks the deep poverty and highly inequitable distribution of wealth in Mexico. Indeed, the gaps between the wealthy and the poor in Mexico are among the largest in the world (Hernandez and Córdova 1979). Nowhere are poverty and inequity more apparent than in the country's rural areas where about 40 percent of Mexico's 70 million people resided in 1980. A study carried out in 1979 estimated that nearly 70 percent of the rural workers were unemployed or underemployed, while estimates for 1970 indicated only 40 percent of the workers in these categories (LAER, Vol. 7, no. 2; LAER, Vol. 7, no. 30). To acquire enough income to feed and clothe their families, many rural inhabitants must migrate to urban areas or to the United States to look for temporary or permanent work (Dinerman 1982). Moreover, rural wages have not kept pace with the growth of urban wages, a condition that widens the gap between the countryside and the cities (Bailey and Link 1980). Levels of education, health, nutrition, and housing are also extremely low in rural areas.

Inequity is revealed also in the distribution of landholdings in the countryside. Approximately half of the land is distributed in the form of *ejido* grants to groups of peasant farmers. An *ejido* is Mexico's form of communal landholding system. Generally, plots on *ejidos* are exploited individually rather than collectively, even though access to many state services, such as credit and irrigation, is available only to formal groups of *ejidatarios* (those who have the right to farm *ejido* land). *Ejido* land cannot be sold and, until 1980, could not be legally rented. Much of the land distributed to *ejidatarios* is of poor quality and is located in areas of inadequate and unpredictable rainfall. Over the years, *ejidos* have tended to exhibit both fragmentation of parcels and concentration of land in the hands of more wealthy or powerful *ejidatarios*, trends that increase both poverty and inequity. Another 7 percent of the land belongs to independent smallholders. While some of these individuals own sizable plots of good quality land, most are subsistence farmers who are unable to eke out a living from tiny plots of inaccessible and poor quality land. The best 45 percent of the cropland in the country belongs to a small group of large landholders, who control most of the irrigation in the country and who use modern production and marketing techniques. The crops they grow— among them, high-quality fruits and vegetables—are usually destined for export markets, primarily in the United States. It is these farmers who have benefited most from the government's programs to build infrastructure such as roads, railroads, storage facilities, and irrigation works, and to supply credit and technology such as fertilizer, high-yielding varieties of seeds, pesticides, and agricultural extension services (Hewitt de Alcántara 1976; Yates 1981). These farmers have also benefited from a subsidized supply of energy that has allowed them to mechanize their production successfully.

As a result of these characteristics, the Mexican farm population is clearly divided between the majority of subsistance-oriented producers who have little access to profitable markets and government services and a minority of successful commercial farmers who own a disproportionate amount of land, who produce crops primarily for export, and who use capital-intensive production techniques. Rapid population growth and a process of concentration of land-holdings has also meant that the number of landless rural families has increased. It is estimated that about half of all rural families are landless (Lassen 1980). These are usually among the poorest of rural inhabitants. Rural Mexico is therefore characterized by a clear division between the "haves" and the "have nots." To a large extent, these conditions are the result of policies pursued by the government from the Revolution of 1910 to the early 1970s.

THE REVOLUTION AND THE AGRARIAN REFORM

The Mexican Revolution of 1910 was the first great social revolution of the twentieth century. It erupted from a variety of grievances, but central to the uprising was a dispossessed peasantry whose objective was to obtain the land and livelihood that the country's previous development process had wrested from it (Womack 1968; Wolf 1968). Rural inhabitants suffered most from the massive violence of the bloody years after 1910. Their sacrifices were important, however, because the fight for the land largely destroyed the power of the traditional landed elite in the country. The Constitution of 1917 recognized peasant claims by enabling the state to expropriate private land and to distribute it to individuals and collective groups.

However, the spirit of the 1917 constitution was not lived up to in the period that followed. Although some land was distributed to politically important or well-organized peasants, administrations in the immediate postrevolutionary period were more interested in acquiring and promoting the health of large landholdings as a basis of economic and political power than they were with benefiting the peasant masses who had fought the revolution (Hamilton 1982; Hellman 1978). Thus, for almost two decades, the revolutionary political elite pursued policies to stimulate agricultural development on large landholdings. Agrarian reform was undertaken only when peasants seized the land unilaterally.

In 1935, however, under the skillful leadership of President Lázaro Cárdenas, the agrarian spirit of the revolution was strongly revived. Between 1935 and 1940, more than 20 million hectares of land were distributed to 770,000 peasants, primarily in the form of *ejido* grants (Cornelius 1973; Hamilton 1982). By 1940, half the cultivated area of the country had been distributed in *ejido* grants and the number of landless laborers had been reduced from 68 percent of the rural workforce in 1930 to 36 percent a decade later. At the same time, Cárdenas established a rural credit bank and initiated infrastructure projects to respond to peasant needs and increase their capacity to produce efficiently. Health and education services were also extended greatly in rural areas. In addition, the Cárdenas *sexenio* was noted for the efforts to organize peasants at the local, regional, and national levels so that they could become a more effective political force in the country (Hamilton 1982; Ronfeldt 1973; Sanderson 1981; Warman 1980).

Unfortunately, the distribution of land and the organization of the rural population made it possible for administrations after 1940 to control the political activities of the peasants so that development policies could be turned to other goals, notably the encouragement of large-scale commercial agriculture. Gradually, then, the *cardenista* organizations, incorporated into the PRI through the National Peasants' Confederation, were transformed from effective vehicles for grass-roots political activity to vehicles for top-down control and cooptation of dissent (Craig 1983; Hellman 1978). In the period after 1940, when Cárdenas left office, policies toward rural areas were clear evidence of the failure of the peasants to achieve political influence in the authoritarian system.

THE REFORM BETRAYED

Between 1940 and 1970, the structure of inequitable rural conditions took firm shape (Hewitt de Alcántara 1976; Centro de Investigaciones Agrarias 1974; Esteva 1980). The government continued to distribute land to *ejido* groups and small landholders, but primarily in order to coopt peasant beneficiaries and to discourage independent political activity. At the same time, it began a process of stimulating agricultural modernization on large landholdings through the provisions of credit, infrastructure, and green revolution technology. The *ejido* sector was largely ignored as a recipient of these goods and services, and the gap between subsistence and commercial farmers widened. By 1970, 12 percent of Mexico's farmers owned 42 percent of the farmland, 48 percent of its irrigated land, 73 percent of its farm machinery, and 61 percent of its green revolution technology (LAER, Vol. 7, no. 20). Irrigation programs, which received between 75 and 85 percent of all investment in agriculture during these years, were directed at large landowners who were then able to take better advantage of state-subsidized green revolution technology and extension services. Irrigation districts were the focus of agricultural development policies after 1950, and by 1970 irrigated districts accounted for 93 percent of all official credit, as well as 70 percent of mechanized farming. Not surprisingly, this sector of the agricultural economy grew in productivity and gained considerably in political power, while the subsistence farm sector failed to prosper and peasants became the real orphans of the state development policies (Hewitt de Alcántara 1976; Sanderson 1981). These characteristics increasingly concerned administrations after 1970.

PUBLIC POLICY RESPONSES TO RURAL PROBLEMS

In Mexico, each new *sexenio* is accompanied by a massive turnover of personnel within elective positions, the party, and the bureaucracy (Grindle 1977a; Smith 1979). The beginning of a new *sexenio* generally offers opportunities to reorganize the bureaucracy and provides ambitious advisers and other officials with the chance to influence presidential decisionmaking and even to experiment with new policy solutions. Therefore, when Luis Echeverría assumed the presidency in late 1970, changes in public policy were widely expected. The new administration was particularly concerned about agriculture and rural areas for a number of reasons. First, high-level officials were aware that agricultural production was failing to contribute effectively to national development and was falling well behind rates of population increase (see Table 5.1). In addition, they became aware that the government's emphasis on the expansion of a modern export-oriented agriculture had meant ignoring or discriminating against the production of crops for domestic consumption such as corn and beans. By 1965, Mexico found it necessary to begin importing corn and other basic foods even though the country had been self-sufficient in these crops for many years. By 1970, these imports were costing Mexico considerable amounts of foreign exchange and government planners were duly alarmed about this condition.

TABLE 5.1

Average Annual Growth Rates, Mexico 1940-1979
(Percentages)

	1940-1950	1950-1960	1960-1970	1965-1970	1970-1979
Gross Domestic Product	6.7	5.8	7.1	7.1	5.4a
Population	2.8	3.1	3.5	3.5	3.3
Per Capita Product	3.9	2.7	3.6	3.6	1.8
Agricultural Production	8.2	4.3	3.6	2.2	2.0
Manufacturing Production	8.1	7.3	8.9	9.0	6.8a

Source: Grindle, 1977a: p. 77; Interamerican Development Bank, 1979, based on official statistics. a1971-1979.

In addition, a number of high-level officials who accompanied Echeverría into office were concerned about the inequitable distribution of wealth in the country. There was growing evidence that the poorest 50 percent of the population was beng left behind in the country's impressive economic growth. Politicians and planners worried about what this meant for social unrest, particularly in the countryside. During the presidential campaign, Echeverría had traveled to remote rural areas and had been confronted with the reality of rural poverty; he saw why so many rural Mexicans were migrating to large urban areas and causing concern about urban congestion, unemployment, and the rapid expansion of shantytowns (Esteva 1980; Hewitt de Alcántara 1976; Warman 1980). Finally, urban areas were growing rapidly and officials were concerned about being able to supply low-income families with sufficient corn, beans, rice, cooking oil, and other staples to forestall the possibility of urban unrest. All of these conditions indicated to officials that they needed to determine what was going wrong in agriculture and rural areas.

Their analysis soon led many of them to the conclusion that if they wanted to increase the production of basic foodcrops, then those responsible for these crops—the peasants—would have to receive much more assistance from the government. In their discussions and studies, officials concerned with agriculture and agrarian policy began to argue that there was a clear connection between poor yields in basic foodcrops and levels of poverty in the countryside. Because of poverty, they claimed, peasant crops had to be sold at low prices before they were harvested; credit had to be obtained on usurious terms from local moneylenders; markets were distant and transporters charged high prices; storage facilities were rare; and middlemen of all types siphoned off any profits the peasants might earn. Poverty made them extremely vulnerable to exploitation. As a result, the argument developed, peasants tried to protect themselves against being exploited by producing primarily for their own subsistence without the use of technological innovation that would increase their productivity.

Given the new interpretation of the problem, Echeverría's closest advisers were convinced that the solution was to direct toward rural areas efforts that would allow peasants to make agriculture a more profitable activity. The advisers' task was to gain the strong support of the president for a new policy orientation. Without this support, it was unlikely that those with vested interests in long established policies could be challenged, that sufficient public resources to fund a variety of new rural programs could be secured, or that middle- and lower-level bureaucrats would be motivated to work hard to implement the new policies.

Among the most important officials who spoke repeatedly with Echeverría about the problems in rural areas and the new solution to them were two of the president's closest advisers, the minister of the presidency and the finance minister. In addition, the director of the government's large marketing agency (CONASUPO) was very active in presenting arguments to the president about the need for a new approach to rural poverty and underdevelopment. Within these three groups, middle- and upper-level officials worked diligently during the first year and a half of the *sexenio* analyzing information about rural areas and the agricultural sector in general. They helped put together information and proposals that were then presented by cabinet and subcabinet officials in a series of meetings with the president.

These officials argued forcefully that the government had to change the policies that discriminated against peasant producers; the low support prices for many agricultural commodities offered by the government in an effort to keep urban food costs low were singled out as particularly important (Esteva 1976). More importantly, the solution implied the need for structural changes in the rural economy so that peasants would no longer be so easily exploited. Technical teams within the ministries and CONASUPO identified specific instruments to bring about these structural changes: higher support prices for basic crops; consumer and production credit; more infrastructure such as storage facilities, feeder roads, extension services, and small irrigation works; subsidized clothes, food, fertilizer, improved seeds, tools, and medicines; and medical and educational services. The argument that all of these had to be delivered widely and effectively to peasant producers was crucial to this policy advice. The *ejido* sector in particular would be a focus for a wide variety of new government services.

Echeverría, who had developed great concern for the rural and agricultural sector, was persuaded by the analysis of the problem and the solutions proposed by his top officials. The success of the ministers of finance and the presidency and the head of CONASUPO in their policy advocacy is evident in budgetary allocations. By the mid-1970s, Mexico was directing more than 15 percent of public sector investments toward rural areas. This was a very significant increase over previous administrations that had targeted 10 percent or less of public investments toward agriculture and rural development. Not only was the percentage of investment growing, but also the total amount of government investment grew very rapidly, paralleling a great expansion of the size and spending habits of the public sector (Bailey and Link 1980).

A policy redirection and higher levels of funding were not all that was needed for more effective programs in rural areas. Coordination among official agencies was also vital to ensure that "packages" of appropriate goods and services reached rural inhabitants. As a result of the influence of policy supporters within the government, Echeverría created the Agricultural Sector Coordinating Committee in 1973 in an effort to bring together the most important ministries and agencies with responsibilities in rural areas. In addition, he consolidated three rural credit banks into one in 1975 and began a major integrated rural development program known as PIDER, which brought together the activities of a number of public agencies (Cernea 1979).

The president, with the aid of the Ministry of the Presidency and the Department of Agrarian Affairs, introduced into congress new legislation to stimulate the development of the *ejidos*. Considerable efforts also to distribute land were undertaken by the Department of Agrarian Affairs (Sanderson 1981). However, the greatest contributions of the Echeverría administration were the "rediscovery" of the importance of the peasantry for national development and the public attention given to the rationale for directing resources to this sector of the rural economy. Formulating this policy was almost exclusively a task pursued by middle- and top-level officials in a few important ministries and agencies.

In late 1976, the *sexenio* of José López Portillo was inaugurated. Close advisers within his personal staff were joined by officials from the Ministry of Agriculture and Hydraulic Resources and the Ministry of Planning to study the problem of rural poverty and low productivity. Their new analysis stressed a number of the problems that had concerned the previous administration— the stimulation of export production at the expense of domestic crops, the favoritism in government policy toward the irrigated zones, the urban bias in pricing policies for basic crops, and particularly, the problem of Mexico's food dependency on the United States. Agricultural imports grew rapidly after 1976, and planners were visibly alarmed about the amount of money that was being spent to import food that Mexico should be able to produce itself (see Table 5.2). They were adamant that they did not wish to see the new wealth that was coming from discoveries of oil being spent to import food (Oficina del Asesores del C. Presidente 1980; Luiselli 1982).

The planners and policymakers in the new administration also accepted the importance of directing government resources toward peasant agriculture. But when they asked why the peasants don't produce more, they came to a different conclusion than the policymakers of the previous *sexenio*. Rather than

TABLE 5.2

Value of Agricultural Trade, Mexico 1967–1978
(Thousands of U.S. Dollars)

	Total Merchandise Trade		Food and Agricultural Products		Ag. Imports as Percent of All Imports
	Imports	Exports	Imports	Exports	
1967	1,745,852	1,103,814	118,147	639,355	6.8
1970	2,460,811	1,372,957	216,277	694,505	8.8
1971	2,407,277	1,473,665	192,918	699,503	8.0
1972	2,718,480	1,674,080	269,314	861,312	9.9
1973	3,813,400	2,070,480	543,662	956,288	14.3
1974	6,056,700	2,850,100	1,054,618	1,015,062	17.4
1975	6,580,156	2,858,625	989,834	949,323	15.0
1976	6,029,589	3,264,186	563,335	1,329,144	9.3
1977	5,487,500	4,064,800	769,931	1,418,164	14.5
1978	7,560,742	5,437,900	1,078,526	1,656,152	14.3

Source: Statistical Abstract of Latin America, 1980: FAO, Trade Yearbook, 1979.

the broad structural constraints considered important under Echeverría, the new team of administrators and policymakers argued that peasants were not more productive because the regions they lived in were poorly serviced with basic infrastructure and because subsistence farmers were unable to take the risks necessary to adopt new technologies. After a series of meetings and consultations, the president was convinced by his agricultural policy advisers that the solution to this problem was to expand infrastructure in zones of peasant agriculture and make incentives to adopt new technologies more available to peasants. In their presentations, little importance was given to the role of intermediaries and the question of exploitation. In fact, the Echeverría policies had tried to exclude middlemen from their traditional roles, but López Portillo's advisers promoted efforts to incorporate them and also to respond to the concerns of large landowners with favorable legislation (Redclift 1981). Similarly, Echeverría, who had links to the country's agrarian past and the dominant party, was concerned about the economic rejuvenation of the *ejidos*; López Portillo's closest advisers, in contrast, were inclined to view the *ejido* sector as an economic white elephant with little productive potential. Instead, it was the independent small farmers who were considered to be the most likely beneficiaries of the new policies. The advisers were also skeptical about the availability of land for distribution and the utility of continuing the agrarian reform. As a result, during his term of office, the president emphasized repeatedly the need to bring the distributive phase of the 1917 agrarian reform to an end.

Once again, the president's support of the new policies was evident in increased budget allocations. By the early 1980s, public spending on agriculture and rural development was nearly 25 percent of all investment, reflecting an explosion of new programs and legislation dealing with the rural sector. In accordance with the new analysis of the constraints on peasant agriculture, the Ministry of Agriculture and Water Resources created rainfed districts to serve as the loci of public investment in infrastructure and the promotion of green revolution technology. A program for marginalized areas and groups, known as COPLAMAR (Coordinating Program for Marginal Zones), was also initiated and became a competitor for funding and personnel to the PIDER program, which had been established by the Echeverría planners. In 1980, the major effort of the López Portillo administration, known as the SAM (Mexican Food System), was unveiled (Meissner 1982; Luiselli 1982; Redclift 1981). The SAM, stressing food self-sufficiency for the country, was a strategy for increasing the efficiency of food production, marketing, processing, and consumption in Mexico, largely through the use of subsidies (Oficina de Asesores del C. Presidente 1980). This massive effort was planned almost exclusively by the president's personal staff responsible for agricultural policy.

The policymaking for agriculture and rural development during the 1970s and 1980s indicates how the process works in Mexico when the welfare of relatively powerless groups is involved. Under both Echeverría and López Portillo, agricultural sector studies were widely known among policy analysts. However, these perspectives did not become influential in shaping public policy until they achieved presidential support. In both cases, those who argued for the new policy approaches were presidential advisers or officials within the cabinet or the bureaucracy. Under Echeverría, the peasant sector of the PRI was consulted and informed of the thrust of the new policy, but it was not involved in the actual formulation of the policy (Grindle 1977a). Under López Portillo, a small group of advisers close to the president was responsible for the planning, without much participation even from officials in the ministries or agencies. In this case, the peasant sector of the PRI was not even consulted about the SAM (Redclift 1981). Thus, the policy changes that channeled more resources toward the rural poor did not result from the mobilization of peasant demands but from decisions at the top to address the problem. This suggests that how responsive the government is to specific problems of low-income groups depends considerably on the sensitivity and political astuteness of a handful of individuals who occupy the pinnacle of power within the political system.

The Politics of Policy Implementation

In contrast to policy formulation, the policy implementation process in Mexico tends to be much more flexible, open, political, and competitive. There are two general areas where policy implementation is most susceptible to political pressure and competition and that pose considerable problems for achieving policy goals. The first area concerns the institutional constraints to policy implementation and the willingness or ability of various ministries, agencies, or departments to carry out presidential initiatives. Centralized policymaking often results in public programs that are established without a clear concern for their administrative feasibility. Programs may envision goals that bureaucratic organizations are incapable or unwilling to pursue, perhaps because of poorly trained administrators, lack of knowledge about how to achieve the goals, or refusal to alter familiar behaviors or comfortable organizational structures. In addition, when bureaucratic agencies have not been deeply involved in formulating policy, they may simply resist having changes imposed on them. In other cases, of course, individual agencies, ministries, or departments can become enthusiastic policy supporters, especially if they can anticipate an expansion of their budgets, personnel, power, or programs from jumping on the policy bandwagon.

Policy implementation becomes highly political also when government activities directly affect individual citizens and groups. Indeed, because so few are involved in policy formulation, if citizens are to influence the policy process at all, they must direct their efforts at the allocation of public resources and the decisions made by a variety of middle- and lower-level administrators (Grindle 1977a). This kind of political activity is particularly difficult to document because so little of it is public. It takes place through private conversations, over a "friendly" lunch, during extended negotiations over the telephone to Mexico City headquarters, or by way of subtle hints from bureaucratic superiors to subordinates that this individual or that group should be favored over others.

Both institutional and political constraints on policy implementation were important in the rural development initiatives of the 1970s and 1980s. To begin with, achieving the new rural development goals required considerable coordination and cooperation among a variety of government agencies. The PIDER program of integrated rural development that was initiated under Echeverría, for example, called for the coordination of fourteen different national agencies by a staff within the Ministry of Planning and Budgeting and by committees within each state and each region where the program was to be implemented. Centralized decisionmaking and different levels of commitment to the program made it extremely difficult for these agencies and committees to work together. The SAM, pursued under the López Portillo administration, required the commitment and cooperation of an even larger number of official agencies.

The policies of both administrations also depended upon the reorientation of bureaucratic behavior to be more responsive to low-income groups in rural areas. In practice, it was often the case that cooperation among official agencies was conspicuously absent. Some agencies were more willing to commit themselves to the new priorities than others because they expected to gain politically from them. One of the more eager public organizations, for example, was the marketing agency, CONASUPO. This agency anticipated, quite realistically, that the new rural development initiatives would lead to a great expansion in its resources and power. The Ministry of Agriculture, in contrast, was a large and fragmented organization that had long been committed to the development of the modern, capital-intensive form of agriculture that had emerged in the irrigation districts. It also had a politically influential clientele among the large commercial farmers. In addition, ministry officials were not eager to collaborate actively with other agencies because they feared that they would lose influence and prestige to other, more active and enthusiastic organizations. As a variety of individual agencies and ministries such as these two pursued their own priorities, there was frequently little incentive for them to collaborate with each other.

As the number of programs dealing with rural underdevelopment expanded, the problems of coordination and competition became more widespread. A good example of this was the tension that emerged between the PIDER program, initiated under Echeverría, and COPLAMAR, established by López Portillo. By the late 1970s, they were competing intensely with each other for presidential support and resources, and officials of the two programs continually sniped at each other and sought to denigrate the work of the other. As they had somewhat similar goals, PIDER and COPLAMAR regions often overlapped; duplication and planning errors were reported frequently. One widely cited anecdote drew attention to the COPLAMAR health clinic. Followers of COPLAMAR argued that it was carrying out the original goals of PIDER, whose officials were incapable of achieving them. Partisans of PIDER, however, argued that COPLAMAR programs were poorly planned and unrealistic. Competition and conflict did little to overcome frequent problems of poor planning, lack of information, duplication, and waste of effort.

Other problems resulted from the *sexenio* change of 1976. When presidential administrations change in Mexico, most public programs are temporarily suspended and then redesigned, renamed, cut back, or abolished as the new team seeks to place its stamp on public initiatives. This happened to the rural development activites of CONASUPO. The agency had been catapulted into a greatly expanded role in the early 1970s under Echeverría. Its rural activities were cut back drastically by López Portillo in early 1977 and then encouraged to grow again after 1979. These changes in the agency not only impaired the stability and continuity of its efforts, but also seriously affected its capacity to inspire confidence among its low-income clientele. Waste of effort and resources and public cynicism were an inevitable result of its waxing and waning popularity with policymakers.

Moreover, because of the six-year limit to each administration, many policies were abandoned before they had a chance to prove themselves. As a result, Mexico lost valuable opportunities to test the longer-term viability of various approaches to the problem of rural development. The attempt of the Echeverría *sexenio* to address structural conditions of exploitation in rural areas is a good example; in 1977 it was replaced by a different perspective and a different set of programs. The SAM strategy was pursued for only twenty-two months under the López Portillo administration before it was scrapped by the new *sexenio* of Miguel de la Madrid.

Institutional constraints on effective policy implementation were complemented by the realities of political power in the country. In the 1970s government development policies had so strengthened the modern agricultural sector that is was able effectively to act as a constraint on the implementation of policy, if not on its formulation. This became clear in 1975 and 1976 when the Echeverría administration attempted to expropriate and distribute lands in the irrigation districts of northwestern Mexico. The economic power of the large landowners was great because of the foreign exchange they generated through agricultural exports; the government ultimately had to bow to their demands for a "stabilization" in the agrarian reform (Sanderson 1981). It is interesting to note that the peasant sector was not able to make equally strong demands for attention from the government because it lacked an independent base of political or economic power. The López Portillo administration and that of his successor, Miguel de la Madrid, were willing to accept the idea that the large landowners who might be affected by expropriation were too important to the economic development of the country to confront with such efforts. Both therefore stressed that land distribution was not a feasible solution to the rural problems of the country.

In spite of the efforts of the government to direct public resources to rainfed agriculture, the large landowners were able to continue to demand more than their share of public benefits. This was true of the SAM strategy, which helped raise production of basic crops significantly during its first full year of implementation. The SAM, although primarily directed toward zones of rainfed agriculture, offered generous subsidies to any farmers who would grow appropriate crops, corn and beans above all. Producers in the irrigated districts quickly took advantage of this offer and the amount of corn and beans grown in these regions increased markedly in 1981. In zones of rainfed agriculture corn and bean production declined in the same period. This suggests that a significant portion of the SAM subsidies were captured by the most advantaged farmers. It also suggests that the institutional and political constraints to reaching peasant producers and the rural poor more generally had still not been overcome. In the following years, when subsidies were significantly curtailed, the problems of insufficient production recurred and the country returned to importing large amounts of basic grains from the

United States. In spite of its initial success, the SAM did not really offer a significant solution to the problems of rural poverty and underproductivity because it did not address the issue of political and economic power in the countryside.

Implementation of the rural development initiatives was also limited by the economic and political power of the middlemen in the rural economy. Often, they were the real beneficiaries of programs directed toward the rural poor, even under the Echeverría administration when attempts had been made to exclude the intermediaries. The middlemen, or *caciques* (bosses) as they are often called, were able to use their connections to state and national politics and the PRI to halt the expansion of programs that would hurt their vested interests or to take charge of resources meant for the poor (Grindle 1977a). The allocation of public resources was therefore often diverted from policy and program goals in order to keep the political peace with the most influential local inhabitants.

Finally, the rural poor were not asked to participate actively in the implementation of the new programs. In rural areas, the PRI has been especially successful in maintaining a supportive but inarticulate base among the poor through the National Peasants' Confederation (CNC) and the loyalty of local *caciques* (Hansen 1971). Therefore, mobilizing the peasants to make effective demands on the political system was a political impossibility for the implementers of the new policy. As a result, the power of the *caciques* could not be effectively countered; cooperation among peasants was limited; programs suffered from lack of communication between beneficiaries and administrators; and the politically and economically influential were able to siphon away benefits intended for the poor.

The Impact of Rural Development Policies

Given the institutional and political constraints to effective implementation, it is not surprising that greatly expanded public investment in rural areas had little evident impact. Overall levels of agricultural production did not increase significantly during the 1970s and early 1980s. The growth rate averaged 1.7 percent from 1971 to 1975; was 1.2 percent in 1976; rose to 5.1 percent in 1977; and declined to 3.6 percent in 1978 and −0.4 percent in 1979. The average growth rate was about 2 percent a year, and imports of food in 1980 amounted to a third of all imports, costing about $3 billion. Some of this disappointing experience is the result of capricious weather conditions. Droughts in 1975–1976 and 1979 were particularly devastating to peasants; commercial farmers with access to irrigated land were much less affected. Even taking weather into account, however, it is important to note that until 1981, the area dedicated to basic crops—the target of the rural development programs—declined slightly each year, while the area for export crops such as fruit and vegetables increased considerably, as did forage cropland. Production of basic crops increased only slightly. We have already seen that unemployment and underemployment worsened during the period, and levels of social welfare did not improve for the rural poor. Thus, in spite of massive new resources directed to rural areas during the 1970s and early 1980s, conditions of rural underdevelopment actually increased.

Conclusions

Rural development emerged as an important goal in Mexico in the 1970s and 1980s. The ways in which the policies were formulated and implemented indicate much about the political system of Mexico. In that period, Mexico's large population of peasants was "rediscovered" and extensive rhetorical commitment was given to revitalizing the revolutionary "alliance between the state and the peasantry." The subsequent interpretations of what was wrong with rural areas were based on extensive data collection and thoughtful analyses of the underlying causes of rural underdevelopment. The formulation of the policies revealed the highly centralized nature of decisionmaking in Mexico, and their implementation provided some insight into the basis of its authoritarian control over low-income groups. The policies were established in Mexico City by a small group of influential public officials who managed to gain presidential support. The policies were then translated into specific programs and projects and introduced into rural areas in largely "top-down" fashion. As a result, peasants were not able to become effective participants in the programs that were to benefit them, and many of the benefits were actually channeled to those who helped keep the peasants politically unmobilized and inarticulate—the *caciques*—or those who had the greatest economic power—the large landowners.

Ultimately, these development initiatives failed to address the problems of poverty and rural underdevelopment because of the characteristics of the political system. Given the realities of Mexican politics, it is difficult to envision how these problems can be more effectively addressed in the future. A variety of initiatives are needed, including those (1) to reverse the concentration of landholdings; (2) to discourage technologies that are inappropriately capital-intensive; (3) to make better quality land and water resources available to the rural poor; (4) to break the power of the *caciques* and other intermediaries within the rural economy; (5) to confront the growing power of large landowners and agribusinesses; (6) to increase the availability of infrastructure, technology, credit, and jobs to rural people. These may imply a new agrarian reform for Mexico. But such a reform would be a difficult, if not impossible, undertaking for politicians and bureaucrats who value the relative political peace that has been a central characteristic of Mexico's postrevolutionary and authoritarian regime.

CASE STUDY

Revolution and Foreign Policymaking: How Cuba Influences Nicaragua

JUAN M. DEL AGUILA

Cuba in the 1980s is a society where revolutionary changes affecting all areas of national life and governmental policymaking have produced a fairly egalitarian social order, economic austerity, and stable politics. The establishment of formal executive, legislative, and judicial institutions in 1975–1976 changed the character of the Cuban state, formalizing roles and investing them with legal authority. In turn, the hegemonic role of the Cuban Communist Party (PCC) is sanctioned by the "socialist constitution" of 1976, which certifies Marxism-Leninism as the official ideology and defines the limits of political participation.

The global reach of Cuba's foreign policy became evident even as the reorganization of the state advanced, and its regional dimensions are in line with the regime's world view. Of particular significance is the fact that Cuba's armed forces are relied upon in the pursuit of "internationalist" commitments and that military features shape the regime's foreign policy outputs. The military is in turn fully integrated into the political elite, and its interests are presumably taken into account when routine as well as major foreign policy decisions are made. Though the military is subordinate to the party and the political leadership and fails to assert autonomous decisionmaking power in foreign policy, its role involves much more than the defense of the country (Domínguez 1979).

An important issue treated in studies of policymaking in Cuba is the role that the Soviet Union (not individual Soviet advisers in Cuba) plays in the process. It is generally held that the Soviets were instrumental in encouraging

Cuba's leaders to "institutionalize" the revolution, partly to increase the system's managerial and administrative capabilities and bring greater rationality to bear on the policy processes, and partly to bring Cuba closer to the Soviet bloc's political and military models.

Granted that the Soviet Union influences Cuba's foreign policy more than any other external actor, decisions involving Cuba's fundamental security interests are in all likelihood made in Havana (LeoGrande 1981:187–206). Cuba's leaders may decide that it is in Cuba's interest to support the Soviets on East/West or North/South matters, but it is unlikely that they are forced to do so. The outcome may be the same, but who controls the process is also crucial. Horowitz has described that condition as "authenticity without independence" (1981:4), in the sense that Cuba must take into account what the Soviet national interest is before choosing its own option(s). Thus the Soviet Union places objective limits on Cuba's foreign policy, without controlling the foreign policymaking process, because Cuba's policymakers are well aware of what is or is not acceptable. At the margins, Cuba also has some flexibility.

The Nicaraguan revolution of 1979 created promising opportunities for low-risk expansion of Cuba's influence, and the latter is an actor whose policies towards Nicaragua have an impact in several areas. In this essay, I will examine why foreign policymaking in Cuba is restricted to a few decisionmakers, and why the process of institutionalization has not increased institutional or popular pressures or control on the foreign policymaking elite. The focus is on Cuba's efforts to shape the Sandinista revolution and secure certain political objectives, but some observations on the relationship between values and foreign policy will also be made.

Institutions and Foreign Policy

One of the principal features of the process of institutionalization was the creation of national institutions designed to bring Cuba into a period of stable, if not legitimate, rule. A host of ministries and state agencies carry on the work of government, but the state bureaucracy has been reorganized along functional lines. In part, the creation of national institutions stemmed from the need to expand popular participation and at the same time maintain central control. As a consequence, the regime went from a period where charismatic authority and "revolutionary" legitimacy shaped its character to one where formal processes are observed. As a revolutionary regime, its legitimacy stems not from direct popular consent, but from the fact that its performance in critical domestic areas has been credible, and because tacitly or otherwise, most Cubans consider its authority to be properly exercised. A brief review of the central institutions of the state is necessary; however, one needs to emphasize the fact that foreign policymaking responsibilities are outside these institutions' purview.

The National Assembly, which has been the country's "socialist parliament" since 1976, is not autonomous and does not discharge any responsibilities either in foreign policymaking or in overseeing Cuba's foreign relations. Its executive committee, the Council of State (SC), is a permanent body whose members are the highest representatives of the state and government. The council consists of a president (Fidel Castro), a first vice-president (Raúl Castro), five additional vice-presidents, and twenty-three others. The council is invested with legislative authority, and its president also commands wide appointive and executive powers. For example, Fidel Castro can assume the leadership of any ministry or central agency of the administration if it should be decided that poor performance, or other deficiencies, warrant it. In 1979, Castro took over four portfolios, including Interior and Defense, in a sweeping shake-up. He has since given these up (Domínguez 1981).

The executive branch of government has also been restructured. The Council of Ministers (CM), is the highest administrative and executive organ, and it constitutes the government of the republic. The CM has the power to set and oversee domestic policies; it is also charged with the conduct of foreign policy and relations with other governments. Its executive committee, made up of the president (Fidel Castro), the first vice-president (Raúl Castro), and other vice-presidents, "controls and coordinates the work of the ministries and central organizations" by sectors (Cuban Constitution 1976). Fidel Castro himself is the principal decisionmaker in the foreign policy field, along with a few trusted associates in the political and military leadership.

The PCC, since 1976 defined in the Constitution as "the organized Marxist-Leninist vanguard of the working class," and as the "highest leading force of the society and of the state," is the only party in existence. As is the case with other ruling communist parties, its highest organs are the Political Bureau, the Secretariat, and the Central Committee, with the first constituting the ultimate and most powerful decisionmaking body. For all practical purposes, policies set by the fourteen-member Political Bureau are followed down the line, both through the party and through the governmental hierarchy. In the foreign policy field, the Central Committee's General Department of Foreign Affairs and the America Department maintain liaisons with ruling communist parties elsewhere, and with revolutionary groups in Latin America and throughout the Third World (LeoGrande 1980:410–411). Jesús Montané, an alternate member of the Political Bureau and a loyal Castroite, is the director of the General Department of Foreign Affairs. Major Manuel Piñeiro, longtime operative in Cuba's intelligence and espionage services, heads the America Department. The department is the coordinating agency for Cuba's covert operations, possessing operational and logistical capabilities that respond directly to the wishes of top policymakers. In all likelihood, these staff agencies follow policies set by the Political Bureau; as such, they are not centers of decisionmaking, but of implementing and subsequently overseeing policies. But since they are party agencies, they probably exercise greater influence over policy than the Foreign Ministry itself. Incidentally, Cuba's foreign minister, Isidoro Malmierca, is not a member of the Political Bureau, and his powers therefore cannot compare with those of, for example, Mexico's foreign minister, Bernardo Sépulveda, who is also a member of Mexico's dominant party, the PRI. Malmierca is subordinate to Castro and, ultimately, to the political leadership, and he is probably not a powerful decisionmaker. Not much is known regarding how the party's top echelons relate their views to lower party bodies and to state agencies. According to LeoGrande, the Central Committee "seems to be emerging . . . as the principal locus of intraelite communication and coordination," and as the entity through which party policy preferences are disseminated (LeoGrande 1980:409). In all likelihood, orientations for the two Central Committee departments involved in foreign policy come from the top policymakers. As is the case with other bureaucrats, it is possible that organizational prerogatives may produce tensions between party representatives and those charged with implementation, but it is extremely unlikely that the party's views would be rejected by strictly administrative personnel.

This brief discussion has already pointed out a crucial feature of institutionalized communist systems: overlapping membership in top state and party organs, with the latter exercising supreme policymaking authority. In effect, the party sets policy and the state bureaucracy implements it. Fidel Castro, as first secretary of the PCC, president, and commander-in-chief, is the final source of domestic and foreign policy authority; unquestionably, he is the top policymaker. However, Castro in the 1980s is less preoccupied with agriculture, trade, or education (his concerns in the 1960s) than with foreign policy matters. The process of institutionalization has itself created demands for technocrats, specialists, and "socialist managers," and Castro has delegated authority in such areas to competent and loyal subordinates. Temperamentally, Castro is also better suited to waging war in Angola or uniting guerrilla factions in Central America than to setting production goals for cement or managing the tobacco crop. The big challenges remain in foreign affairs, and that is where Castro is at his best, where he focuses his energy and talent, and where he exercises near-absolute authority. In short, the demarcation of where Castro's authority ends and institutional-bureaucratic rule begins is more explicit in domestic than in foreign policy matters. Cuba's foreign policy still has a dominant Castroite character. To that extent, it has not been "depersonalized"; the *process* of policymaking is therefore unified and centrally controlled to a high degree, rather than thoroughly bureaucratized (Ferguson 1980:323).

Decisionmaking and Values

If centralization is the hallmark of policymaking in communist systems (and in Cuba's case charismatic authority adds a crucial element) then the process of decisionmaking has to take into account not only external stimuli, but also contextual values. So while Castro and his small coterie of leaders retain supremacy in the policy process, institutionalization has in no small measure curbed the ad hoc impulses of Cuba's top decisionmakers, who must operate in a more structured context. That fact has probably also introduced a greater sense of rationality to the process and a heightened awareness that some decisions are unwise because Cuba lacks the capabilities to see them realized. Being aware that constraints (domestic and external) impinge on capabilities makes for sounder foreign policy decisions.

Making foreign policy, however, especially in a revolutionary state committed to transformations *beyond* its borders, involves questions of value, as well as matters of *Realpolitik*. Cuba's policymakers may at times pursue pragmatic policies, such as maintaining cordial relations with noncommunist, democratic nations like France or Spain, but that in no way constitutes an abdication of their reolutionary goals. Pragmatism and ideology are not irreconcilable, and Cuba's foreign policy blends the two effectively.

One must look at the substantive focus of a policy in order to determine the balance between revolutionary values and objective national interests. For instance, the Constitution itself "recognizes the legitimacy of the wars of national liberation" and considers Cuba duty bound to "help those under attack and the peoples that struggle for their liberation." From that standpoint, Cuba's commitment to "proletarian internationalism" means that it will be active in regions where its leaders perceive "progressive forces" waging anti-imperialist struggles. That may be in Africa, the Middle East, or in Central America. If the call comes, and Cuba's own security is not directly jeopardized as a result of its forays, the nation—or so its leaders proclaim—is ready to go to the barricades. The policy process itself is shaped to produce that outcome, should it be decided at higher levels to do so.

Such a view permeates the foreign policymaking process, making it more than a series of rational calculations involving gains or losses. In fact, some of Cuba's foreign policy successes, especially its African campaigns, once appeared irrational acts from the standpoint of small-state theory. In the past, states like Cuba rarely entertained extending their influence far from their immediate region, and they were often incapable of doing so even if the will to do it was present. Cuba's overseas commitments, considering its size and estimated power, would be incomprehensible if one did not take into account the leadership's serious commitment to revolutionary causes or failed to appreciate why smaller states are able to exercise leverage over more powerful actors. The point here is not to dismiss the fact that Cuba's initial victories in Angola and Ethiopia have led to a protracted occupation, or that its "becoming stuck in an African quagmire," with weak clients unable to provide for their own security, cannot be credibly described as a major political success (Segal 1983:144). What is important is that the calculations that preceded Cuba's involvement correctly assessed the potential political and strategic payoff, especially in terms of Cuba's own leadership in the Third World.

In Central America, and especially in revolutionary Nicaragua, Cuba projects its value preferences abroad through its foreign policy in an effort to enhance its own security (by cultivating allies), strengthen its regional position, and expand its influence, sharply curtailed following the U.S. invasion of Grenada. Cuba's relations with Nicaragua are thus shaped by its leaders' view that a sound foreign policy must articulate a definition of national interest that conforms with the values of a revolutionary political culture. Insofar as Cuba can influence the path of change in Nicaragua away from reformism, capitalism, and "bourgeois democracy" and towards a unitary socialism, its policies will have succeeded. However, if Managua rejects political sectarianism, complete "statization," partial satellization by the Soviets, and a penchant for insurgency and revolutionism beyond its borders, Cuba will have failed to achieve most, if not all, of its major objectives.

Decisionmaking: Influences and Constraints

Foreign policymaking in Cuba takes place in a restricted space. Few are privy to major decisions on matters of security, on relations with the Soviets, or on what policies to pursue in Central America. Popular pressures do not affect decisionmaking in any fundamental way; mass organizations do not raise questions regarding the wisdom of the regime's external commitments. No rival centers of power exist that might conceivably challenge Cuba's posture in Central America. The government presents a united front at home and successfully projects that image abroad.

Institutions like the National Assembly hardly shape Cuba's foreign or regional policies. Debate in the assembly is tightly controlled, and the 499-member body routinely supports the political leadership's views on foreign policy. All deputies are Communist party members, assuring that no dissent—if it exists in someone's mind—becomes public. Altogether, there is no evidence that serious public debate on foreign policy issues takes place in any national forum, and it is likely that even members of the political subelite do not have available to them the kind of accurate information that would enlighten them about their country's actions abroad. None of the formal leaders of the National Assembly is a member of the PCC's inner circle.

Rather, the pattern is one where the political leadership decides what policies the regime will follow, what specific objectives it will pursue, and what costs it will tolerate. Castro's own public pronouncements, couched in the principles of revolution, "internationalism," or "proletarian solidarity," are meant not so much for public information purposes as for telling the people why Cuba *must* support revolutionaries the world over.

In contrast, the regime's mobilizational capabilities are impressive, constituting a major asset when the citizenry is urged to support foreign policy moves. For instance, Cuba's defeat in Grenada was portrayed at home not as a blow for the regime's regional ambitions, but as a cause worth fighting and dying for. Colonel Tortoló, returning to Grenada on Castro's orders on the day before the invasion to assume command of Cuban forces, was subsequently welcomed in Havana, not as a leader who had failed, but as a national hero. Nevertheless, one suspects that his military career will not be as successful from here on.

What is therefore crucial, from a policymaking standpoint, is the virtual absence of countervailing pressures on decisionmakers, either of an institutional, bureaucratic, or popular nature. The media is, of course, not a source of criticism, and its politically mandated task is to reaffirm the regime's policies and speak of triumphs rather than failures. Insofar as one is able to determine, the foreign policymaking process remains nearly insulated from "checks" within the regime, as well as in the political system, and the leadership can frame policies that may have dire consequences, without fears of public or institutional retribution. If a policy turns sour, as it did in Grenada, or a relationship produces higher-than-expected security costs, as may be happening with Nicaragua, accountability is exercised inside the ruling elite itself. Usually, top policymakers call subordinates on the carpet, but that is done secretly and without fanfare. Purges and sweeping changes in personnel are indications that something has gone wrong, and in a regime that prizes unity "in the face of imperialist aggression," dismissals have to be carried out carefully. There is no way to know when and if the assumptions of a particular policy are reconsidered, until the shift is manifest.

Finally, members of the Political Bureau, the "superelite" ultimately responsible for Cuba's overall policies, are at once the most responsible, most secure, and least vulnerable actors. The Castro brothers are immune, even if they are not infallible, and their mistakes litter the record of the past three decades.

Although the regime appears to act as one, there is reason to believe that its alleged homogeneity is subject to some divisions. Gonzalez (1979) has identified three foreign policy tendencies in the leadership, namely: (1) the pragmatic economic tendency, (2) the revolutionary-political tendency, and

(3) the military mission tendency. Personalities, corporate interests, and ideological origins partly shape each tendency's role in the policy process, and the extent of each tendency's influence is determined by the nature of the foreign policy problem (or opportunity) at hand. The pragmatists are presumably "led" by Carlos Rafael Rodríguez, now seventy years old, a leading member of the pre-1959 Communist party (PSP), and a classic survivor of internecine policy battles and ideological confrontations. An economist with administrative expertise, something of a "practical Marxist theoretician," and a man with vast diplomatic experience, Rodríguez has been a member of the Political Bureau since 1976 and is now a vice-president of the Council of State and Council of Ministers. By some accounts, he is Cuba's third most powerful man, is on very good terms with the Soviets, is familiar with the socialist world's bureaucratic milieu, and is involved in diplomacy and state-to-state relations.

The radical tendency is personified by Fidel Castro and "is backed by veteran Fidelista revolutionaries and close associates who occupy top leadership posts in the party, state and government" (Gonzalez 1979:19). Since Castro is its de facto leader, this is the dominant faction. A third group is headed by Raúl Castro, minister of the Revolutionary Armed Forces, Havana's link to the Soviet military, and the man responsible for national defense. Presumably, these tendencies lend balance to the ruling coalition and attempt to integrate views and interests prior to reaching decisions on questions of foreign policy, security, and national defense. All told, these tendencies represent, respectively, pragmatism and the interests of a "stable technocracy"; that brand of radical politics stemming from Castro's charisma and *caudillismo*; and the military's recognized participation in policy matters.

Cuba and Nicaragua: The Context of Decisions and Their Possible Impact

The Nicaraguan revolution presented an opportunity for the dominant tendency to reassert itself. Promoting radical revolution and maintaining an unflinching anti-U.S. posture is Castro's game, because from his (and therefore the regime's) standpoint, that is the best strategy for extending Cuba's influence. There is little doubt that the Sandinistas look to Cuba for guidance; during the insurrection, they followed Castroite and Guevarist tactics. Some among the nine commanders (Tomás Borge, Bayardo Arce) wish to repeat the Cuban experience in Nicaragua, though that appears more and more unlikely partly because no one in the leadership comes near Castro either in political savvy, charisma, or nerve. Nonetheless, the prospect of building up a clientelistic relationship with a nationalist, neo-Marxist regime in Central America is very much in Cuba's interest, especially at a time when the hostility of the United States is directly felt. In effect, the times demand bold action rather than circumspection. Castro, "unlike the pragmatists who emphasize economic strategies" for building bridges to the outside world, "employs leverage politics as the principle means through which his otherwise vulnerable, dependent island is to be made secure and great" (Gonzalez 1979:20). Seizing the moment, Cuba quickly moved in with a formidable physical presence, and I have little doubt that it remains the most influential external force shaping the Sandinista revolution.

That does not mean that Cuba is unaware of its limitations or that deepening radicalization in Nicaragua means fewer worries for Cuba. Unquestionably, Cuban policymaking elites feel political and psychological pressure. The threat that the Sandinistas pose to their neighbors has energized regional resistance to what is also perceived as Cuba's geopolitical offensive. Cuba and its immoderate protégés may have overestimated their ability to exploit vulnerabilities in the region, but they still hold many bargaining cards. Rather, it is precisely because Cuba is limited in what it can accomplish regionally that makes it take the initiative, carefully calculating where to stake resources, prestige, and credibility. And its political system is especially well suited for quick responses to unfolding situations. In turn, its centralized policymaking process, with focused participation from top policymakers, responds well to shifting trends in the region.

However, such a process may fall prey to ad hoc decisions, and the system's ability to process information reliably is bound to be affected by ideological considerations and errors of fact. Misperception and miscalculation plague the foreign policymaking process of most states, and one must not assume that Cuban policymakers read all the signals correctly. It is not inconceivable that if Castro misreads a situation, and the process under way in Nicaragua is full of contradictions that even experts cannot fathom, then others in the political hierarchy will fail to challenge Castro's mistaken notions. All the talk about "collective leadership" aside, who among the members of the Political Bureau is going to tell Castro to his face that his assessments are flawed? Even if discussion and debate take place within the top ruling circle, prevailing *against* Castro is not an easy task. In fact, if a majority in the Political Bureau is ever fashioned in opposition to a Castroite position, no one knows about it. While one does not doubt that the leadership prefers a consensual model to one where confrontation and division create considerable "decisional conflict" (Janis 1982), pressures within the top elite may make the latter unavoidable. Contextual errors may thus be compounded insofar as group dynamics lead some policymakers to go along with decisions that they know may be flawed. Finally, neither Castro nor those around him can escape the fact that "the evidence available to decisionmakers is almost always very ambiguous, since accurate clues to others' intentions are surrounded by noise and deception" (Jervis 1969:243). Although Cuban intelligence is known to be very good, blunders, such as that evident in its failure to detect the disintegration of Prime Minister Maurice Bishop's regime in Grenada, suggest that in some cases policymakers may operate in the dark.

In addition, misperception due to ideological distortions can occur. Revolutionary regimes tend to view the world ideologically and to interpret reality in accordance with specific "historical laws." According to Ole R. Holsti, that has a direct bearing on the policy process, since an ideology such as Marxism-Leninism: (1) establishes the intellectual framework through which policymakers observe reality, (2) prescribes for policymakers both national roles and an image of the future state of the world, (3) serves as a rationalization and justification for the choice of more specific foreign policy decisions, (4) defines the moment in history in which policies are likely to be more or less successful, and (5) posits an absolute moral system defining what is right and wrong (1983:325–326). If Havana's policymakers view the process of change in Nicaragua as a form of class struggle, which is necessary in order to break the power of traditional bourgeois interests, then their policy options take on a more radical character. In contrast, if the situation is seen as one in which structural changes can accommodate the interests of various contenders, then the options suggest moderation and pragmatism.

I have little doubt that Cuba's own revolutionary legacy shapes its policies toward Nicaragua. Both revolutions are built on nationalist sentiments focused against authoritarian rule backed up by an imperial power. Both revolutions have adopted Marxism-Leninism substantively and for its intrinsic symbolic value. Both are anticapitalist and favor "statization" over private initiative. Other similarities exist, especially in the area of political organization and mass mobilization, where the Sandinistas have borrowed freely from the Cuban model. Obviously, Cuba is an institutionalized communist society while Nicaragua has failed to establish legitimate rule. And it is not inconceivable that the Sandinistas will be swept from power or end up rejected by their own people. Nonetheless, much evidence suggests that Cuba has influenced the path of revolution in Nicaragua to a considerable degree, "in ideological persuasion, structures, modus operandi, and even in intangibles such as political and revolutionary style" (Jorge 1983:219).

The presence of large Cuban contingents (despite recent reductions in nonmilitary personnel) is felt in education, health care, social work, construction, and administration as well as in political, ideological, intelligence, and security matters. Such an effort is designed not only to assist Nicaragua in reconstruction and development, but more importantly, to support consolidation of power by the Sandinista National Liberation Front (FSLN). It is politics that matter, and Cuba's overseas missions never lose sight of what is crucial. As Coleman and Quirós Varela point out, a "revolutionary alliance" exists between Havana and Managua, "in which the Cubans are the 'experts' on literacy campaigns and on their potential for revolutionary politicization" (1981:47). Cuba's "expertise" is already evident in the creation and function of Sandinista Defense Committees (CDS); in the 1980 literacy campaign, where ideology dramatically shaped the selection of educational materials; in the colors (red and black), tone, and symbolism of Sandinista marches, rallies, and demonstrations; in popular sloganeering; and in the personal demeanor of Nicaragua's new leaders whom former Sandinista commander Edén Pastora derides "as nine little Castros."

Contacts between Sandinista leaders and Cuban officials add to the closeness of governmental relations. This is a crucial element of policymaking, often overlooked by approaches that stress process, roles, and procedures. In a fluid revolutionary environment exacerbated by political conflict and military tensions, frequent contact among top policymakers or their trusted subordinates is often necessary in order to expedite the transfer of information. This is particularly necessary when governments face a protracted crisis, as is now and likely to remain the case in Nicaragua. Castro visited Managua in 1980, and other high officials like Raúl Castro and Armando Hart have gone there since. In return, Daniel Ortega, Tomás Borge, Sergio Ramírez, and other Sandinistas have visited Cuba. Delegations from both countries are also in contact at the United Nations, at meetings of the nonaligned nations movement, and at other regional and international forums. Information coming into the policy process is thus likelier to be "fresh," since conventional exchange mechanisms or normal diplomatic channels are frequently bypassed. This may compensate for other flaws.

If Cuba's policies are to have a lasting impact on the process of restructuring Nicaragua's polity and sociocultural systems, the security aspect cannot dominate the bilateral relationship. Granted that security is crucial—the Cubans know what it takes to survive in a hostile environment. But if the process of change is to reach into the social fabric and endure, then the reshaping of individual attitudes is as important as acquiring military capabilities. In other words, assuming that ideas matter, the presence of Cuban teachers in the Nicaraguan hinterland preaching the virtue of Marxist socialism may be more politically effective than the transfer of arms from Cuba to Nicaragua. Havana's policymakers know this. And the absence of a democratic tradition in Nicaragua, or the lack of a sense of national community, favors those who would lose if genuine pluralism were to emerge. Cuba's leadership knows the value of language and ideas, and it deploys Marxism-Leninism in a particularly appealing way, simplifying history to suit its purposes.

Cuba has been training personnel for overseas duty for years. It is a wise investment in human capital that many developing countries welcome. But one should not view such efforts as either humanitarian or altruistic. They are intended to advance Cuba's political objectives abroad, because Havana's leaders know that a bridge, or a hospital, or a school built by its minions may bring political payoffs. To put it differently, Cuba's policymakers face opportunities as well as limitations in their attempt to stand their ground in Nicaragua. Governing a resource-poor, indebted, and dependent society means that Cuba must rely on means other than economic or financial largesse if it is going to compete with wealthier donors. Communicating political knowledge and experience in situations where power is at stake may be as valuable as giving millions in aid or transferring technology. What good is the latter if your political clients are driven from power? In other words, if Cuba falls short on economic assistance, its political handbook does contain valuable lessons on what is necessary for the maintenance of a revolutionary dictatorship: political will tested during crisis and confrontations, ruthlessness towards one's opponents, a skillful use of national symbols as rallying points against foreign aggression, and an uncanny ability to disguise weaknesses and vulnerabilities.

It is not certain that Castro's protégés in Managua can live up to their mentor's exploits, and they have committed blunders (such as insulting the Pope) that make one wonder how much longer Havana is willing to associate with such political primitives. Poor leadership in Managua, stemming from the ill-advised conviction that civil strife is preferable to power sharing, may undo Havana's painstaking work and leave Managua in a more precarious position. In the meantime, Havana will sustain an integrated policy, one in which the realization of its objectives can be achieved through concerted action in different tracks.

Conclusions

The institutionalization of the revolution in Cuba has affected foreign policymaking to the extent that responsibilities for implementing policies are now structured in a more rational manner. Enough time has passed for cadres to be trained in various aspects of the policy process, though it is difficult to assess just how competent such specialists, technocrats, and socialist bureaucrats are.

The "inner circle" of decisionmakers is small, however, and Fidel Castro is much more than *primus inter pares*. He is the intellectual force behind Havana's foreign policy, particularly in its regional manifestations. In a totalitarian state, systemic pressures hardly affect the context of foreign policy decisions, which are made far removed from popular view. Public debate on issues of war and peace is nonexistent, and the function of national institutions and the media is to praise the wisdom of decisions, not to question their merits. Top policymakers may be accountable to each other, but the Castro brothers are politically immune. Fealty to Fidel Castro's views is still the best way to avoid being purged, even if the policy becomes too costly or fails. Fundamental disagreements with Castro may be politically fatal.

Foreign policymaking involves not only rational calculations, but also ideological criteria. Presumably, a balance is struck between ideological zeal, capabilities, and organizational imperatives. Policymakers do face constraints, especially when assessing what responses to Cuba's moves adversaries might contemplate. In Nicaragua, Cuba is aware that radicalization raises the risk to its own security; it has therefore embarked on a policy of integrated support for the Sandinistas and a willingness to cooperate in a regional settlement.

Lastly, Cuba's policies have had an impact on the course of events in Nicaragua, though it is unlikely that the Cuban experience could be replicated there. Cuba's contributions in the area of education and political socialization may be as significant as its role in improving the Sandinista regime's repressive capabilities. But the Sandinistas' blunders, and their failure to establish a one-party state committed to authoritarian socialism, suggest that Cuba has found objective resistance to its designs.

[6]
Patterns of Public Policy

To this point, we have concentrated our attention on understanding how policy is made in various Latin American countries. We have examined different kinds of regimes and have explored the differences and the similarities among them. Our analysis has provided a close look at the functioning of the political structures and the roles of various actors in the making of public policy. Two critical questions remain to be examined. Do differences in the process of policymaking lead to any significant differences in the content of public policy? To put the questions in somewhat more academic language, we ask: Is there a relationship between regime type, policy output, and policy impact?

The term *policy output* actually is a redundancy. If we define policy as what the government does, then output refers to what "comes from" government action. We use the phrase, nevertheless, to distinguish it from the phrase *policy impact*. We should be able to determine policy output by a careful examination of the process of policymaking, including the formulation, adoption, and implementation of policy. Government's actual expenditures for higher education, or the number of people covered by social security are policies, or policy outputs. But what is the societal impact of these policies? Are people more literate and smarter as a result of educational policy? Do retired workers live a longer, or more secure, or happier life as a result of social security policies? Is the economy growing or stagnating, and is this a result of government policy? These are the kinds of questions one ultimately asks when analyzing the impact of public policy.

In Chapter 7, we confront the issue of policy impact. In this chapter, let us focus our attention on the problem of determining whether or not there is a relationship between a regime type and a pattern of public policy. Necessarily, our analysis is rather broad and sweeping. We attempt to provide a few details and specifics, but in the main we seek to characterize the nature of government policy in three areas. The first area to be examined is economic policy; then we describe the nature of social policy, and finally we describe political and civil rights policy. As you read this chapter, keep in mind that

177

to a large extent this exercise is necessarily interpretive. You may wish to consider alternative interpretations based on additional statistical and case study information. Ours is certainly not the final word, for example, on Cuban economic policy or Brazilian social policy.

Economic Policy

Government leaders in each of the six countries, and in most of Latin America, have expressed concern over the principal economic issues of growth, distribution, and dependency. For a variety of reasons, achieving economic growth is one of the higher priorities for policymakers in Latin America. Population increases require some growth of the economy just to keep from falling behind. While population pressures are mild in some countries—Argentina, Chile, Costa Rica, and Uruguay have population growth rates between 1 and 2 percent annually—in others, population increases present an acute problem. For instance, in Mexico the economy must grow by about 3 percent each year just to keep things even. If Mexican leaders wanted to aim for a net (per capita) economic growth rate of 3 percent per year, their economy would actually have to grow by 6 percent.

Rising expectations is another very important reason why political leaders must concern themselves with economic growth policies. Because of the exposure to advertisements, to those who live well, and to the exhortations of various political and educational leaders, people in rural areas, the poor in the cities, workers, and even middle-class individuals are no longer satisfied with their material conditions. Governments either must work to make their economies grow to meet some of these expectations or use repression to minimize unrest. But leaders are finding that repression has its limits and, in any event, is a very expensive means by which to keep things peaceful.

The need for economic growth also is related to the problem of distribution. There are two ways to provide more for those in society who have little. Through economic growth, more is made available to society in general, and some of that increase in wealth can be made available to the less well-off. Alternatively, various policies, such as progressive taxation or land redistribution, can be used to redistribute wealth from the well-to-do to others. This alternative is extremely difficult to employ, since the people with the wealth frequently are those making the decisions or those who have the ability to influence decisions. Cuba's case is typical in that massive redistributive efforts occur only when preceded by a revolution, which allows a set of redistribution-oriented leaders to assume control of government.

The problem of distribution is not solely a matter of economic growth and, in fact, it would be misleading to suggest too intimate a relationship.

Certainly, it is politically easier to give the poor (or any one group) more by giving all more. For several reasons though, the problem of distributing a nation's wealth goes beyond striving for economic growth. Because of the limitations of resources, the limitations on access to what resources do exist, the nature of international trade and economic competition, and the distribution of international power, there are very real limits to what any country, and especially any Latin American country, can hope to achieve by way of sustained economic growth. To put it more bluntly, economic growth rates will not be very high for the foreseeable future. Therefore, to provide for the less well-off, policymakers must pay attention to means by which some redistribution can occur.

Whatever the limits on economic growth, a notion of justice also requires that some attention be paid to distributive policy issues. Admittedly, in most Latin Ameican countries, very few policymakers or other politically influential individuals see much need to achieve economic equality in order to have social justice. The concept of equality of opportunity would suffice for some, and, in fact, probably would be too radical for many. Nevertheless, all but the most traditional and reactionary recognize it is unjust to maintain a society in which a very few are quite wealthy and the vast majority quite poor. So while notions of economic justice may be limited, they do exist and must be considered by policymakers.

How to achieve and sustain economic growth and how to provide for an acceptable and just distribution of a nation's wealth are issues facing government policymakers everywhere. In Latin America these two critical economic issues are joined by a third—the problem of dependency. Actually, there are two kinds of dependency, and most Latin American countries are affected by both. Product dependency occurs when a nation depends very heavily on only a very few commodities to earn most of its foreign trade money. Historically, Cuba has been extremely dependent on sales of sugar for export earnings; Costa Rica depends on coffee and bananas, Brazil has depended on coffee, Chile on copper, Bolivia on tin, and so on. Even where the basic export commodity is valuable, dependency can be a real problem. Venezuela depends on oil. Oil dependency is much better than banana dependency but still permits the same problem. When the international price of that one commodity goes down, so does the economy in general. Any given product runs the risk not only of a drastic fall in price, but also of wild price fluctuations. When either occurs, it becomes impossible to engage in any kind of meaningful economic planning. Thus, the Mexican and Venezuelan economies grew when the price of oil was booming, and as the price went down both economies began to suffer trade deficits, increasing unemployment, and rising inflation.

A second form of dependency occurs when a nation depends very heavily upon one, or a very few, other nations for most of its trade and foreign investment. When the countries of Latin America once were colonies (primarily of Spain or Portugal, though France, England and the Netherlands did have small colonial possessions in Latin America), they were almost totally dependent upon the mother country. When the international power of Spain and Portugal waned, first Great Britain and then the United States moved in, not as colonial powers, but as the principal trading partner and investor. More recently, in the case of Cuba, the Soviet Union has become a principal investor and trader. Where this kind of trade and investment dependency exists, as it does to some extent for virtually all Latin American countries, it means that many important economic decisions are made outside of the country. As we have seen, foreign private capital and foreign governments play very important roles in policy-making in the Latin American countries. This is the problem of dependency, and it must be met by policies to diversify export products and trading and investment partners—or the country will never be fully independent and able to make its own decisions.

Leaders in each of the Latin American countries have acknowledged current and long-term needs in the areas of economic growth, distribution and dependency, but the extent of concern for each of the issues and the willingness to utilize the resources of the state to tackle the issues vary from country to country. Perhaps of all the countries in Latin America, the military regime in Brazil since 1964 has most unequivocably concerned itself with achieving economic growth. Following the military coup, economic policy was put under the direction of planning minister Roberto Campos and a group of experts. According to their plan, the new regime first would have to tackle the problem of inflation and then pursue a policy of stable, economic growth (Skidmore 1973:12–13). After Campos was replaced and control over economic policy-making was shifted to the Ministry of Finance, headed by Antônio Delfim Netto, economic policy focused almost exclusively on growth. Dr. Mario Henrique Simonsen, a regime theorist and policymaker, summarized the regime's economic philosophy as one that "establishes as a basic priority the accelerated growth of the GNP, accepting as a short-term liability the corollary of an appreciable imbalance between individual rates of income . . ." (Flynn 1978b:258).

Several elements constituted the growth policy. The state significantly increased its extractive capability through raising taxes and, especially, increasing its ability to collect taxes. The total burden rose from 18 percent of gross domestic product in 1963 to 30 percent of GDP by 1970. The total number of taxpayers during this period increased from 470,000 to some 4 million (Skidmore 1973:22, 39–40). Government-established institutions, such as the National Housing Bank, collected funds from employees and employers, and then used the funds to help finance construction and other economic activities.

A second part of the growth policy involved the extension of various tax credits to those willing to expand significantly their productive capacity. Tax write-offs given to individuals to invest in industry, excise tax rebates given to spur the development of manufacturing exports, and a variety of tax benefits to foreign industries willing to help Brazilian export markets were some of the benefits tendered.

Finally, the government spent sizable sums of money on various projects to expand the ability of the country to house modern industry and meet its various needs in communication, transportation, and energy, that is, those things typically referred to as part of the infrastructure. These projects involved such activities as building or improving roads, dams, and telephone and electricity lines. The government also has been willing to nationalize businesses or industries, or allow them to go under, if such action is believed to be necessary to remove hindrances to further industrial development.

Although Brazilian economic policy has emphasized expansion since 1964, most of that effort has been concentrated on industrial expansion. The agricultural sector has not received as much attention. Some incentives, including tax benefits and the threat of land expropriation, have been used in the hope of spurring productivity. In general, though, most funds and projects have been used to aid the industrial sector. In fact, by 1969 the budget for the Ministry of Agriculture had been cut substantially (Ayres 1975:21).

While significant efforts were being expended on economic growth activities, much less concern was evinced with regard to problems of distribution. To a large extent, as Dr. Simonsen's statement indicates, the regime felt that growth had to be achieved, at virtually any cost. One way of accomplishing rapid, short-term growth was to hold down benefits to the working class and the poor. Thus, for example, between 1964 and 1967 the real minimum wage was down 20 percent. Though there have been some upward wage adjustments since, the real minimum wage in the early 1970s was still only about what it had been in the mid-1950s (Fishlow 1978:255). Nor did government policy attempt to deal with problems of distribution in the rural areas. Though some attempts were made to expand development of the chronically poor northeast area, government action here, as elsewhere, was aimed at industrial expansion and the export market, not at alleviating suffering and poverty or the great disparities of wealth.

Government action in the area of dependency policy resembles action in the distributive area. On the one hand, military leaders have constantly evoked symbols of Brazilian nationalism and have engaged in the rhetoric of independence. On the other hand, the government has been quick to court foreign capital. This has been true particularly where foreign investments and foreign firms have been involved in developing both the most modern sectors of industry and Brazilian exports. For example, Brazil has attracted a number of automobile manufacturers and has been working with several West German firms to develop an atomic energy industry. If anything, trade and especially investment dependency have increased under the military regime. U.S. direct, private investment in Brazil is one good indicator of increased dependence. It increased from a fairly sizable $1 billion in 1964 to a staggering $7 billion by 1978 (Hewlett 1980:228). By 1981, the figure climbed to $8.3 billion (*LAWR* 1983:9). As we noted earlier, those in the military who have disagreed with such a pro-foreign capital policy, such as former Minister of Interior Alfonso Albuquerque Lima, have not been well received by the dominant power coalition. On the other hand, product dependency has been attacked. Though Brazil still receives a substantial portion of foreign earnings from the export of coffee, manufactured exports have increased greatly, including armed tanks and computer parts to the United States and watches to Switzerland.

The nature of Peruvian policy during the 1968–1975 period is more difficult to characterize than Brazilian policy. First, this so-called radical or revolutionary military regime was in power a short time. Many policies were not fulfilled. Whether this was due to the fact that rhetoric outstripped intent or to insufficient time for full implementation we will never know for sure. Another problem that makes accurate assessment difficult is that the military leadership itself seemed somewhat unsure of the precise direction it wanted. Some leaders clearly favored a radical restructuring of social, economic, and political relations. As we have seen, this was particularly true of most members of COAP and of many leaders of SINAMOS. In contrast, most of the early cabinet members, as well as others, obviously favored a more conservative approach.

For these military leaders, the goal was not a radical restructuring of Peru, but rather some limited social and economic tinkering to generate more efficacious conditions for economic growth. Inevitably, given this diversity within the military, policy decisions would evidence some contradictions and ambiguities. Finally, it is difficult to characterize the 1968–1975 period because the military regime that continued to govern Peru from 1975 until 1980 was, on balance, a more conservative group. Thus, policy decisions taken during the Velasco period often were altered, reversed, or ignored. This means that often the data that have been used to assess the impact of the Velasco period are tainted because much of the legislation necessarily had to be implemented during the ensuing period. With these caveats in mind, we present what seems to be the predominant view of economic policy during the years of President Velasco.

In comparison to the economic policies of the military in Brazil, the Peruvian military focused their policy less on economic growth and more on modernizing and restructuring the economy. When the military took power in 1968, Peru possessed one of the poorest and least developed economies in Latin America. Along with widespread poverty, there was a handful of individuals who possessed great wealth. The result was a tremendous gulf separating the rich and the poor. For instance, just under 2 percent of the landed estates controlled something on the order of 85 percent of the land. The top 1 percent of income earners possessed some 31 percent of the nation's income; the bottom 25 percent of the population then had to try to get by on an incredibly meager 3 percent of the nation's wealth (Lowenthal 1975:23). In addition, trade and investment dependency were quite high. Not only was a good deal of the economy (and the polity) controlled by a few wealthy, landowning families but also most of the relatively small but dynamic modern sector of the economy was controlled by foreign capital. President Velasco summarized his view of the problems facing Peru this way: "The structural root of the great problems that beset Peruvian society . . . arises in final analysis from its double, inter-related condition of being a society that is underdeveloped and subject to imperialist domination. . . . For this reason it is not possible to resolve any of our major problems without confronting the crucial questions of dependence and underdevelopment" (Hunt 1975:310–311).

To attack these causes of Peru's economic difficulties, the regime seems to have established four general policy goals: (1) break the dependency of Peru; (2) destroy the dominance of the landed oligarchy; (3) assign to the state a major role as a leader of economic development; and (4) develop an economy in which individualist capitalism is only one element, along with various forms of cooperatives, workers' communities, and state-owned enterprises (Gorman 1978:289–290). Several measures were implemented with respect to the de-pendency issue. A number of foreign, particularly U.S., companies were taken over, though usually under terms acceptable to the company. Among the firms expropriated were the International Petroleum Company (IPC—a subsidiary of Standard Oil of New Jersey), the Peruvian Telephone Company (an affiliate of IT&T), the W. R. Grace Company, and the landholdings of the Cerro De Pasco Corporation (a U.S.-controlled firm). In addition to expropriations, the Velasco administration attempted to expand the range of countries with which it engaged in trade and investment ventures. The Peruvians tried to broaden economic relations with Western Europe, and sought new relationships with the Soviet Union, China, and Japan.

The primary weapon used to destroy the dominance of the landed oligarchy was the Agrarian Reform Law of 1969. Although estimates vary, we can say conservatively that 18 million acres of land were expropriated and redistri-buted. The impact of agrarian reform on the oligarchy was so devastating that, in effect, the oligarchy was eliminated. However, a few wealthy, individual landowners remained, while some simply moved their wealth abroad or into the industrial sector.

Of all the economic policy areas, the one pursued most vigorously and most successfully was the expansion of the economic role of the state. At the time of the military coup of 1968, the Peruvian state played a relatively small part in economic development, far less than was typcially the case in the economically more developed countries of Latin America. Under the lead-ership of President Velasco, the government moved quickly to control a wide variety of resources and to put itself at the center of most economic relationships. By the end of the Velasco period, the state controlled forty-five enterprises, including those active in oil, mining, sugar exports, electric supply, fertilizers, and banking. In 1965 the state accounted for only about 19 percent of the GNP; by 1975 it accounted for almost 50 percent (Cleaves and Scurrah 1980:72).

The final policy goal, the development of economic forms and relationships other than the individual, capitalist one, was pursued with less consistency and vigor than the previous area. Although cooperatives were established and industries were required to institute one or another form of workers' participation, this was an area where the government often altered course when faced with strong criticism from industrialists and middle-class entrepreneurs. By the end of the regime, the amount of workers' participation was weakened. In the countryside, the cooperatives sometimes came to be a kind of rural industry run by a new group of middle-class technicians and managers.

Whatever the limitations of the economic restructuring achieved under the Velasco regime, it is clear that a good deal of restructuring did occur. But restructuring is not a goal itself; it is merely a means to accomplish some end or ends. What was the purpose of all these structural modifications? It seems clear that Peruvian leaders were not attempting to emulate Cuban governmental leaders. Economic rebuilding in Cuba was designed to achieve socialism; in Peru, however, it was designed to achieve greater economic growth within a modified capitalist framework. This is not to say that the Peruvians, like the Brazilians, were uninterested in issues of distribution. The Agrarian Reform Law and the General Industrial Law of 1970, which established such practices as workers' participation and profit sharing, contained obvious redistributive consequences. Some other steps were taken that provided real, if limited, benefits to the less well-off. For instance, though housing policy was still biased toward middle- and upper-class needs, a fairly large number of land titles were given to families in urban squatter settlements. In fact, more of these titles were given between 1970 and 1972 than in the previous decade (Collier 1976:114).

In spite of the fact that there was some concern for issues of distribution, the primary focus was on eliminating obstacles to growth. What was clear to the military was that the old semifeudal agricultural system, which prevented both agricultural development and sufficient industrial investment, had to be destroyed. It was also clear to the military that the state had to be a major partner in the economic game, as the state already was in countries like Argentina and Brazil. A clear indication of the military's intent, and perception of the problem, can be seen in the decisions adopted to compensate expropriated landowners. When the government took an estate, it provided for compensation by a combination of cash payments and bonds. The bonds constituted the primary means of payment and were to mature over a long period of time (about 20 years) at a very low rate of interest (about 6 percent). Given the rate of inflation, averaging about 25 percent annually between 1969 and 1978, these bonds would not be worth a great deal when fully matured. However, the government was willing to increase significantly the value of the bonds if the holder was willing to invest in industry. In fact, the regime's tendency to publicly disparage the landed oligarchy was not meant to disparage all wealthy investors. President Velasco himself made this quite clear when he said: "When we speak of 'oligarchy' we are not referring at all to the industrialists and entrepreneurs who contribute to the creation of wealth in this country . . ." (Jacquette 1972:653–654).

We have already seen that with respect to the area of dependency, the Peruvian regime pursued a policy of diversification in terms of the numbers of trading and investment partners. In particular, the government clearly sought to break the very heavy dependency of Peru upon the United States. This policy, however, did not mean that Peru was anti–foreign investment or even anti–United States. On the contrary, the military sought a wide range of investments from a wide range of countries. For instance, at the 1972 meeting of the "Paris Club," the Peruvian government presented a project of industrial development that included $3 billion of international financing (Colter 1975:55).

On balance, the Peruvian government emphasized an economic policy of immediate restructuring in order to obtain long-term growth. In this respect, policy was designed to bring Peru "up to" the structural conditions extant in a country like Brazil. However, even given comparable structural conditions, the Peruvian regime under Velasco was somewhat more attentive to distributive and dependency issues than was its counterpart in Brazil.

In 1935, the Mexican government created *Nacional Financiera* as a primary means by which the state would help finance economic development, through low-interest-rate loans to private industry. Between 1934 and 1940, during the presidency of Lázaro Cárdenas, the state took over the oil industry and became active in the electric power field. In 1959, almost 2,000 new enterprises were being developed in Mexico (Cline 1963:282). In the early 1970s, the government launched SICARTSA (the Lazaro Cárdenas Steel Production Center), a project to gain self-sufficiency for Mexico in steel production (Johnson 1978:119). What these examples illustrate is the commitment by the Mexican government to achieve economic growth. Unfortunately, Mexican policy, much like Brazilian policy, has placed a heavy emphasis on growth but shown little interest in how that growth is distributed throughout the various income groups. Jesús-Agustín Velasco, a scholar and participant in Mexican policymaking, put it this way: "The thirty-year period between 1940 and 1970 was, in essence, a phase of economic growth characterized by a long-term policy of industrialization via import substitution . . . and without meaningful development. During this period, although national economic growth took place, the gap between rich and poor increased" (1983:27).

For at least the past two or three decades, then, Mexican economic policy has resembled very closely economic policy in Brazil. Under the very active and firm guidance of the government, great emphasis has been placed upon achieving high and sustained rates of industrial growth. To this end, the government has engaged in a wide range of measures to aid economic development. A standard package of tax incentives and subsidies exists to spur productivity in several areas of industrial exports. The government has spent heavily over the years on a variety of infrastructure projects, increasing energy available to industry and improving transportation and communication systems. In addition, the government has created and lavishly funded a number of institutions designed to provide funds and technical advice for many industrial projects, such as *Nacional Financiera*. Finally, the government itself has taken over several different kinds of enterprises. As we saw in the case of Peru, this has been done not to achieve socialism, but to break up structural obstacles to sustained growth. As Clark Reynolds (an expert on the Mexican economy) wrote: "Beginning with the administration of Lázaro Cárdenas and particularly since the presidency of Miguel Alemán, government and private industry have cooperated to mutual advantage in what might be termed an 'alliance for profits'" (1970:186).

In its development of agricultural policy, particularly from the 1950s to the early 1970s and again in the early 1980s, Mexican government action also has resembled Brazilian policy. In general, the agricultural sector has received less attention. In particular, this sector has received an insufficient input of capital and has been increasingly incapable of feeding the nation's population. However, as was true in Brazil, the few modern and highly capitalized farms have benefited from government policy (Thompson 1979:191–192).

Another area of similarity between Mexican and Brazilian policy concerns trade and investment dependency. Mexican government leaders consistently issue expressions of nationalism and of the need to ensure economic independence. Legislation exists that denies to foreign firms majority control of most enterprises in Mexico. In spite of all this, foreign industry, and especially U.S. industry plays an important role in the Mexican economy. As an example, U.S. direct investment in plants and equipment in Mexico rose from $35 million in 1957 to $250 million by 1975 (Kaufman 1977b:219). By 1981 total direct U.S. investment in Mexico had reached $7 billion (*LAWR* 1983:9). Thus, while the level of investment is not quite so high as it is in Brazil, it has been growing as rapidly and plays as strong a role in certain key sectors of the economy. Statistics on trade between the United States and Mexico provide additional evidence of Mexican dependence. In trade with its fourteen leading partners, approximately 73 percent of Mexico's imports came from the United

States while almost 80 percent of Mexico's exports went to the United States (*LAAR* 1979:165).

Economic policy in postrevolutionary Mexico has not always resembled the policy of the post-1964 military regime in Brazil. Following the conclusion of the violent part of the revolution (1910–1917) and especially during the years of President Lázaro Cárdenas, economc reform policies roughly comparable to Velasco's policies in Peru were pursued. Under President Cárdenas the oil industry was nationalized, the educational system was reformed, the state significantly increased its role in guiding the economy, and some 40 million acres of land were redistributed to peasant farmers. Though on a less grand scale, the administrations of Aldofo López Mateos (1958–1964) and Luis Echeverría (1970–1976) engaged in a range of economic reform decisions. In both cases, rather significant efforts were launched to do something about rural poverty. Nevertheless, as was true in Peru between 1968 and 1975, Mexican economic reforms have been taken not so much to improve problems of distribution as they have been to break up bottlenecks or sources of significant disaffection.

Pause for a moment and visualize the chalkboard in the classroom. On the board we draw a line with a point at each end. The line represents a continuum of economic policy. The point at the left end of the line represents a policy concerned solely with achieving economic equality; the point at the right end of the line represents policy solely concerned with achieving rapid economic growth. Let us now place three dots on the line to represent the economic policies of Brazil, Peru, and Mexico. What we should find is that the three dots cluster close together toward the right end of the line. Brazil would be farther to the right than Peru or Mexico. We probably would get more of an argument about the proper location of Peru than of the other two since, as we noted earlier, Peru in the 1968–1975 period was seen by some as embarking on rather radical changes in economic and social policy. However, if we now add a fourth dot to our line, representing Cuba, we provide a clear contrast with the other three country-dots. Cuba would be placed far to the left.

Since Fidel Castro and his revolutionaries marched into Havana in 1959, Cuban economic policy has undergone a radical transformation from the pre-1959 period, and, until quite recently, has been radically different from almost every other regime in Latin America. On the one hand, Brazil and Mexico, and to a lesser extent Peru, have concentrated on economic growth; and on the other, Cuban policymakers have concentrated on redistributing its product. One of the first major policies of the revolutionary regime was to redistribute land. Initially the redistribution was rather modest; soon, it became quite radical. Later, the government went on to nationalize virtually all aspects of the Cuban economy (though some private ownership has always existed). These nationalizations then allowed the government to establish wage policies directly.

As a rule, wages were set so as to minimize the differential in minimum and maximum wages. According to one study, the typical ratio of lowest to highest wage was 1:3.5 (MacEwan 1976:87). This may be a bit low, but it is generally recognized that wage, and wealth, inequality in Cuba is dramatically lower than anywhere else in Latin America (and probably among the lowest in the world). Other government policies were implemented in order to further reduce inequities: an extreme reduction in rents in the cities, expansion of health care and educational systems, and their provision without cost.

Although policymakers in Cuba focused their attention on distributive policy issues, they either neglected or failed to meet adequately the problem of economic growth. Of course, this is not to say that policymakers were oblivious to the need for economic expansion. Castro's stated intent of achieving a 10-million-ton sugar harvest is one of the more notable contributions to the gallery of misplaced hopes and misguided policies of growth ever announced anywhere. It is not accurate, then, to say that the Cuban government followed a policy of total concern for equality and of no concern for growth—we cannot put Cuba at the extreme left end of our line on the blackboard—but it is fair to say that from 1959 until the mid-1970s Cuba has emphasized issues of redistribution. One ironic consequence of these policies is that even though many more people have much more money than before, they find significantly fewer goods on which to spend that money. The ration card is a result. To insure that everyone has some access to goods that are in limited supply, especially certain foodstuffs like meat, rationing has existed for some time now. As one writer put it, "the ration card summarized the twin aspect of revolutionary economic performance: success in redistribution, failure in growth" (Domínguez 1978:186).

Precisely because Cuban policy has focused so heavily on distributive issues and has paid insufficient attention to the problem of growth, with the predictable consequences, the government recently has redirected some of its economic policies. Now greater effort will be expended on raising production levels. Among other changes, the government has announced it is abandoning its reliance upon moral incentives to spur productivity and will now return to greater use of wage and other material incentives. One obvious result is an increase in wage inequality, as is reflected in Table 6.1. Another consequence has been a rise in unemployment. Employment statistics are almost impossible to come by, but it appears that although overt unemployment once was virtually eliminated, this new policy emphasis on growth and efficiency has created some real and noticeable unemployment (Mesa-Lago 1981:31). In spite of these changes, which are too recent to analyze fully, Cuban policy has been significantly different than Brazilian, Peruvian, or Mexican in terms of the policy areas of growth and distribution.

When we consider the policy area of dependence, we note the lack of any clear differences with respect to the other three countries. Although it once

TABLE 6.1

Selected Actual Incomes in Cuba, 1977-1979

Occupation	Income (Pesos per Month)
Highly Skilled Technician	700 - 1,000
Sugar Cane Cutter	800
Physician	300 - 600
University Professor	325 - 500
Engineer	300 - 400
Mid-level Bureaucrat	200 - 300
Schoolteacher	100 - 190
State Farm Worker	80 - 100
Cleaning service personnel	75 - 80

Source: Mesa-Lago, 1981: p. 154.

may have been Castro's desire to achieve full economic independence, at the moment it can be no more than a wistful dream. Two sets of statistics clearly demonstrate the continuing dependence of the Cuban economy. In 1959, just under 69 percent of Cuba's total trade was with the United States. For 1978, preliminary figures indicate that 69 percent of Cuba's total trade was with the Soviet Union (Mesa-Lago 1981:93). Data on product dependency indicate the same situation. Prior to the revolution, the Cuban economy depended very heavily upon sugar for its foreign currency. Today, the extent of dependence upon sugar is virtually unchanged—about 70 to 80 percent of foreign earnings derives from sugar (*LAAR* 1979:196).

The democratic regimes of Costa Rica and Venezuela generally have followed a path more in the middle than have the strongly growth-oriented administrations of Brazil and Mexico or the redistribution-oriented regime in Cuba. In the case of Costa Rica, the "balanced" economic policy has been tipped to the left, or distributive, side of our line on the chalkboard. As you can see from the figures provided below, in the section on social policy, Costa Rican administrations have been devoting an extremely large proportion of government expenditures to health, education, and welfare. Administrative costs also are very high, in large part because the government tends to be a primary employer of well-educated, middle-class people (Denton 1979:386–387). Further attempts to deal with problems of distribution can be seen in the various efforts to make the income and social security taxes more progressive. In sum, Costa Rican economic policy clearly has been biased toward meeting distributive needs.

Policymakers in Costa Rica, however, have not been unmindful of growth needs. Public investment in Costa Rica has increased consistently during the 1960s and most of the 1970s and the great majority of investment funds has gone into infrastructure and production projects. Moreover, the Costa Rican government actively has sought international financing for a variety of development projects (DeWitt 1980:74). The government also has engaged in the traditional mechanisms of tax incentives to expand existing industries and develop new ones.

Costa Rican policymakers have had little success in reducing dependency. Relying heavily upon a limited number of agricultural products, especially bananas and coffee, Costa Rica also has a limited number of significant trading partners. In fact, only five countries, the United States (with the most), West Germany, Guatemala, El Salvador, and the Netherlands, account for the bulk of export earnings (*LAAR* 1979:149). Moreover, the economic difficulties Costa Rica experienced in 1982 have made it even more dependent on the United States and a few international financial agencies, especially the International Monetary Fund (IMF).

Perhaps more so than any other country in this study, Venezuela has formulated an economic policy explicitly designed to minimize conflict with the economic elite. As we noted in Chapter 4, a democratic regime came into being following a coup led by the military and *Acción Democrática*. But a "heavy-handed and occasionally somewhat authoritarian reformism" alienated a sizable portion of the economic elite. Alienation of the elite in turn contributed to the downfall of democracy in 1948. When AD regained power in 1959, its leadership vowed "to avoid redistributive pressures, instead allowing economic elites to retain their prerogatives and protected status" (Tugwell 1977:238, 239).

A second feature of economic policy has been its heavy reliance on oil as the cornerstone of economic development. Until massive oil discoveries by Mexico in the 1970s, Venezuela held a unique position in Latin America with its abundant holdings of such a valuable resource. How to control the development and marketing of this resource and how to use it to maximize economic development have been the principal issues of Venezuelan economic policy. In contrast to Costa Rica then, the "balanced" economic policy of Venezuela tends to be biased toward the side of growth and industrial development.

Following the revival of democracy in 1959, the government, under the leadership of President Rómulo Betancourt, pursued fairly conservative monetary and fiscal policies. Since then, the government has been willing to spend more, especially to promote economic development. As a percentage of gross domestic product, public sector spending increased from 39 percent in 1971 to 61 percent by 1975. Following the boom in oil prices in the early 1970s,

Venezuelan policymakers have had sizable sums of money to pour into industrial projects.

Unlike Brazil, though, Venezuelan governments have not neglected the problem of distribution. In 1960, a law was passed to redistribute land to landless peasant families. The intent of the initial law was to give land to about one-half of the 300,000 landless families. By the 1970s, about 166,000 families actually had received titles (Wilkie 1974a:63). It should be noted that this program was far more a distributive than a redistributive one. Though a few large, privately owned estates were expropriated and redistributed, most of the land given to peasants was government-owned land, much of it previously unused. Besides the agrarian program, the government has spent extensively on education and has been slowly reforming the income tax structure to make it more progressive.

Venezuela has attempted to achieve economic independence; yet the country still relies heavily upon petroleum for its export earnings. Policymakers have been trying to guide investments so as to promote greater industrial diversification. Given its continued reliance upon petroleum, Venezuela's most significant move to independence was taken in January 1976 when President Carlos Andres Pérez announced the nationalization of the oil industry. Venezuela has been attempting to diversify not only its list of exports, but also the country to which it sends those exports. It is still tied quite strongly to the United States, but policymakers have been working to increase trade relations with Western Europe, Japan, and Eastern Europe.

Social Policy

Economic policy is not the only category of policy that concerns government leaders. Policymakers also must be attentive to the needs and demands of the disabled, the old, and the unemployed, as well as to demands for housing, and for all those things we think of under the heading of social policy. Social policy tends to be much like the distributive side of economic policy in that the bulk of actions taken in both areas is designed to improve conditions for those who are not rich. Wealthy people can provide for their own housing, can take care of their own medical bills, can send their children to private schools or hire tutors. But people in the lower economic groups, including much of the middle class, cannot provide for all of these needs or can do so only partially. In general then, an assessment of a regime's performance in the social policy area is also an assessment of its concern for these classes. However, we must express caution in this type of interpretation of social policy. The redistributive impact of social policy depends significantly upon the nature of the tax burden. Because a fairly high percentage of government revenue in Latin America is derived from indirect taxes rather than from income and other direct taxes, taxation in Latin America is not progressive. Instead, taxation tends to be proportional and, in some cases, literally regressive. To put it another way, most people in the middle and working classes who receive social benefits from government policy are paying for those benefits. This brings us to our second point. Social policy does have a definite redistributive effect to the extent that it benefits the very poor. But, we shall see, it is the very poor who rarely benefit from government policy. Finally, we must note that educational policy, particularly when measured simply in terms of total government expenditures, is difficult to interpret in distributive (or redistributive) terms. The extent to which the less well-off benefit from government educational policy depends less on the amount spent by government and more on how and where government spends the money. Since most public schools tend to be located in the cities and large towns, it is children in urban areas (and usually from the middle and more prosperous part of the working class) who tend to benefit.

Since the coup of 1964, Brazil's social policy has not had a very high priority: Economic growth has been of paramount concern. According to one study, "In the years immediately following the military coup, spending on social development was cut sharply" (Hayes 1975:32). Those who tend to be or are projected to be the primary beneficiaries of most social legislation have been hurt by many of the military's policies. For instance, the military, like several previous regimes, has been concerned about the *favelas*, the large urban slums. For many years since 1964, the military's policy was to eliminate the problem by eradicating the slums and then permitting the development of housing only affordable to middle- and upper-income families. Though some of the government's decisions have been redirected since, public housing policy in general has benefited the middle class, not the poor (Portes 1979).

In the early years after the military takeover, the declining attention to social policy occurred not only because of the military's desire to emphasize economic growth policy, but also because the military was concerned for its own economic well-being. Thus, for 1965–1966 the military budget increased 50 percent (as a percentage of GDP) from the previous period (Weaver 1973:79). Since those early years, the relative size of the military budget has decreased, as its needs have been met quite adequately. Lowered defense allocation needs and increasing dissatisfaction in the early 1970s with the government's treatment of many working-class and some middle-class groups led the military to increase some areas of social spending. In particular, expenditures on education and social security increased. Table 6.2 indicates that government spending on education rose from 2.7 percent of GNP in 1970 to 3.7 percent by 1977. Though official statistics on social security spending are incomplete, it appears that Brazilian policymakers have provided for some expansion of coverage among the better-paid workers.

TABLE 6.2

Government Expenditures on Education

	As Percent of GNP		As Percent of Total Expenditures	
	1970	1977	1970	1977
Argentina	3.3a	2.7	16.0	10.9
Bolivia	3.3	4.1	28.4	25.4b
Brazil	2.7	3.7	10.6	
Costa Rica	5.2	6.6b	31.8	30.1b
Cuba	4.2	7.2	18.4	32.4b
Mexico	2.6	4.8	8.5	11.7
Peru	3.8	3.4	18.8	14.7
Venezuela	4.8	5.1c	22.9	8.2

Source: UNESCO, Statistical Yearbook, 1981: pp. iv-10, iv-12,13.

[a]1971.
[b]1976.
[c]1978.

Not long after the military in Peru took power, it increased the defense budget. Sizable increases in 1970, 1971, and 1972 inevitably led to some trade-offs with social expenditures, as was true in Brazil. But in Peru, social policy did not suffer quite so much. The Peruvian military government believed that future economic growth and social stability required certain immediate structural transformations. In particular, most leaders of the military regime under Velasco desired the destruction of the old oligarchy. This necessarily meant that at least some middle- and/or lower-income groups would benefit from government action. The military reinforced the likelihood of these outcomes by drawing much of its support from the organized Left. By the end of 1971, some 1,700 rural cooperatives with some 600,000 members had been established (Palmer 1974:53). As we noted earlier, a large number of land titles were given to families in urban squatter settlements. Expenditures for health increased, especially in the urban areas, while the government expanded social security coverage (Webb 1975:113, 115).

Social policy under the Peruvian military was more extensive and certainly helped workers more than was the case in Brazil, but Peruvian policymakers could not be called aggressive in pursuing social policy. In spite of the cooperatives and the fanfare following Velasco's agrarian reform, agricultural workers were not aided very greatly by the military regime. Nor were the very poor in the urban areas. Housing policy under the Velasco regime, though it probably benefited a somewhat broader range of people than has Brazilian housing policy, still was rather traditional and tended to favor middle-income groups and the better-off sector of the working class (Collier 1976:114–115). Significant expenditures for education were maintained though there was a slight decline from what was spent in the years 1965–1967; a good deal more could have been done to expand educational facilities in the rural areas (Webb 1975:117; Drysdale and Myers 1975:258).

Officially and rhetorically, the Mexican government is committed to extensive activities to provide benefits to the poor and to rural and urban workers. Among other documents, the 1917 Constitution (put into effect at the end of the revolutionary war) dedicates Mexican policymakers to improvements in education, to a better distribution of land, to greater benefits for urban workers, and to an upgrading of the social conscience in Mexico. Every six years, during the campaign for the presidency, the dominant political leaders renew their dedication to the goals of the revolution and the Constitution of 1917. Though practice almost never coincides with rhetoric, there have been times since the revolution when social policy has moved toward meeting stated goals. We have already noted the massive land distribution programs under Presidents Cárdenas and López Mateos. Both leaders engaged in social reform measures in other areas as well. The educational system was revised and expanded, and under López Mateos, significant headway was made in the provision of welfare benefits, social security coverage, and inexpensive foodstuffs to workers and the poor (Padgett 1976:286–294).

More recently, under President Echeverría, there was a reinvigoration of social policy. Significant attempts and modest gains were registered in reform of the tax structure (Shapira 1977:572). Government spending for education increased 23 percent from 1971 to 1972 and expenditures for higher education were three times more in 1973 than in 1970 (Padgett 1976:288). There has been a further expansion of social security and, as we noted earlier, the Echeverría administration moved to reform government assistance to the agricultural sector. In addition, over the last few decades, the government has benefited some urban, low-income groups through public housing and medical clinics.

In spite of all this, social policy in Mexico still has a long way to go. The provision of benefits has been far greater to urban than rural areas. One result of this has been a huge increase in rural violence. According to one study, between 1970 and 1973 there were some 600 peasant invasions of large estates in just the three states of Guanajuato, Michoacan, and Tlaxcala (Montes de Oca 1977:58). Even in the urban areas, the distribution of social services is quite uneven. Generally, the better organized and paid workers, including government bureaucrats, tend to receive the lion's share while the very poor receive next to nothing.

Three factors seem to be primarily responsible for the government's poor record in the social area, in spite of periodic attempts of impressive magnitude. First, political leaders in general have been more concerned with achieving economic growth than with attaining distributive justice. While social development long has been an articulated goal, virtually a motif of all incoming administrations, the reality is a commitment to economic development defined as the expansion of industry and manufacturing. Secondly, Mexico has been saddled with population growth of startling proportions. Though recent figures indicate the growth rate may be slowing down, for several decades the population has increased at about 3.4 percent each year. In absolute numbers, this means that Mexico's population grew from 36 million in 1961 to 47 million by 1968 and is now around 70 million. Even more dramatic, and more serious, has been the mushrooming of Mexico City. From an almost manageable 5 million in 1968, Mexico City has grown to a staggering 14 million and could easily reach 20 million by the turn of the century. In other words, population growth is outstripping the provision of social benefits; even if more attention and more resources were devoted to social development, the growth would still probably be greater than the social services could handle.

Corruption is the third principal reason why apparent government efforts in social policy result in so little for the poor. Long claimed by government officials to be nothing more than an inevitable and minor nuisance, both governmental and business corruption have become pervasive and serious. The use of government funds for private enrichment has assumed a startling magnitude and is eroding not only the financial base of government but also its base of legitimacy (Johnson 1978: esp. Chaps. 5 and 7). The extent of corruption, and public awareness of it, have become so broad that government officials finally have been forced to admit that it is a problem.

Cuban social policy stands in marked contrast to social policy developments in Brazil, Mexico, and Peru. Clearly, the hallmarks of the Cuban revolution, to date, have been the amount of resources devoted to redistribution of income and wealth and the provision of basic social services to all. Of all social policy areas, educational policy has received the greatest attention of Cuban policymakers. Under the leadership of Fidel Castro, the number of students enrolled in all levels of schooling grew from about 838,000 in 1958 to over 3.3 million in 1978, a fourfold increase (Brundenius and Lundahl 1982:151). Of even greater significance than the total educational effort has been the work by policymakers to equalize the provision of education between urban and rural areas. Although higher education still is offered primarily in the cities, at other levels the rural areas have caught up. Just prior to the revolution, rural areas accounted for approximately 40 percent of the population but only 30 percent of public primary enrollment. By the mid-1970s rural population as a percentage of total population and as a percentage of primary enrollment were equal (Domínguez 1978:168).

Health policy has been another area of great effort by the Cuban revolutionary regime. Cuba had one of the best health-care systems in Latin America prior to the revolution; the Castro government has also devoted large amounts of resources to this field. In spite of the mass emigration of physicians following the revolutionary takeover, there were significantly more doctors in Cuba in the early 1970s than there had been in the late 1950s. The number of hospital beds also was increased (Bray and Harding 1974:693). In general, government policy led to the doubling of the health-care system between 1958 and 1978. Once again, though, what has been particularly remarkable about Cuban health policy is that it has greatly expanded the availability of good health care to the countryside. Few countries in the world can now match the Cubans in this area.

Other areas of social policy have received some attention. Expenditures for social security increased from 114.3 million pesos in 1959 to 647.6 million pesos in 1978, thereby achieving almost universal social security coverage in Cuba (Brundenius and Lundahl 1982:148, 149). Recreational facilities are available for most, and day care for children is widespread. Moreover, until recently, these benefits have been provided without charge. As we noted earlier, however, the Cuban government has begun to concentrate more resources in the area of economic growth. One result is that many once-free social goods now must be bought. In most cases, the fees are still very low and are usually scaled to one's income level (Domínguez 1978:179; Mesa-Lago 1981:31).

As was true in the area of economic policy, in the area of social policy the democratic countries of Costa Rica and Venezuela fall somewhere between the strongly socially oriented regime in Cuba and the industrial growth-oriented regimes of Brazil and Mexico. Since the late 1950s, Costa Rica has moved toward becoming a welfare state. As can be seen from the data in Table 6.2, Costa Rican governments have spent a high proportion of government revenues on the educational system. In fact, relative to the GNP only Cuba outspends Costa Rica on public schooling. Health and social security is another area in which the Costa Rican government has expended great efforts (see Table 6.3). According to one source, about 26 percent of the budget goes to expenditures for health, social security, and welfare (World Bank 1980: 209). When we add them to expenditures for education, we can see a very sizable proportion of the nation's resources go to social policy. Unfortunately, social programs and administrative costs have taken such large quantities of money that they have been a principal factor in Costa Rica's economic malaise of the early 1980s.

Venezuelan policymakers have shown somewhat less commitment to social policy than have their Costa Rican counterparts but have not been insensitive to social needs. As with Cuba, the government felt the need to devote significant resources to education for political purposes. In the case of Venezuela, the politicization concern was less total and less radical, but real nonetheless. Leaders were convinced in 1960 not to make the mistakes that brought such a short life to democracy in the late 1940s. Consequently, the educational

TABLE 6.3

Percentage of Economically Active Population Covered by Social Security

	1960	1966	1971
Brazil	19a	20b	
Costa Rica	25	31	54
Cuba	63c	100	100
Mexico	12	20	25
Peru	25	32	36

Source: Rosenberg, 1979: p. 127.

a1962.
b1967.
c1959.

system was used to try to widen the base of democratic values and to deepen the commitment to them. As a result, school enrollments increased from under 483,000 in 1949–1950 to almost 2,600,000 by 1972–1973. As a percentage of the total government budget, educational expenditures rose from 12.3 percent in 1957 to 25 percent in 1972 (Ruscoe 1977:261, 263). Since 1972, expenditures (as a proportion of the budget) have fallen off as the expansionist phase has drawn to a close.

Health care is reasonably good in Venezuela. About 18 percent of the government's budget is devoted to public health, compared to only about 1.5 percent in Brazil (Sorkin 1976:18). About three-fourths of the physicians in Venezuela devote some of their time to the public health-care system, thus increasing both the availability and quality of health care (Wiarda 1974:331). Expenditures on public housing and related amenities also are relatively high in Venezuela, while social security and welfare expenditures are relatively low (World Bank 1980:366).

Political and Civil Rights Policy

Finally, we briefly review the policy areas of political and civil rights. Under the heading of political rights we are concerned with such things as the ability to vote in competitive elections in a free and uncoerced fashion and the ability to voice disagreement with the system or with particular policies without suffering recriminations such as beating or jailing. By civil rights we are referring to, in a general sense, the concepts of due process of law, equality of treatment in the legal process, and the respect for certain fundamental individual protections, such as habeas corpus.

Costa Rica clearly possesses the best record in the policy areas of political and civil rights. Citizens are allowed to participate freely and may criticize, assemble, and protest without fear of government reprisal. Elections are held on schedule, competition is open and without significant fraud. The court system seems to be adequately independent of influence from the executive (a situation not typical in Latin America). Civil rights are fully protected, as due process and habeas corpus seem to be fully established.

This is not to say, of course, that the influence of everyone in the political system is equal or that the wealthier do not have some advantages in the legal system. Political power is unequally divided, as we have seen. As every citizen in the United States knows, wealthier people can afford better legal assistance than can poorer people. Less prosperous rural people, in particular, suffer both in their attempts at political participation and in being fully equal in a courtroom. In spite of all this, Costa Rica, by Latin American, and indeed by international, standards, has done a remarkable job in protecting and expanding fundamental political and civil rights.

As a reasonably democratic and peaceful country, Venezuela also has developed policy to promote widespread political participation and to protect civil rights. A highly competitive multiparty system exists in Venezuela, and all adults are expected to vote in national elections. In fact, it is illegal not to vote, though this is not fully enforced. There is no press censorship (at least not obviously) and freedom of speech and of assembly generally have been well protected by government policy. Fundamentally then, political leaders in Venezuela have achieved a good record in political and civil rights. However, at times, decisions have been taken that have made the Venezuelan record somewhat less positive than the record in Costa Rica.

In the early 1960s a good deal of violence erupted throughout Venezuela. Fearful that unless the violence were controlled quickly and fully the newly established democratic regime would give way either to revolution or to a military coup, government leaders acted forcefully. Troops were called out, the leash on the police was loosened, and several fundamental constitutional guarantees, such as habeas corpus, were suspended. Inevitably, police brutality increased and a number of innocent people became its victims. Though this episode turned out to be brief, it indicated a willingness to set aside policies protecting political and civil rights (Blank 1973:112–124).

Policy toward the native peoples of Venezuela also has evidenced some disrespect for political and civil rights. To a large extent, Indians in Venezuela have been treated in a manner similar to the treatment of Indians in the United States, i.e., as second-class citizens. Until Indian rights are better protected, Venezuela's record in these policy areas will continue to be spotty.

Generally, though not completely, the shortcomings that exist in political and civil rights policy in Costa Rica and Venezuela result not so much from authoritarian behavior or consciously discriminatory policies as from the unequal distribution of wealth and status. Such, however, is not the case in Brazil and Cuba, two countries where political and civil rights have been severely restricted.

In Cuba, citizens are allowed some very limited freedom to criticize. As a rule, complaints must be limited to those of a personal nature rather than those that imply criticism of the system. For instance, I could publicly accuse the managers of a restaurant of providing poor food or service. I could even go so far as to accuse a local politician of poorly representing my interests or the interests of my town. I could not imply that the style of governing, or the values of the political leaders, had anything to do with bad restaurants or with the laziness of my politician.

The pattern is similar with respect to elections in Cuba (Domínguez 1978:243–247). At the local level, elections are held and some competition among candidates does exist. Local politicians must report periodically to their constituents and probably are as accountable as, if not more so than, politicians anywhere. However, electoral policy in Cuba is such that elections do not affect the principal policymakers. Although provincial and national assemblies do exist, they are not directly elected by the people, as we have seen, nor, in any event, do they perform policymaking functions.

Like electoral activity, action by workers' organizations is circumscribed and the freedom to strike is severely limited. Nevertheless, strikes have occurred (Domínguez 1978:275). Similarly, though not viewed with favor, religious activities are tolerated and a kind of détente exists between church and government leaders.

Some rights, then, do exist in Cuba. It would be wrong to portray the social and political systems in pure Orwellian terms. By the same token, it would be terribly misleading not to recognize the severe limitations placed on political and civil rights. Press censorship is almost total. Freedom of assembly and of the right to protest are virtually nonexistent. The use of identification cards, in fact, presents the government with a mechanism for extensive control of the population. In sum, public policy in Cuba is a long way from permitting much freedom of expression, political competition, or political protest.

Political and civil rights policies in Brazil since 1964 have been similar to Cuban policies. As in Cuba, government leaders have been intolerant of any opposition to the regime. Beginning soon after it took power, the military issued a number of Institutional Acts (decrees with the status of constitutional articles). Most of the early acts were designed to set limits on individual political rights, focusing especially on members of congress and other politicians. Most infamous of the decrees was Institutional Act Number Five, issued in December 1968. Among other things, this act allowed the president to close congress, to run the state and local governments, and to deprive a person of all political rights for a period up to ten years. The act did not stop with establishing limits on political rights. It went on and slaughtered civil rights as well. In particular, habeas corpus was suspended, thus giving legal sanction to arbitrary arrests, secret jailings, and the like. Indeed, during the 1960s and at least the early 1970s, police and military officials engaged in almost wanton torture. Treatment of political prisoners was particularly vicious and included continual beatings, electric shocks to the genitals, and rape (Flynn 1978a:436–437).

Besides these gruesome means of dealing with the problem of opposition, Brazilian government leaders used more typical and milder policy instruments. Political parties were banned and replaced by ones acceptable to the government. Labor unions were placed under strict control and quickly suppressed when they threatened any serious protest. The press was censored, the clergy muzzled and, generally, a climate of fear created. By the latter part of the 1970s, however, the military regime came to realize it could not continue all these policies indefinitely. If nothing else, its international image had been blackened by reports of torture (including torture of priests and nuns) and massive, arbitrary arrests. In recent years, large numbers of political prisoners have been released and many exiled political figures allowed to return. Government leaders claim they no longer engage in torture; arbitrary arrests have at least been limited, if not stopped. Some press criticism has been tolerated, but the government is still willing to suspend a newspaper if it goes beyond what the government leaders consider acceptable. Some opposition now operates openly. In general, there has been a relaxation in the military's extremely tough policies on political and civil rights.

In broad terms, we may characterize political and civil rights policy in Mexico and Peru as lying somewhere in between the relatively open and tolerant policies of Costa Rica and Venezuela and the harsh and repressive policies of Brazil and Cuba. As military institutions are wont to do, the Peruvian military from 1969 to 1975 acted in an authoritarian manner. Except for a few organizations of the Left, the military suspended or banned the traditional political parties, interest groups, and legislative bodies. In their place, the new political policymakers created agrarian cooperatives, workers' collectives, and attempted a new, corporatist form of representation under the umbrella of SINAMOS. The press was censored and then taken over, and, on occasion, differences of opinion between the military and workers, students, and teachers resulted in violence.

In spite of these various attempts to control political opposition and carefully manage the direction of change, the Peruvian regime under President Velasco was not an extremely repressive regime. Protest did occur and was not always resisted by armed force. In fact, protest and criticism led the military to revise a number of policies and government actions, as we saw earlier. The large-scale arrests of political opponents, which occurred in Brazil and Cuba, did not take place in Peru. Nor did the military move to suspend basic guarantees of personal liberty for any length of time. Some individuals were indeed maltreated, and prison conditions in Peru traditionally have been quite poor (Owens 1963:69), but military policymakers did not attempt their version of Institutional Act Number Five.

Political and civil rights policy in Mexico is harder to summarize, not because its nature is not clear to those who have studied it, but because many apparent contradictions and paradoxes make it difficult to present an adequate picture to those less familiar with Mexican politics. In contrast to Brazil and Cuba, Mexico does not openly recognize its authoritarian and frequently repressive character. In fact, government leaders have gone out of their way to convey an image of Mexican politics as democratic, based upon full political freedom and competition. And there is some truth to these claims. Opposition parties do exist, are allowed to campaign and even to hold seats in the national legislature. Criticism of the government by some organs of the press is frequent. One can easily move about within the country without observing any obvious signs of repression or authoritarianism. Not only has the government not suspended basic rights on any general basis but also it is proud of having developed (at least in theory) a very broad instrument for the protection of individual rights. Known as the writ of *amparo*, this sweeping legal device includes such protections as habeas corpus, mandamus, and injunction.

There is unfortunately a darker side to Mexican political and civil rights policy. As we have noted, appearances notwithstanding, party and electoral competition do not exist. Only members of the dominant PRI win presidential elections; only the PRI has ever had a majority of the national legislature; only the PRI controls the vast majority of state and local governmental positions. If the press moves too far in its criticism, especially when it details any significant case of corruption or abuse of authority by top government officials, it will be censored or closed down. Such, for instance, was the fate of the journal *Por Que?* in 1974 when it detailed a number of human rights violations and the use of secret, right-wing, paramilitary terrorist groups by the government (Johnson 1978:97).

The government also has been willing to resort to violence openly when it feels threatened. This was the case when police and military troops shot several hundred protesting students in 1968, and such has been the case repeatedly as the government's most frequent means of responding to peasant land invasions. Mexico's deserved reputation for government corruption and its equally deserved reputation for squalid prisons and ill-treatment of prisoners also are parts of the darker side of Mexican political and civil rights policy. It is possible that some corruption and some police violence occur in spite of official policy to the contrary. Corruption has such deep roots in the Mexican social system that only the most extensive of efforts could begin to correct the problem. Nevertheless, some of these actions exist because, at the least, they are tolerated, and to that extent they help define not only behavior but also policy. In sum, there is a little more tolerance in Mexico than in Cuba and Brazil. A bit more opposition is allowed to survive; individual rights generally are somewhat more protected. But there are very real limits to political opposition, and the penalty for transgressing these limits can be harsh.

Regime Type and Policy Output

Now we come to the most difficult question. Does the type of regime make any difference in policy output? Or, in other terms, is there a correlation between the type of regime and the pattern of policy outputs? If we turn to the existing literature there appears to be a great deal of disagreement. No simple, straightforward answers to our question will be found. In a broad, comparative study of industrial countries, Groth believes he has found significant differences, at least in certain policy areas (1971). Clearly in the area of political rights and civil liberties there are differences between democratic countries and authoritarian ones. Similarly, in an even broader study, which included a number of developing countries, McKinlay and Cohan found consistent differences between military and nonmilitary regimes in political rights policies but found no significant differences in the level of military spending (1976:853, 856).

A larger number of studies, at least in the Latin American area, have concluded that no meaningful differences exist between regime types and policy patterns. According to one study, the pattern of government spending for education and defense was essentially the same for both military and civilian regimes (Ames and Goff 1975:186–188). Another study found no consistent differences between military and civilian regimes with respect to government spending for social services and public health (Weaver 1973:91–92). In an article reviewing the literature on the policy impact of military regimes, Karen Remmer demonstrates that a larger body of scholarship argues the case against significant differences than for significant differences between civilian and military regimes (1978:39–54).

In our brief review of some of the literature on the relationship between regime type and policy output, you may have noticed some patterns that suggest there might be less disagreement among scholars then is first apparent. We shall return to that shortly, after taking a summary look at our information. Our response to the question is, unfortunately, rather complex. We argue that the answer to whether there is a relation between regime type and policy output is yes, no, or it depends.

First, for the "yes" part. Comparing the democratic regimes with the others shows a very clear difference in policy output in the area of political and civil rights. Whether we examine policy toward political opposition, or the right to political protest, or basic civil liberties, distinctions between democratic and nondemocratic countries are obvious and predictable.

A comparison of economic policies produces at least one difference, though it is less clear-cut. In general, it appears that the democratic countries tend to pursue a series of economic policies that are more balanced in meeting both growth and distributive needs than are Mexico and Brazil, which have placed a heavy emphasis on growth, or Cuba, which has put most of its emphasis on distribution. However, we now begin to see that regime categories are less helpful in sorting out economic policy patterns than was the case with political and civil rights. Although it is true that both postrevolutionary regimes have tended toward an unbalanced economic policy pattern, the nature of the imbalance is different. The picture is confused further if we concentrate our attention on Cuba after 1975. Since that year, the previous extreme devotion to distributive policies has been replaced by a more balanced concern for growth and distribution. Finally, the military regime of Peru seems to have exhibited a fairly balanced economic policy.

As our clear "yes" answer begins to get fuzzy we move to some clear "no's." Certain specific economic and social policies cannot be correlated with particular regime types. All six countries have spent comparable sums on higher education, and all but Brazil and Mexico have spent comparable sums on education in general. All except Cuba use a similar package of tax incentives and government development of infrastructure to attract industrialists and spur economic growth. All rely heavily on foreign investment capital. In the area of social security policy, Costa Rican efforts seem more similar to Cuban than Venezuelan policy actions, and Cuba is certainly closer to Costa Rica than to her categorical partner Mexico.

ᵀn some areas of public policy, the correlation between type of regime and pattern of policy output seems to be quite close. When this occurs, particularly in the case of political and civil rights policies, we are inclined to say that the policies differ, in part, because of the type of regime. However, it appears that in some areas of public policy there is little if any significant difference between the types of policies pursued by different regime types. If we return for a moment to our brief review of the literature and examine the findings of several scholars, we can formulate a conclusion very similar to the one based on the information of this study. When political scientists analyze the relationship between regime type and policy output in the category of constitutional or political rights, they invariably find that regime type makes a difference. When the researcher concludes with a statement that no differences exist, it typically is the case that the policy areas examined were military and education expenditures (though it is always gross expenditure levels that are compared rather than the particular objects on which the money is spent). In sum, it appears that the extent to which there exists a meaningful relationship between regime type and policy outputs depends on the policy area examined.

If we look closely at the patterns of policy outputs that emerge from a comparison of our six countries, we may notice yet another problem. On a number of occasions policy patterns for Mexico are much more similar to Brazil's than they are to Cuba's. Significant differences also occur in policy patterns between the two military regimes, Brazil and Peru. What seems to be happening is that our concepts for labeling the different types of regimes are too imprecise. It is true, for instance, that Cuba and Mexico represent the only two countries in Latin America that have undergone a thorough social-political revolution (some would add Bolivia, and, as noted above, Nicaragua is in the process of revolution). In a very general sense then, it seems to be logical to refer to them as postrevolutionary. But on closer inspection, one is struck by the differences in the nature of the revolutions. To put it in broad terms (and admittedly a bit superficially), the Mexican revolution could be defined as a middle-class, capitalist, developmental revolution while Cuba has undergone a radical, socialist transformation. The fact that Cuban economic and social policy is so different from the policy of the other Latin American countries is more easily explained by referring to Cuba as socialist, rather than as postrevolutionary. Socialism obviously cannot explain the similarity in problems of dependency, yet it is a concept that is quite useful in explaining the other policy differences.

Similarly, we need more powerful, more precise categorical names for other countries. Substantial enough differences between Brazilian policy outputs and those of Peru ought to lead us to question the utility of the "military" label. The fact that Mexico is a postrevolutionary society and governed by civilians, and that Brazil has not had a revolution and is governed by the military, seems to be less consequential than the fact that both regimes are authoritarian, dedicated to economic, and especially industrial, growth, and tend to be ruled by an alliance of upper-level bureaucrats and industrialists.

It may have occurred to you that all this labeling and conceptualizing might not be very important. It might be just a game of semantics played by academics and have little bearing on reality. Unfortunately, this does happen sometimes. Moreover, as Robert Ayres once pointed out, broad, regime-level distinctions might be too general, too crude to yield significant differences in patterns of policy outputs (1975:18). To the extent that concern for proper labels for types of regimes serves to distract us from understanding what is happening in a country and what all that has to do with the way people live, then we should abandon our search for labels. Our contention, however, is that this does not have to be an abstract game but a very real need to understand the extent to which different types of governments and different ways of processing demands yield significant differences in types of policy. If such variations exist, then we want to know what kind of system is most likely to meet our needs. If such variations do not exist, then we can cease worrying about things like democracy and authoritarianism and concentrate on whatever does make a difference.

[7]
The Impact of Public Policy

To describe the nature of a country's public policy is a tricky, but not impossible, task. One must avoid the common pitfall of associating statements by high-ranking government officials with actual policy. Additionally, one must be careful not to assume that any particular decision represents a policy pattern or tendency. With these guidelines and much hard work, it is certainly possible to present a clear and accurate picture of a regime's policies.

This chapter, however, deals with a topic that is equally important, yet more elusive. For our final question, we ask: What is the relationship between a government's policies and the behavior of the society? In other words, what are the consequences of public policy?

It is common for us to assume a rather close tie between policy output and policy outcome or impact. If inflation increases, and unemployment increases, and interest rates are high, we tend to blame the government for its stupidity, callousness, and incompetence. If inflation, unemployment, and interest rates fall, government leaders will congratulate themselves for their marvelous economic policies, and we are inclined to concur, though usually with less zeal. If the economy is humming, but large numbers of people live in squalor, we may praise the government for its economic policies while criticizing its social policies. These all seem to be reactions common to the citizenry of most countries. But are the sentiments sound? Is it possible to find a vibrant economy in spite of government policy? Is it possible for inflation and unemployment to increase even though the government is making serious efforts to attack the problems?

In general, it seems fair to believe there is a link, though perhaps a tenuous one, between what governments do and what economies and social systems do. To assume there is no connection is to render the human situation extremely ludicrous, given the energy expended on conflict over who should govern or what type of government is best. But precisely what effects do public policies have? Just exactly what do government subsidy programs produce? What are the consequences of government expropriations of large estates and their transformation into cooperatives? It seems that we cannot adequately answer such questions. At this state of our knowledge and understanding we cannot fully appreciate all the effects of a policy or all the causes and linkages involved in unemployment or inflation or the many fundamental problems facing societies. But we can look for patterns, for correlations. This is the approach taken in this chapter. For each of the countries studied in the previous chapter, we provide information about economic growth, the distribution of wealth, social outcomes such as health and education, and the extent of political freedom and civil liberties. For each of these we then describe the extent to which there appears to be a correlation between outcomes and the government's policies.

Economic Performance and Policy Impact

During the first few years of the military dictatorship in Brazil, the economy grew little. In 1968 the economy surged forward, and from then until 1973 real annual increases in the GNP averaged about 11.5 percent, a staggering rate of growth (Hewlett 1980:46). More specific economic indicators also demonstrated impressive increases. Manufacturing, for instance, witnessed average annual rates of increase of 10.5 percent between 1965 and 1970 (World Bank 1980:374). After 1973, the rate of growth fell off but still continued at a respectable 5 percent annual average throughout the 1970s. By the end of its first decade in power, the military regime appeared to be a model for achieving rapid economic and industrial development.

As the decade of the seventies drew to a close, so too did the marvelous improvements in the Brazilian economy. By the early 1980s growth rates for the GNP were falling to 3 percent and less, bankruptcies were multiplying alarmingly, and productivity was being threatened by a surge of labor strikes. (See *LAWR*, December 18, 1981 and September 17, 1982.) Moreover, inflation, which once had been brought under control, was hovering at the triple-digit level by 1981.

During the years of rapid economic growth, the distribution of the nation's wealth had become more unequal. By 1967 the real minimum wage was 5 percent less than it had been twelve years earlier. The Gini index of income distribution moved from a figure of 0.49 in 1960 to 0.56 in 1970 (the higher the index number, the greater the inequality) (Fishlow 1973:85–86, 94). In 1960, the top 1 percent of income earners possessed 11.7 percent of the nation's income. By 1970 they had increased their share of national income to 17.8 percent. Meanwhile, the bottom 80 percent of income earners saw their share of national income drop from 45.5 percent to 36.8 percent (Evans 1979:97).

TABLE 7.1

Per Capita Gross Domestic Product (Constant U.S. dollars of 1978)

	1960	1970	1978	1979
Argentina	1313	1740	1892	2004
Bolivia	322	408	505	499
Brazil	571	781	1266	1310
Costa Rica	709	973	1287	1312
Cuba	850a,d	977b,d	1462c,e	1404c,e
Mexico	764	1037	1166	1215
Peru	798	972	984	992
Venezuela	1566	1998	2399	2416

Source: Statistical Abstract of Latin America, 1981: p. 14.

[a] Gross Social Product, 1965 prices.
[b] Gross Social Product, 1970 prices.
[c] Gross Domestic Product, current prices.
[d] Domínguez, 1978: p. 177.
[e] Adapted from Latin America Weekly Report, 17 September 1982: p. 9.

TABLE 7.2

Index of Per Capita Food Production (1961-1965 = 100)

	1953	1971	1976
Argentina	98	98	116
Bolivia	66	110	124
Brazil	88	112	128
Costa Rica	123	134	140
Cuba	114	100	93
Mexico	78	110	104
Peru	100	102	102
Venezuela	82	120	124

Source: Statistical Abstract of Latin America, 1981: p. 9.

The data in Table 7.1 show that the rate of growth in Peru under General Velasco was very low. However, from 1969 to 1973 the gross national product did increase by over 6 percent annually, though the rate of increase fell to 4 percent by the latter part of the Velasco years (Fitzgerald 1976:17; *LAAR* 1979:124). Food production was up only very slightly (see Table 7.2), though between 1971 and 1973 manufacturing grew by almost 8 percent (*LAAR* 1979:126).

During the Velasco years, significant growth occurred not in the economy, but in the state's role in the economy. From the nationalization of sugar plantations and the fishmeal industry to various forms of intervention in the agricultural sector, energy production, and so on, the government greatly expanded its role as entrepreneur and manager.

As far as distributive measures are concerned, the Velasco government seems to have done less than it initially appeared. The principal effort of the regime was the redistribution of some 18 million acres of land. This was no mean feat but it benefited only about one-quarter of the peasant families (McClintock 1980:68). The other principal distributive accomplishment was to have given vast numbers of land titles to urban squatters. Nevertheless, as Table 7.4 indicates, these activities seem to have had little impact upon income distribution. By the end of the Velasco period, Peru still had one of the most unequal distributions of income of any country in Latin America. For instance, while the bottom 40 percent were getting only some 9 percent of the nation's income, the top 5 percent received 39 percent (Fitzgerald 1976:16).

Recent Mexican economic experience roughly parallels that of Brazil. Though its rate of economic growth has not been dramatic, for the better part of the last three decades Mexico has enjoyed annual growth rates of about 6 percent. Manufacturing growth was somewhat over 8 percent annually from 1950 to 1970; it fell off a bit in the early 1970s, and then recovered in the late 1970s (World Bank 1980:374). In contrast, agricultural production is a far different story. Although certain products have shown production increases, notably those for export, overall per capita food production has been consistently declining since the early 1970s (see Table 7.2).

Moreover, like Brazil, Mexico in 1982 has been experiencing severe economic difficulties. The country is deeply in debt to a number of private foreign banks; the currency has been devalued dramatically; and inflation, once almost unnoticeable in Mexico, pushes toward the triple-digit level.

The pattern of economic distribution in Mexico also resembles the Brazilian pattern. In spite of significant growth of the economy, the bottom half of the income earners has not seen any benefit. Over the past few decades, according to Evelyn Stevens, the top 5 percent of income earners held their position, those in the 80th to 95th percentiles increased their income, those in the 40–80 percentile range saw their relative share decline slightly, while the bottom 40 percent have been hurt substantially (1979:403).

The uniqueness of contemporary Cuba, in having undergone a socialist revolution, is reflected in the data on the state of its economy. From the capture of the government in 1959 until about the mid-1970s, Castro had seen very little growth in the Cuban economy. For most of the postrevolutionary period, economic growth has crawled along at about 4.5 percent, though during the period 1970–1974 the social product grew by about 12 percent each year (*Granma* 1/6/80:2; *LAAR* 1979:196, 198). Data on product output show that between 1960 and the early 1970s there was little growth in sugar, little in cement production, none in tobacco, and a decline in milk (Mesa-Lago 1981:41).

Although growth figures generally are unimpressive, data on changes in the patterns of distribution are very impressive. Table 7.4, for instance, illustrates the point. In the immediate prerevolutionary period, the poorest 40 percent of the population received only slightly more than 6 percent of the national income. By the 1970s their share of national income had more than tripled to over 20 percent. In fact, this figure understates the comparative position of the lower-income earners of Cuba because so many services are available either free of charge or with only nominal charges.

The figures in the preceding two paragraphs adequately reflect the nature of the Cuban economy from the revolution to the latter 1970s, but they convey a misleading picture as we move to the early 1980s. The distribution of income and wealth remains essentially unchanged; the economy, however, has been growing at higher, though not dramatic, rates. Growth rates seem to be moving up to the 6 percent figure and the output of certain products seems to have jumped forward. To what extent this will continue remains to be seen. Nevertheless, it is important to note that Cuba does indeed seem capable of sustaining at least moderate levels of economic growth.

For the better part of the last two decades, the Costa Rican economy has grown consistently (Table 7.1). The per capita gross domestic product increased from $709 in 1960 to $973 in 1970 and by 1979 had reached $1312. This was a moderate rate of growth when compared to Brazil, but a quite substantial growth rate when compared, for example, to Peru. During the period 1960 to 1977, the average annual rate of growth for gross domestic product per capita in Costa Rica was just under 6 percent (DeWitt 1980:69).

Table 7.2 provides another illustration of substantial growth in the Costa Rican economy, this time measuring increases in per capita food production. Another source cites an industrial growth rate figure of about 7 percent (*LAAR* 1979:148). However, for the latter part of 1981 and for 1982, Costa Rican growth has been reduced to a trickle and inflation, once negligible, was in the neighborhood of 60 percent for 1981.

While Costa Rica has enjoyed good, if not spectacular, rates of economic growth (at least until the latter part of 1981), the country also has experienced a comparatively well distributed income. Table 7.3 shows that Costa Rica possesses one of the lower Gini coefficients for Latin America, and Table 7.4 suggests that the poorer people in Costa Rica are better off than their counterparts in most other Latin American countries. Clearly there are individuals in the country who suffer the consequences of living in squalid conditions. Yet, relative to most other countries at comparable levels of industrialization

TABLE 7.3

Distribution of National Household Income (Gini Coefficients)

	Year	Gini Coefficient[a]
Argentina	1970	.44
Brazil	1972	.66
Costa Rica	1971	.49
Mexico	1967	.59
Peru	1972	.60
Venezuela	1971	.50

Source: Statistical Abstract of Latin America, 1981: p. 192.

[a]The computation of the Gini Coefficient is such that the higher the coefficient, the greater the inequality.

TABLE 7.4

Income Share of the Poorest 40 Percent (Percentage of Nation's Income)

	1955-1960	1970-1977
Argentina	16.6	16.2
Bolivia		13.0
Brazil	11.5	7.9
Costa Rica	13.7	14.7
Cuba	6.2	20.4
Mexico	10.9	10.5
Peru	10.0	9.0
Venezuela	14.5	13.0

Source: Adapted from Brundenius and Lundahl, 1982: p. 4.

and gross national product, Costa Rica has done quite well in matters of economic distribution.

Throughout most of the 1960s, the Venezuelan economy grew consistently, but at only quite moderate rates. For instance, gross domestic product grew at an average annual rate of about 5.5 percent and agriculture at about 6 percent (Hanson 1977:81–82). With the great increase in the price of petroleum in the early 1970s, the growth rates increased significantly. GDP growth rates went up to an average of about 7.5 percent while agriculture and industry grew at about 8 percent each year. By the early 1980s the growth rate once again slowed as the world witnessed a significant drop in the price of oil.

Although Venezuela has had an enviable record in economic growth, and although it has experienced less inequality in income distribution than many other Latin American countries, significant inequalities persist and, as Table 7.4 suggests, may be getting worse. The comparison between Venezuela and Argentina is instructive. In spite of having possessed authoritarian, repressive, and economically conservative governments for most of the last two decades, Argentina's national income is more equally distributed than is Venezuela's. In Venezuela about 5 percent of the population live on some 710,000 bolívares per month (on the average) while three-quarters of the population try to get by on less than 700 bolívares each month (QER 1977:7).

Having taken a summary look at economic performance in our six countries, we can now reflect upon the relationship between what we have considered in this chapter and that in the preceding chapter. This reflection, we believe, leads to two general conclusions. First, there does seem to be some correspondence between government policy and economic performance. Brazil's strongly growth-oriented policy correlates rather highly with an economy that, until the early 1980s, grew rapidly, but also one in which income concentration worsened. Essentially the same can be said for Mexico. The structural reformism of the Velasco government in Peru was associated with moderate to low levels of economic growth, with little change in income distribution, but with significant changes in the economic activities of the state. The revolutionary socialist regime in Cuba has corresponded with moderate rates of economic growth but dramatic changes in the patterns of distribution. The government's attempts at striking a balance between growth and distribution demands in Costa Rica seem to correlate quite nicely with an economy that has achieved a fairly good record of distribution. Much the same can be said of Venezuela, though we would characterize its growth record in somewhat more positive terms and its distributive record in more negative terms.

The second general conclusion is that significant deviations from our first conclusion also occurred. First, we saw in the last chapter that our regime categories were not always helpful in explaining or predicting the policies of certain countries. Mexico, for instance, pursued a pattern of economic policies far more similar to Brazil's than to Cuba's, though Mexico categorically is placed with the latter. Though less drastic, there were also substantial dissimilarities in economic policy between Brazil and Peru, though both were placed in the same category. As we suggested in the last chapter, however, we do not believe this is a theoretically destructive admission. Using our study as a starting point, we can begin the task of developing more sophisticated and valid categories.

A second set of deviations, however, does suggest limits to the theoretical utility of regime categorizations. In a number of cases there seems to be little relationship between policy outputs and system performance. Venezuelan economic growth correlates reasonably well with government policy, but correlates even more highly with the value of oil exports. All of the countries, but most especially Mexico, Costa Rica, and Brazil, suffered dramatic economic reversals in 1982. Yet there are significant differences in either policy or domestic economic conditions. One could argue that Costa Rica's heavy spending on social policy undermined its economy. If that is the case, how do we account for the troubles in Brazil and Mexico where policy has long emphasized growth and where social spending is relatively low. We could argue that the Mexican economy has been hurt by a drop in world oil prices and a dramatic and sudden increase in international borrowing. But then why hasn't the change in the oil market helped Brazil and Costa Rica, two heavy importers of oil? Clearly, there are answers to these questions, and extensive borrowing is one all have in common. Just as clearly, however, many important factors are quite local and thus suggest we must be wary of attempting to explain too much by such concepts as regime type or pattern of policymaking.

Social Conditions and Policy Impact

One indicator of a country's social well-being is the state of its people's health. Three useful, though not exhaustive, measures of people's medical well-being are infant mortality rates, life expectancy rates, and the number of physicians per capita. As the data in Table 7.5 demonstrate, health conditions in Latin America vary dramatically. Health care in Cuba is excellent. It is good in Costa Rica, less good, though generally adequate, in Argentina, Mexico, and Venezuela, and rather poor in Brazil, Bolivia, and Peru.

In Cuba, the physical well-being of the people has been, relatively, quite good for some time and is continuing to improve. As noted earlier, Cuba is reputed to have one of the best health-care systems in the world; the data in Table 7.5 lend credence to that view. Health conditions in Costa Rica are also noteworthy. Life expectancy is almost as high as in Cuba and the infant mortality rate, though higher, has been dropping faster. Perhaps the most significant difference between Cuba and Costa Rica is that in the former there are far more physicians per capita. As of 1960, health conditions in Venezuela were slightly better than those in Cuba and Costa Rica. But since 1960, Venezuela has experienced no improvement in life expectancy or infant mortality despite possessing a sizable number of medical doctors.

Statistics for Mexico indicate significant improvement in the health of its people over the past two decades, with a substantial increase in life expectancy

TABLE 7.5

Indicators of Health Care

	Life Expectance At Birth		Infant Mortality Rate (Age 0-1) Deaths per 1,000		Inhabitants per Doctor
	1960	1977	1960	1977	1970
Argentina	66	71	59	59	521
Bolivia	42	52		158	2174
Brazil	56	62	180	110	1918
Costa Rica	61	70	69	38	1804
Cuba	62	72	35	23	1123
Mexico	56	65	74	52	1726
Peru	49	56	93	65	1917
Venezuela	66	66	54	53	1115

Source: Brundenius and Lundahl, 1982: p. 4; Statistical Abstract of Latin America, 1981: p. 7.

and a substantial decrease in mortality rates. Peru and Brazil also witnessed significant improvements in people's health but still experience infant mortality rates that are high and life expectancies that are low.

We should note that the data on health conditions do not address the issue of how those conditions are distributed in terms of social class or geographical area. In most cases, infant mortality and life expectancy rates are good for those in the urban upper and middle classes while they are quite poor for those in the lower classes, especially those who live in the countryside. Only in the case of Cuba is this not so true. There, as we pointed out in the previous chapter, quality health care is readily available to virtually all. Perhaps in Costa Rica the disparities are less drastic than in most other Latin American countries, though this assertion is based on impressionistic rather than hard data.

Another social area for which sufficient comparative data are available is that of education. The supply of teaching personnel and the rate of literacy give us some clue as to how countries are faring in this area. The data in Table 7.6 illustrate that the pattern in educational conditions is quite similar to that for health conditions. Cuba leads the way, with Costa Rica and Argentina not too far behind. The worst conditions, once again, are to be found in Bolivia, though conditions in Mexico and Peru also need much improvement. The principal difference between the pattern in education and the one in health is that the Brazilian record is fairly good in the former. Though the literacy rate in Brazil is still relatively low, substantial improvement has been

TABLE 7.6

Indicators of Educational Conditions

	Teachers Per 10,000 People, Ages 7-14		Adult Literacy Rate	
	1960	1975	1960	1977
Argentina	343	525	91	93
Bolivia	146	240	39	63
Brazil	126	288	61	76
Costa Rica	223	251	84	89
Cuba	144	366	80	98
Mexico	113	170	65	76
Peru	166	222	61	72
Venezuela	177	224	65	82

Source: Brundenius and Lundahl, 1982: p. 4; Statistical Abstract of Latin America, 1981: p. 138.

achieved over the past two decades. This is most noticeable when comparing the 1960 and 1975 figures in Brazil on the number of teachers per capita.

Again, we emphasize the fact that the data do not address the issue of distribution. What was said of the distribution of health care can be said of the distribution of educational facilities: Except for Cuba and to a lesser extent Costa Rica, it is biased heavily to upper- and middle-class, urban areas.

Statistics on health and education provide us with some useful indicators about social conditions and the extent to which these conditions have improved. They do not, of course, tell us anything about how workers, compared to professionals, in an urban area live, or how the urban ghetto resident lives, or the construction worker, or the teacher, or the manager at a factory. Data of this kind of detail do not exist in anything approaching reliably comparative statistics. As we have shown, however, all countries except Cuba contain extreme disparities of living standards between rich and poor, urban and rural areas. Of the nonsocialist countries, only in Costa Rica do we find less extreme disparities in living conditions.

Data in Table 7.7 offer two additional indicators of social conditions. On the one hand, we see that all of the countries need improvement in the provision of safe water. People living in urban slums and those in poor housing conditions in the rural areas, where such diseases as amoebic dysentery can be widespread, suffer most from unsanitary water. On the other hand, the data show that survival is not a basic problem in most of the countries. Of course, the information on caloric intake, as opposed to the information on safe water access, says nothing about the distribution of those calories among

TABLE 7.7

Provision of Safe Water and Caloric Requirements

	Percent of Population With Access to Safe Water 1975	Daily Caloric Supply, Percent of Requirements 1974
Argentina	66	129
Bolivia	34	77
Brazil	77	105
Costa Rica	77	113
Cuba		117
Mexico	62	177
Peru	47	100
Venezuela		98

Source: Stewart, 1982: p. 63.

the population. Clearly the figures are averages, which include people who eat far too much and those who eat too little, or whose diets are unbalanced. Nevertheless, although problems of nutrition are significant in Bolivia, Mexico, Peru, and certain sizable areas of Brazil, only in a few countries in Latin America (and only in Bolivia among those surveyed here) is the level of caloric supply a real problem.

To what extent do the data presented on social conditions and changes in social conditions correspond to what we know about social policy in each of the countries? We are struck by what appears to be a high correspondence between social policy efforts and social conditions. Of the countries for which we have presented data, Cuba clearly outranks all others in government policy to provide educational and health-care facilities, and the data just as clearly demonstrate that Cuban health and educational statistics are impressive. In fact, relative to its level of industrialization and gross national product, Cuba has been very successful in achieving low rates of infant mortality, long life spans, and high rates of literacy (see Stewart 1982:59).

Though Costa Rica's statistics on health and education are not quite as impressive as Cuba's, for a country as rural as Costa Rica life expectancy is quite long and infant mortality quite low. As with Cuba, we noted that the government in Costa Rica has devoted significant portions of the budget to education and, in general, has sought to achieve a balance between spending for economic development and social development.

At the other end of the spectrum, we note that the more industrialized and growth-oriented countries like Brazil have a significantly poorer record in the areas of health and education. Infant mortality rates are substantially higher, compared to Costa Rica and Cuba, life expectancy is substantially lower, and literacy is lower. Venezuelan results also seem to parallel closely government efforts in the significant increase of teachers and the substantial improvement of literacy during the 1960s and 1970s. But the lack of improvement in health statistics partially confirms our earlier statements that Venezuelan governments have paid insufficient attention to social policy areas. However, one would have expected at least a little improvement in health, given the increase in the public health-care system; thus, the health situation partially disconfirms the notion of a straightforward relationship between policy output and policy impact.

More interesting anomalies occur. Though Brazil's infant mortality rate is still appallingly high, that nation has experienced quite significant improvement in the situation during the past two decades, this in spite of a regime hardly known for its social concerns. In fact, the Brazilian case suggests a general conclusion about social policy for the six countries, plus Argentina and Bolivia: With the exception of Costa Rica and Cuba, there is a fairly strong positive correlation between social outcomes and levels of industrialization and gross national product. For instance, most of the indicators for health and educational attainments are better for Argentina than for Venezuela and, in general, as good or better for Argentina than for Costa Rica, in spite of the relatively retrograde administrations that have governed Argentina for quite some time. But Argentina is wealthier and more industrialized than Costa Rica, and more industrialized and, until quite recently, wealthier than Venezuela. Brazilian statistics reflect rather nicely a country that has been relatively poor for some time but now is becoming significantly wealthier and more industrialized. Data for Peru and especially Bolivia suggest countries that have been and still are rather poor, which indeed is the case. Thus, just as in the area of economic policy, so in social policy we find some evidence that clearly seems to link policy outcomes with societal performance and other evidence that suggests that policy has less direct impact than do general levels of urbanization, industrialization, and gross national product. In short, the wealthier the country, the more likely that its people's level of education and the quality of health care will be high, despite the nature of that country's political regime.

Political and Civil Rights and Policy Impact

To a fairly significant extent, one's political and civil liberties are defined by government policy. Where governments choose to censor the press, to deny the right to strike, to vote, to organize opposition political parties, and to criticize policy publicly, and where governments engage wantonly in torture, one's rights and liberties are circumscribed accordingly. Conversely, where government policy protects the right to strike, to criticize, to vote for whomever one wishes, and so on, one's liberties and rights are expanded accordingly. The former situation adequately characterized both policy and results in Brazil from the coup of 1964 until the mid- to late-1970s. It also characterizes Cuba in terms of political rights, though the Cuban government does not engage in torture nor, usually, does it engage in arbitrary and capricious behavior.

The situation of expanded rights and liberties generally characterizes Costa Rica and Venezuela. As noted earlier, government policy in Peru and Mexico falls somewhere in between the more authoritarian regimes of Brazil and Cuba and the democratic regimes of Costa Rica and Venezuela.

We can in many cases trace clearly the linkages between policy and societal performance in the area of political and civil liberties, but to suggest a completely straightforward relationship would be quite misleading. Even when governments aggressively seek to protect liberties for all citizens, inequalities in the distribution of political resources and the nature of dominant values and attitudes inevitably create some inconsistencies between governmental policy and actual behavior. For instance, as we suggested in Chapter 1, Fidel Castro seems to have been frustrated in bringing sexual equality to Cuba. In all countries, but especially in capitalist ones, inequalities in income distribution will lead to certain inequalities in the practice of justice (due, generally, to the unequal ability to hire good quality legal assistance), even if it is the intent of public policy to ensure an essentially equal and fair treatment. Even in this policy area, then, government action does not completely define or control social and individual behavior, though it does more so than in the previous two areas.

Perhaps a final consideration that we might touch upon only briefly is the question of whether some types of regimes are more effective than others in doing whatever policy they set out to do. Some contemporary writers and political actors have suggested that with the generally limited resources available to less-developed countries and the complexity and enormity of many of their developmental problems, the democratic regimes are too *unwieldy* and "costly." Instead, authoritarian, nondemocratic regimes of either a military or nonmilitary nature are what these countries need. Specifically, one argument along these lines is that authoritarian regimes are better equipped than are democratic ones to manage and direct economic development. This was certainly the position of the Brazilian military junta.

A related argument might be that although democratic regimes may be more effective in successfully implementing political and civil rights policies, they are significantly less effective in generating economic growth. Does our study shed any light on this issue? If the arguments are valid, we could expect that the regimes that we characterized as more authoritarian in nature and that have emphasized economic growth as a central policy goal would have a better record in this area than the other regimes. The evidence we have is ambiguous. Authoritarian regimes in Latin America do not clearly have an edge over democratic regimes in successfully pursuing policies of economic growth. As discussed previously, Venezuela's growth, while clearly not so rapid as that of Brazil, was moderate and consistent throughout the 1970s. Moreover, both Venezuela and Costa Rica, the two democratic regimes in our study, maintained overall growth rates in the 1970s that were virtually identical to those of more authoritarian Mexico. That all six countries in this study have been experiencing economic difficulties since the beginning of this decade is more likely a result of international financial dependence shared by all of them and less likely related to the disparate natures of their particular regimes.

Similar limitations to the main argument—that is, the alleged *inherent* policymaking superiority of authoritarian regimes—can be seen in the mixed record of these countries' redistributive social policies. Cuba remains a deviant case here, in that it is both postrevolutionary and generally authoritarian and it has been more successful than any of the six regimes in implementing effective redistributive social policies. The only other authoritarian regime that consciously pursued redistributive social policy in a somewhat vigorous manner was Peru under the Velasco-led junta. As our figures demonstrated, these policies had relatively little impact on society. Peru, in fact, looks much worse in this respect than either Venezuela or Costa Rica, which have both implemented redistributive policies in more democratic contexts.

Conclusions

By now, you will probably agree with us that making accurate and meaningful generalizations about how government policymaking is conducted, and what it produces, is no easy task. At least since the time of Aristotle, political scientists have been interested in determining those characteristics of a political system that are critical to its structure and behavior. To a very large extent, this study falls into that tradition.

In this analysis, we have categorized six countries according to three types of regime: military, democratic, and postrevolutionary. Both of the last two types of regime are led by civilians. We have found enough consistent differences in styles of policymaking to suggest some conceptual validity to our categories. For instance, legislative bodies play a role in policymaking in democratic regimes, but not in military or postrevolutionary regimes. Postrevolutionary regimes effectively use mass organizations for purposes of control and mobilization; military regimes do not, while democratic regimes utilize smaller, competitive parties and are generally characterized by more autonomous interest group activity.

Nevertheless, there are many similarities among the regimes in policymaking, especially between military and postrevolutionary regimes. In all cases, public policy, or at least major policy decisions, tend to be formulated by an elite. In all cases, it appears that middle- and upper-level bureaucratic officials play a critical role in developing policy. In both postrevolutionary and military regimes, the style of policymaking can be characterized as authoritarian. Although elites also dominate the policy process in democratic societies, some greater competition and conflict is allowed, and a greater variety of avenues are open for the expression of individual or group values.

The picture gets more confused when we turn to policy outputs and to system performance. For instance, in economic policy Mexico behaves more like Brazil than like Cuba, while in social policy Mexico has behaved more like Peru than like Cuba. All but Cuba share many similarities in economic policy, though Costa Rica and Venezuela do seem to have more in common with each other than with Brazil, Mexico, or Peru. The same, in general, is true with respect to social policy. In particular areas, however, the pattern dissolves. Brazilian and Peruvian expenditures on education, for instance, place them closer to the democratic regimes than to Mexico.

These general analyses suggest several important lessons to be learned about the comparative study of public policy. When comparing the policies of one country with another, one must do more than compare a single indicator. Even two or perhaps three indicators are insufficient. What do we mean? An indicator of a country's policy in a particular area could be the amount of money a government spends. It is possible that two very disparate types of government might very well spend similar amounts in one area of policy but very different amounts in all or most others. Moreover, one has to be very careful about inferring too much from any one indicator. For example, even if we find that two countries spend the same amount for education, that does not necessarily mean their educational policies are at all alike. Under the broad heading of "education," money can be spent for a wide variety of things. Most studies rely heavily upon gross budget expenditures as indicators of public policy. But there is a real problem in doing so. If you have ever looked at a government budget, especially the one that gets published and is available to the public, you will notice that the categories for expenditures (and revenues) are very broad, so broad that they tell us very little.

Our analysis raises another type of conceptual problem. As we have had to admit, though Mexico and Cuba are both postrevolutionary regimes, and though they both have much in common in the process of policymaking, they are quite dissimilar in their patterns of economic and social policy outputs. The difficulty here is not empirical, but conceptual. That is, while we can call them both postrevolutionary, the revolutions were quite different. Put most simply but fundamentally, the people who took control of the Cuban revolution and, afterwards, of the Cuban political system believed in socialism (as they understood it). Therefore, policy in Cuba has been made in accord with the elite's perception of what it is to be socialist. The Mexican revolution was not a socialist one. The people who dominated it and who later came to dominate government in Mexico were capitalists and were solidly tied to the emerging middle classes. What Mexico and Cuba share is an authoritarian tradition, which tends to emerge from a society that has undergone a full-scale revolution. What they do not share is a set of values concerning how the economic and social systems should function and what they should accomplish. Thus, the term postrevolutionary is too broad.

A similar, though less serious, problem arises with respect to Brazil and Peru. Again, policymaking styles were far more similar than dissimilar. Yet policy content was fairly dissimilar. This suggests to us a tentative conclusion about military regimes. In terms of how policy is processed and in terms of policy toward political and civil rights, military regimes tend to be similar. They can be distinguished from civilian authoritarian regimes such as Mexico and Cuba in that they are more antipolitical. They eschew or are uncomfortable with political parties, with mobilizing the masses (even if only for purposes of control), and with ideology, and they prefer a technocratic and bureaucratic style (see Loveman and Davies 1978:3–141). Nonetheless, differences in existing social and economic conditions necessarily generate variations in the content of policy. Thus, for instance, one observer of the military in Latin America referred to the Brazilian military that took over in 1964 and to the Argentine military of 1966 as demobilizing and authoritarian. The Peruvian military of 1968 and the Bolivian military of 1969 were called leftist and developmental (Rouquie 1973:4–5).

Political scientist Robert Ayres has noted that excessively "macro" (general) level distinctions will tend to show few differences in policy outputs by regime type because the distinctions (at the macro level) are too gross (1975:18). Certainly, the distinction between civilian and military is rather too crude, given the wide range of civilian regimes that have existed. Military regimes are authoritarian. Civilian regimes may be authoritarian. Perhaps the term *democratic* is too broad also. Assuming that it is used accurately, however, our analysis suggests that *democratic* may not require further qualification. Clearly, the other categorical terms do require qualification. The notion of socialist seems somehow important in describing and explaining the differences in economic and social policy between Cuba and the others. Perhaps the distinction in types of military regime suggested above will allow us sufficient precision for that category.

Having reviewed some of the analytical issues that have been raised concerning the relationship between policy process and policy output, we can now turn to a review of some critical issues involved in the relationship between policy output and policy impact. General indicators of a nation's economic and social well-being, such as GNP per capita, or increases in energy consumption, or literacy rates, are often used to compare the accomplishments of governments. On the face of it, the comparisons that result from this type of analysis make sense. A relatively high ratio of teachers to children generally means that the government is spending more on education (or at least on teachers) than is a government where there is a relatively low ratio of teachers to children. Low infant mortality rates probably indicate that the government is doing more for infant health care than a government in a country with high infant mortality rates. The problem is, however, that these relationships do not always hold.

Three examples should be sufficient to illustrate our point. Between 1960 and 1970, agricultural production in Brazil consistently improved. With the exception of a few export crops, during this same period the Brazilian government tended to ignore agricultural development in favor of industrial growth. In fact, budgetary allocations to the minister of agriculture were cut by over 50 percent between 1960 and 1970 (Ayers 1975:20–21). The Cuban economy's impressive growth rate between 1971 and 1974 was due in large part to greatly increased revenues from the export of sugar. Yet sugar production was up and down during this time. The apparent anomaly is resolved when we note that world sugar prices were unusually high during those years. Earlier (in Table 7.6) we observed that Argentina has a much higher ratio of teachers per capita than does Cuba, in spite of the fact that the Cuban government has expended much greater effort on education than have recent Argentine governments. In each of these cases, government performance has been quite different than what we might have predicted had we looked only at the general indicator of economic or social outcomes.

There are many reasons to explain why the relationship between government policy and system performance is not what we might have expected. Perhaps most obviously, the existence of accessible natural resources has much to do with the nation's economic performance. Of course, it is not possible to develop steel production without iron ore. But plentiful and easily accessible deposits of iron ore might lead to a booming steel industry as long as the government does nothing to discourage it. We can translate this simple illustration into more academically technical but generally useful language. If we think of government policy as the key independent variable and economic or social performance as the dependent variable, then availability of natural resources is a critical intervening variable.

Almost as important as natural resource availability as an explanation of systemic performance is the history of government action. Far too frequently, when we compare the performance of different regimes in different countries, our historical perspective is too narrow. Before any given government can affect the economic or social systems it may be necessary to bring about structural changes. And these kinds of changes take a good deal of time. To put it another way, a variety of expectations, incentives, and relationships may have been put into motion by previous governments that will control behavior until an entirely new set of expectations, incentives, and relationships can be created. Thus, the longer a regime type has been in existence, the more confident we are that there is some connection between what the government has been doing and what the economy is doing. This is certainly a problem in evaluating the impact of the government of General Juan Velasco in Peru. But it could well be a problem in evaluating the performance of any regime, at least during its early years.

Another important factor in explaining cases where government actions seem unrelated to system performance is the very nature of much government policy. A good deal of public policy operates indirectly. Governments can seek to improve a nation's health by building more hospitals and more facilities to train doctors. But people must use the hospitals and the training facilities before the policy will have any impact. Governments can provide tax incentives to owners of industry to update their equipment or wage incentives to workers to increase their productivity, but unless owners see any real personal benefit in working harder the policy will have no impact. Of course, the problem we are discussing varies somewhat, depending on the degree of government ownership of and control over the economy. The impact of government policy on the economy may ultimately be as strong in the United States as in Cuba. But the route of the policy's impact will tend to be more indirect and circuitous in the United States because private individuals and groups control the U.S. economy, while in Cuba the government controls the economy. Nevertheless, even in Cuba some public policy works indirectly, as our example of women's rights (in Chapter 1) illustrates.

Other explanations may be used to understand why policy may not influence performance or influences it in unexpected ways. Some people, for instance, would argue that Latin American nations are so dependent upon foreign countries that the actions of the Latin American nations' governments are far outweighed by the activities of foreign actors. One might also note the frequent cases in which government policy has been contradictory. One policy cancels the benefits of another, and the result is a good deal of government activity without constructive impact. Even if policies are not overtly contradictory, the successful impact of one often depends upon the complementary implementation of the other. Agrarian reform policies, for example, which involve the redistribution of land to peasants, have frequently failed in Latin America because of governments' failures to implement policies that would guarantee agricultural credits to the newly landowning peasants.

You may have found other reasons to explain the problem. The point is not to convince you of the merits of any particular argument, but to convince you that indeed there are good reasons as to why government policy may have no effect, or an unintended effect, upon a nation's economic, social, or political well-being.

Must we finally conclude that government makes no difference, that it doesn't matter what type of regime governs a country? A cautious conclusion is that we believe that governments do make a difference, though certainly not the only difference or necessarily always the most important difference. Additionally, regime type is a static category and, as we have seen in preceding chapters, regimes can and do vary over time. Cuba immediately following the revolution and Brazil immediately following the coup, for example, were extremely repressive, though they have become much less so since then. Finally, regimes of a particular type also vary among themselves in their policies, but they nonetheless differ significantly as a group from regimes of another type. Brazil has been more repressive of political rights than Peru, for example, but both regimes are more generally repressive than are the democratic regimes of Venezuela and Costa Rica.

At the same time, it should be apparent by now that in policy areas other than political and civil rights, the connection between regime type and policy output and between policy output and system performance is problematical and subject to the impact of other factors, both internal and external to the countries themselves.

Bibliography

Books and Articles

Acción Democrática. *Tesis Petrolera*. Caracas: Editorial Antonio Pinto Salinas, 1958a.
————. *Tesis Agraria*. Caracas: Editorial Antonio Pinto Salinas, 1958b.
Acta 2258. Social Security Institute Board of Directors. September 18, 1959. San José, Costa Rica.
"Acta de la Comisión Asuntos Económicos." No. 56, July 13, 1970. San José, Costa Rica.
Alegrett, J. Raul. "The Venezuelan Agrarian Reform: Impact and Perspectives." In *Venezuela: 1969; Analysis of Progress*, edited by Phillip B. Taylor, Jr. Houston: Office of International Affairs, 1971.
Allison, Graham T. *Essence of Decision: Explaining the Cuban Missile Crisis*. Boston: Little, Brown and Co., 1971.
Almond, Gabriel, and Verba, Sidney. *The Civic Culture*. Boston: Little, Brown and Co., 1965.
Ames, Barry, and Goff, Ed. "Education and Defense Expenditures in Latin America: 1948–1968." In *Comparative Public Policy: Issues, Theories and Methods*, edited by Craig Liske, William Loehr, and John McCamant. Beverly Hills, Calif.: Sage Publications, 1975.
Anderson, Charles W. *Politics and Economic Change in Latin America: The Governing of Restless Nations*. New York: Van Nostrand Reinhold Co., 1967.
————. *Statecraft: An Introduction to Political Choice and Judgment*. New York: John Wiley and Sons, 1977.
Anderson, James E. *Public Policy Making*. 2d ed. New York: Holt, Rinehart and Winston, 1979.
Anderson, James E.; Brady, David W.; and Bullock, Charles, III. *Public Policy and Politics in America*. North Scituate, Mass.: Duxbury Press, 1978.
Araya Pochet, Carlos. "Crisis e Historia Económica y Social en Costa Rica, 1970–1982." In *Costa Rica Hoy*. San José, Costa Rica: Editorial Universidad Estatal a Distancia, 1983.
Astiz, Carlos A. *Pressure Groups and Power Elites in Peruvian Politics*. Ithaca, N.Y.: Cornell University Press, 1969.
Atkins, G. Pope. *Latin America in the International Political System*. New York: Free Press, 1977.
Avery, William P. "Oil, Politics and Economic Policy Making: Venezuela and the Andean Common Market." *International Organization* 30 (4) (Autumn 1976):541–572.

227

Ayres, Robert L. "Political Regimes, Explanatory Variables, and Public Policy in Latin America." *Journal of the Developing Areas* 10 (1) (October 1975):15–36.

Azicri, Max. "The Institutionalization of the Cuban State: A Political Perspective." *Journal of Interamerican Studies and World Affairs* 22 (3) (August 1980): 315–344.

Bailey, John, and Link, John. "Statecraft and Agriculture in Mexico, 1980–1982: Domestic and Foreign Policy Considerations." Paper presented at the meeting of the Latin American Studies Association, Bloomington, Indiana, October 1980, pp. 17–19.

Bennett, Douglas, and Sharpe, Kenneth. "The State as Banker and Entrepreneur: The Last Resort Character of the Mexican State's Economic Intervention, 1917–1976." *Comparative Politics* 12 (12) (January 1980):165–190.

Blank, David Eugene. *Politics in Venezuela.* Boston: Little, Brown and Co., 1973.

———. *Venezuela: Politics in a Petroleum Republic.* Stanford, Calif.: Hoover Institution, 1984.

Blasier, Cole, and Mesa-Lago, Carmelo, eds. *Cuba in the World.* Pittsburgh: University of Pittsburgh Press, 1979.

Booth, John A. *The End and the Beginning: The Nicaraguan Revolution.* Boulder, Colo.: Westview Press, 1982.

Bourricaud, François. *Power and Society in Contemporary Peru.* New York: Praeger, 1967.

Brandenburg, Frank R. *The Making of Modern Mexico.* Englewood Cliffs, N.J.: Prentice-Hall, 1964.

Brasil, República Federativa do. *II Plano Nacional de Desenvolvimento (1975–1979).* Guanabara, Brazil: IBGE, 1974. Brasil, República Federativa do. *II Plano de Desenvolvimento da Amazonia.* Belém, Brazil: SUDAM, 1975.

Bray, Donald M., and Harding, Timothy F. "Cuba." In *Latin America: The Struggle with Dependency and Beyond,* edited by Ronald H. Chilcote and Joel C. Edelstein. New York: Schenkman Publishing, 1974.

Braybrooke, David, and Lindblom, Charles E. *A Strategy of Decision.* New York: Free Press, 1963.

Brundenius, Claes, and Lundhal, Mats, eds. *Development Strategies and Basic Needs in Latin America: Challenges for the 1980s.* Boulder, Colo.: Westview Press, 1982.

Bunker, Stephen. "The Cost of Modernity: Inappropriate Bureaucracy, Inequality, and Development Program Failure in the Brazilian Amazon." *Journal of Developing Areas* 26 (4) (July 1982):573–596.

Caballero, José María, and Álvarez, Elena. *Aspectos Cuantitativos de la Reforma Agraria (1969–1979).* Lima: Instituto de Estudios Peruanos, 1980.

Cabieses, Hugo, and Otero, Carlos. *Economía Peruana: Un Ensayo de Interpretación.* Lima: DESCO, Centro de Estudios y Promoción del Desarrollo, 1978.

Calderón Guardia, Rafael Angel. *El Gobernante y el Hombre Frente al Problema Social.* San Jose, Costa Rica: 1942. (No publisher given.)

Cardoso, Fernando Henrique. *Autoritarismo e Democratização.* Rio de Janeiro: Pax e Terra, 1975.

Cardoso, Fernando Henrique, and Faletto, Enzo. *Dependency and Development in Latin America.* Berkeley and Los Angeles: University of California Press, 1979.

Cardoso, Fernando Henrique, and Muller, Geraldo. *Amazonia, Expansão do Capitalismo.* São Paulo: Brasiliense, 1977.

Carroll, T. Owen; Chatterjee, Romir; and Mubayi, Vinod. "Energy Planning in Latin America: A Brief Review of Selected Countries." *Latin American Research Review* 17 (3) (1982):148–172.

Centro de Investigaciones Agrarias. *Estructura Agraria y Desarrollo Agrícola en México.* Mexico: Fondo de Cultura Económica, 1974.

Cerdas Cruz, Rodolfo. *La Crisis de la Democracia Liberal en Costa Rica.* San José, Costa Rica: EDUCA, 1972.

Cernea, Michael. *Measuring Project Impact: Monitoring and Evaluation in the PIDER Rural Development Project—Mexico.* World Bank Staff Working Paper no. 332, Washington, D.C., 1979.

Chalmers, Douglas A. "The Political State in Latin America." In *Authoritarianism and Corporatism in Latin America.* See Malloy, 1977.

CIDA. *Tenencia de la Tierra y Desarrollo Socio-Económico del Sector Agrícola: Peru.* Washington, D.C.: Pan American Union, 1966.

Cleaves, Peter S., and Scurrah, Martin J. *Agriculture, Bureaucracy, and Military Government in Peru.* Ithaca, N.Y., and London: Cornell University Press, 1980.

Cline, Howard F. *Mexico: Revolution to Evolution, 1940–1960.* New York: Oxford University Press, 1963.

Coleman, Kenneth, and Varela, Luis Quiros. "Determinants of Latin American Foreign Policies: Bureaucratic Organizations and Development Strategies." In *Latin American Foreign Policies,* edited by Elizabeth G. Ferris and Jennie K. Lincoln. Boulder, Colo.: Westview Press, 1981.

Collier, David. *Squatters and Oligarchs: Authoritarian Rule and Policy Change in Peru.* Baltimore and London: Johns Hopkins University Press, 1976.

Collier, Ruth Berins, and Collier, David. "Inducements Versus Constraints: Disaggregating Corporatism." *American Political Science Review* 73 (4) (1979):967–986.

Corbett, Charles D. *The Latin American Military as a Socio-Political Force: Case Studies of Bolivia and Argentina.* Coral Gables: University of Miami, 1972.

Cornelius, Wayne, Jr. "Nation Building, Participation, and Distribution: The Politics of Social Reform Under Cardenas." In *Crisis, Choice and Change: Historical Studies of Political Development,* edited by Gabriel A. Almond et al. Boston: Little, Brown and Co., 1973.

Coronil, Fernando, and Skurski, Julie. "Reproducing Dependency: Auto Industry Policy and Petrodollar Circulation in Venezuela." *International Organization* 36 (1) (Winter 1982):61–94.

Cotler, Julio. "The New Mode of Political Domination in Peru." In *The Peruvian Experiment.* See Lowenthal, 1975.

Craig, Ann. *The First Agraristas: An Oral History of an Agrarian Reform.* Berkeley: University of California Press, 1983.

Deere, Carmen Diana. "Agrarian Reform in Central America and U.S. Foreign Policy: El Salvador and Nicaragua." Paper presented to the Latin American Studies Association tenth annual meeting, Washington, D.C., 1982.

del Aguila, Juan M. "The Limits of Reform Development in Contemporary Costa Rica." *Journal of Interamerican Studies and World Affairs* 24 (3) (August 1982):355–373.

Denton, Charles F. *Patterns of Costa Rican Politics.* Boston: Allyn and Bacon, 1971.

_____ . "Costa Rica: A Democratic Revolution." In *Latin American Politics and Development. See* Wiarda and Kline, 1979.

DESCO. *Estado y Política Agraria.* Lima: DESCO, Centro de Estudios y Promoción del Desarrollo, 1977.

DeWitt, R. Peter. "The Inter-American Development Bank and Policy Making in Costa Rica." *Journal of Developing Areas* 15 (1) (October 1980):67–82.

Dibacco, Thomas V., ed. *Presidential Power in Latin American Politics.* New York and London: Praeger, 1977.

Dinerman, Ina. *Migrants and Stay-at-Homes: A Comparative Study of Rural Migration from Michoacan, Mexico.* Center for U.S.-Mexican Studies Monograph Series, no. 5, University of California, San Diego, 1982.

Domínguez, Jorge I. *Cuba: Order and Revolution.* Cambridge, Mass.: Harvard University Press, 1978.

_____ . "The Armed Forces and Foreign Relations." In *Cuba in the World. See* Blasier and Mesa-Lago, 1979.

Domínguez, Jorge I. "Cuba in the 1980s." *Problems of Communism* 30 (March-April 1981):48–57.

Drysdale, Robert S., and Myers, Robert G. "Continuity and Change: Peruvian Education." In *The Peruvian Experiment. See* Lowenthal, 1975.

Dumont, René. *Cuba: Socialization and Development.* New York: Grove Press, 1970.

Duncan, W. Raymond. *Latin American Politics: A Developmental Approach.* New York: Praeger, 1976.

Dye, David R., and de Souza e Silva, Carlos Eduardo. "A Perspective on the Brazilian State." *Latin American Research Review* 14 (1) (1979):81–98.

Dye, Thomas R. *Understanding Public Policy.* 4th ed. Englewood Cliffs, N.J.: Prentice-Hall, 1981.

Echeverría, Luis. "Second State of the Nation Message." *Comercio Exterior* 8 (10) (October 1972).

_____ . "Fourth State of the Nation Address." *Comercio Exterior* 20 (10) (October 1974).

_____ . "Fifth State of the Nation Message." *Comercio Exterior* 21 (10) (October 1975).

Eckstein, Susan. "The State and the Urban Poor." In *Authoritarianism in Mexico. See* Reyna and Weinert, 1977.

_____ . "The Socialist Transformation of Cuban Agriculture: Domestic and International Constraints." *Social Problems* 29 (2) (December 1981):178–196.

Erickson, Kenneth Paul. *The Brazilian Corporative State and Working-Class Politics.* Berkeley and Los Angeles: University of California Press, 1977.

_____ . "Brazil: Corporatism in Theory and Practice." In *Latin American Politics and Development. See* Wiarda and Kline, 1979.

_____ . "State Entrepreneurship, Energy Policy and the Political Order in Brazil." In *Authoritarian Capitalism: Brazil's Contemporary Economic and Political Development,* edited by Thomas C. Bruneau and Philippe Faucher. Boulder, Colo.: Westview Press, 1981.

Esteva, Gustavo. "Agriculture in Mexico from 1950 to 1975: The Failure of a False Analogy." *Comercio Exterior* 22 (1) (January 1976).

──────. *La Batalla en el México Rural*. Mexico City: Siglo XXI, 1980.

Evans, Peter. "Shoes, OPIC, and the Unquestioning Persuasion." In *Capitalism and the State in U.S.–Latin American Relations*, edited by Richard R. Fagen. Stanford, Calif.: Stanford University Press, 1974.

──────. *Dependent Development: The Alliance of Multinational, State, and Local Capital in Brazil*. Princeton, N.J.: Princeton University Press, 1979.

FAO. *Trade Yearbook*. Rome: Food and Agriculture Organization, United Nations. 1980. Vol. 3.

Farnsworth, Elizabeth; Feinberg, Richard; and Leenson, Eric. "Facing the Blockade." NACLA's *Latin American & Empire Report* 7 (1) (January 1973).

Ferguson, Yale H. "Latin America." In *Comparative Regional Systems*, edited by Werner J. Feld and Gavin Boyd. New York: Pergamon Press, 1980.

Fernández, Lorenzo. *Directrices Para una Acción de Gobierno*. Caracas, n.p., 1973.

Fishlow, Albert. "Some Reflections on Post-1964 Brazilian Economic Policy." In *Authoritarian Brazil*. *See* Stepan, 1973.

──────. "Brazil's Economic Miracle." In *The Politics of Anti-Politics*. *See* Loveman and Davies, 1978.

Fitzgerald, E.V.K. *The State and Economic Development: Peru Since 1968*. Cambridge: Cambridge University Press, 1976.

──────. *The Political Economy of Peru, 1956–1978: Economic Development and the Restructuring of Capital*. Cambridge: Cambridge University Press, 1979.

Fitzgibbon, Russell H., and Fernandez, Julio A. *Latin America: Political Culture and Development*. Englewood Cliffs, N.J.: Prentice-Hall, 1981.

Flynn, Peter. *Brazil: A Political Analysis*. Boulder, Colo.: Westview Press, 1978a.

──────. 1978b. "The Brazilian Development Model: The Political Dimension." In *The Politics of Anti-Politics*. *See* Loveman and Davies, 1978.

Foweraker, Joe. *The Struggle for Land*. London: Cambridge University Press, 1981.

Frohock, Fred M. *Public Policy: Scope and Logic*. Englewood Cliffs, N.J.: Prentice-Hall, 1979.

Gamer, Robert E. *The Developing Nations: A Comparative Perspective*. 2d ed. Boston: Allyn and Bacon, 1982.

Gereffi, Gary. 1978. "Drug Firms and Dependency in Mexico: The Industry." Cited in *Dependent Development*. *See* Evans, 1979.

Gil, José Antonio. 1977. "Entrepreneurs and Regime Consolidation." In *Venezuela: The Democratic Experience*. *See* Martz and Myers, 1977a.

──────. *The Challenge of Venezuelan Democracy*. Translated by Evelyn Harrison I., Lolo Gil de Yanes, and Danielle Salti. New Brunswick, N.J.: Transaction Books, 1981.

González Casanova, Pablo. *Democracy in Mexico*. New York: Oxford University Press, 1970.

Gonzalez, Edward. *Cuba Under Castro: The Limits of Charisma*. Boston: Houghton Mifflin, 1974.

──────. "Castro and Cuba's New Orthodoxy." *Problems in Communism* 25 (January-February 1976):1–19.

──────. "Institutionalization and Political Elites." In *Cuba in the World*. *See* Blasier and Mesa-Lago, 1979.

Gorman, Stephen M. "Peru Before the Election for the Constituent Assembly: Ten Years of Military Rule and the Quest for Social Justice." *Government and Opposition* 13 (3) (Summer 1978):288–306.

Gorman, Stephen M., ed. *Post-Revolutionary Peru: The Politics of Transformation.* Boulder, Colo.: Westview Press, 1982.

Grindle, Merilee S. *Bureaucrats, Politicians, and Peasants in Mexico: A Case Study in Public Policy.* Berkeley: University of California Press, 1977a.

──────. 1977b. "Policy Change in an Authoritarian Regime: Mexico Under Echeverria." *Journal of Interamerican Studies and World Affairs* 19 (4) (November 1977):523–556.

Groth, Alexander J. *Comparative Politics: A Distributive Approach.* New York: Macmillan, 1971.

Gudmundson, Lowell. "Costa Rica Before Coffee: Occupational Distribution, Wealth Inequality and Elite Society in the Village Economy of the 1840s." *Journal of Latin American Studies,* no. 15 (1983):427–452.

Guess, George M. "Recent Public Administration Literature in Costa Rica." *Latin American Research Review* 15 (3) (1980):278–280.

Hamilton, Nora. *The Limits of State Autonomy.* Princeton, N.J.: Princeton University Press, 1982.

Handelman, Howard. *The Struggle in the Andes: Peasant Political Mobilization in Peru.* Austin: University of Texas Press, 1975.

Hansen, Roger D. *The Politics of Mexican Development.* Baltimore: Johns Hopkins University Press, 1971.

Hanson, James A. 1977. "Cycles of Economic Growth and Structural Change Since 1950." In *Venezuela: The Democratic Experience. See* Martz and Myers, 1977a.

Harding, Colin. "Land Reform and Social Conflict in Peru." In *The Peruvian Experiment. See* Lowenthal, 1975.

Hayes, Margaret Daly. "Policy Consequences of Military Participation in Politics: An Analysis of Tradeoffs in Brazilian Federal Expenditures." In *Comparative Public Policy. See* Liske et al., 1975.

Hebette, Jean, and Acevedo, Rosa. "Colonizacao Espontanea, Politica Agraria e Grupos Sociales." UFPa-NAEA, Belém, Brazil: 1977. Photocopy.

Hellman, Judith. *Mexico in Crisis.* New York: Holmes and Meier, 1978.

Herman, Donald L. *Christian Democracy in Venezuela.* Chapel Hill: University of North Carolina Press, 1980.

Hernández Laos, Enrique, and Córdova Chavez, Jorge. "Estructura de la Distribución del Ingreso en México." *Comercio Exterior* 29 (May 1979):507–508.

Hewitt de Alcántara, Cynthia. *Modernizing Mexican Agriculture: Socioeconomic Implications of Technological Change, 1940–1970.* Geneva: UNRISD, 1976.

Hewlett, Sylvia Ann. *The Cruel Dilemmas of Development: Twentieth-Century Brazil.* New York: Basic Books, 1980.

Hilliker, Grant. *The Politics of Reform in Peru: The Aprista and Other Mass Parties of Latin America.* Baltimore and London: Johns Hopkins Press, 1971.

Holsti, K. J. *International Politics, A Framework for Analysis.* 4th ed. Englewood Cliffs, N.J.: Prentice-Hall, 1983.

Horowitz, Irving L., ed. *Cuban Communism.* 4th ed. New Brunswick, N.J.: Transaction Books, 1981.

Hughes, Steven W., and Mijeski, Kenneth J. *Legislative-Executive Policy-Making: The Cases of Chile and Costa Rica.* Beverly Hills, Calif.: Sage Publications, 1973.

Hughes, Steven W., and Mijeski, Kenneth J. "Contemporary Paradigms in the Study of Inter-American Relations," in *Latin America, the United States, and the Inter-American System,* edited by John D. Martz and Lars Schoultz. Boulder, Colo.: Westview Press, 1980.

Hunt, Shane. "Direct Foreign Investment in Peru: New Rules for an Old Game." In *The Peruvian Experiment. See* Lowenthal, 1975.

Ianni, Octavio. *Crisis in Brazil.* New York: Columbia University Press, 1970.

————. "A Luta Pela Terra." CEBRAP, São Paulo, Brazil, 1977. Mimeo.

Incra. Program for National Integration, Colonização da Amazonia, Brasilia. (No publisher given.)

InterAmerican Development Bank. *Economic and Social Progress in Latin America, 1979 Report.* Washington, D.C.: IDB.

Janis, Irving L. *Groupthink.* 2d ed. Boston: Houghton Mifflin, 1982.

Jaquette, Jane S. "Revolution by Fiat: The Context of Policy-Making in Peru." *Western Political Quarterly* 25 (4) (December 1972):648–666.

Jeness, Linda. *Women and the Cuban Revolution.* New York: Pathfinder Press, 1970.

Jervis, Robert. "Hypotheses on Misperception." In *International Politics and Foreign Policy,* edited by James N. Rosenau. Rev. ed. New York: Free Press, 1969.

Johnson, Kenneth F. *Mexican Democracy: A Critical View.* Rev. ed. New York: Praeger, 1978.

Jorge, Antonio. "How Exportable Is the Cuban Model?" In *The New Cuban Presence in the Caribbean. See* Barry Levine, 1983.

Kaufman, Robert R. 1977a. "Corporatism, Clientelism, and Partisan Conflict: A Study of Seven Latin American Countries." In *Authoritarianism and Corporatism in Latin America. See* Malloy, 1977.

————. 1977b. "Mexico and Latin American Authoritarianism." In *Authoritarianism in Mexico. See* Reyna and Weinert, 1977.

Kelley, R. Lynn. 1977. "Venezuelan Constitutional Forms and Realities." In *Venezuela: The Democratic Experience. See* Martz and Myers, 1977a.

Klare, Michael T., and Arnson, Cynthia. *Exporting Repression: U.S. Support for Authoritarianism in Latin American Relations.* Stanford, Calif.: Stanford University Press, 1974.

Kline, Harvey F. "Cuba: The Politics of Socialist Revolution." In *Latin American Politics and Development. See* Wiarda and Kline, 1979.

Knight, Peter T. "New Forms of Economic Organization in Peru: Toward Workers' Self-Management." In *The Peruvian Experiment. See* Lowenthal, 1975.

Lassen, Cheryl. *Landlessness and Rural Poverty in Latin America: Conditions, Trends and Policies Affecting Income and Employment.* Ithaca, N.Y.: Cornell University, Center for International Studies, 1980.

LeoGrande, William M. "Party Development in Revolutionary Cuba." *Journal of Interamerican Studies and World Affairs* 21 (4) (November 1979):457–480.

————. "The Communist Party of Cuba Since the First Congress." *Journal of Latin American Studies* 12 (2) (November 1980):397–419.

————. "Two Decades of Socialism in Cuba." *Latin American Research Review* 16 (1) (1981):187–206.

234   Politics and Public Policy in Latin America

Levesque, Jacques. *The USSR and the Cuban Revolution: Soviet Ideological and Strategical Perspectives, 1959–77.* New York: Praeger, 1978.

Levine, Barry B., ed. *The New Cuban Presence in the Caribbean.* Boulder, Colo.: Westview Press, 1983.

Levine, Daniel H. "Church Elites in Venezuela and Colombia: Content, Background, and Beliefs." *Latin American Research Review* 14 (1) (1979):51–79.

Levinson, Jerome, and DeOnís, Juan. *The Alliance That Lost Its Way.* Chicago: Quadrangle Books, 1970.

Lieuwen, Edwin. *Petroleum in Venezuela: A History.* Berkeley: University of California Press, 1954.

Lindblom, Charles E. "The Science of Muddling Through." *Public Administration Review* 19 (1959):79–88.

———. *The Intelligence of Democracy.* New York: Free Press, 1965.

Liske, Craig; Loehr, William; and McCamant, John, eds. *Comparative Public Policy: Issues, Theories and Methods.* Beverly Hills, Calif.: Sage Publications, 1975.

Lockwood, Lee. *Castro's Cuba, Cuba's Fidel.* New York: Vintage Books, 1969.

Lombardi, John V. 1977. "The Patterns of Venezuela's Past." In *Venezuela: The Democratic Experience. See* Martz and Myers, 1977a.

———. *Venezuela: The Search for Order, The Dream of Progress.* New York: Oxford University Press, 1982.

Lott, Leo B. *Venezuela and Paraguay: Political Modernity and Tradition in Conflict.* New York: Holt, Rinehart and Winston, 1972.

Loveman, Brian, and Davies, Thomas M., Jr., eds. *The Politics of Anti-Politics: The Military in Latin America.* Lincoln and London: University of Nebraska Press, 1978.

Lowenthal, Abraham F., ed. *The Peruvian Experiment: Continuity and Change Under Military Rule.* Princeton, N.J.: Princeton University Press, 1975.

Lowi, Theodore J. "American Business, Public Policy, Case Studies, and Political Theory." *World Politics* 16 (July 1964):677–715.

Luiselli, Cassio. *The Sistema Alimentario Mexicano (SAM): Elements of a Program of Accelerated Production of Basic Foodstuffs in Mexico.* Center for U.S.-Mexican Studies Research Report no. 22, University of California, San Diego, 1982.

McClintock, Cynthia. "Reform Governments and Policy Implementation: Lessons from Peru." In *Politics and Policy Implementation in the Third World,* edited by Merilee S. Grindle. Princeton, N.J.: Princeton University Press, 1980.

———. *Peasant Cooperatives and Political Change in Peru.* Princeton, N.J.: Princeton University Press, 1981.

———. "Post-Revolutionary Agrarian Politics in Peru." In *Post-Revolutionary Peru. See* Gorman, 1982.

———. "After Agrarian Reform and Democratic Government: Has Peruvian Agriculture Developed?" Paper presented at the International Studies Association meeting, Mexico City, April 1983a.

———. "Government Policy, Rural Poverty, and Peasant Protest in Peru: The Origins of the Sendero Luminoso Rebellion." Paper presented at the 1983 annual meeting of the American Political Science Association, Chicago, September 1983b.

———. "Velasco, Officers, and Citizens: The Politics of Stealth." In *The Peruvian Experiment Reconsidered*, edited by Cynthia McClintock and Abraham F. Lowenthal. Princeton, N.J.: Princeton University Press, 1983c.

McCoy, Terry L., ed. *The Dynamics of Population Policy in Latin America*. Cambridge, Mass.: Ballinger Publishing, 1974.

McDonald, Ronald H. *Party Systems and Elections in Latin America*. Chicago: Markham, 1971.

MacEwan, Arthur. "Incentives, Equality and Power in Revolutionary Cuba." In *The New Cuba: Paradoxes and Potentials*, edited by Ronald Radosh. New York: William Morrow and Co., 1976.

McKinlay, R. D., and Cohan, A. S. "Performance and Instability in Military and Nonmilitary Regime Systems." *American Political Science Review* 70 (3) (September 1976):850–864.

Mahar, Dennis J. *Frontier Development Policy in Brazil: A Study of Amazonia*. New York: Praeger, 1979.

Mallet, Alfredo. "Diversification on Standardisation: Two Trends in Latin American Social Security." *International Labor Review* 101 (1970):48–84.

Malloy, James M. "Authoritarianism, Corporatism and Mobilization in Peru." In *The New Corporatism: Social-Political Structures in the Iberian World*, edited by Frederick B. Pike and Thomas Stritch. Notre Dame, Ind., and London: University of Notre Dame Press, 1974.

———. *Authoritarianism and Corporatism in Latin America*. Pittsburgh: University of Pittsburgh Press, 1977.

———. *The Politics of Social Security in Brazil*. Pittsburgh: University of Pittsburgh Press, 1979.

Malpica, Carlos. *Los Dueños del Peru*. Lima: Ediciones Ensayos Sociales, 1968.

María de Jesus, Carolina. *Child of the Dark: The Diary of Carolina Maria de Jesus*. New York: New American Library, 1962.

Martínez, Daniel, and Tealdo, Armando. *El Agro Peruano 1970–1980: Analisis y Perspectivas*. Lima: CEDEP, 1982.

Martins, Carlos Estevan. *Capitalismo do Estado e Modelo Politico no Brasil*. São Paulo, Brazil: Graal, 1977.

Martz, John D. 1977a. "The Venezuelan Presidential System." In *Presidential Power in Latin American Politics. See Dibacco*, 1977.

———. 1977b. "Policy-Making and the Quest for Consensus: Nationalizing Venezuelan Petroleum." *Journal of Interamerican Studies and World Affairs* 19 (4) (November 1977):483–507.

———. 1977c. "The Party System: Toward Institutionalization." In *Venezuela: The Democratic Experience*, edited by John D. Martz and David J. Myers. New York and London: Praeger, 1977.

———. "Approaches to Agricultural Policy in Venezuela." *Inter-American Economic Affairs* 34 (3) (Winter 1980):25–54.

———. "Development and Democracy in Venezuela: Politics and the Management of Petroleum." In *Politics and Economic Development in Latin America*, edited by Robert Wesson. Stanford, Calif.: Hoover Institution Press, 1984.

Martz, John D., and Baloyra, Enrique A. *Electoral Mobilization and Public Opinion: The Venezuelan Campaign of 1973.* Chapel Hill: University of North Carolina Press, 1976.

Martz, John D., and Myers, David J., eds. *Venezuela: The Democratic Experience.* New York: Praeger, 1977a.

Matos Mar, José, and Mejia, José Manuel. *Reforma Agraria: Logros y Contradicciones 1969–1979.* Lima: Instituto de Estudios Peruanos, 1980.

Meissner, Frank. "The Mexican Food System (SAM): A Strategy for Sowing Petroleum." *Food Policy* 6 (4) (November 1982):219–230.

Medonça, Otavio. "Prefacio." In *Legislacão de Terras do Estado do Pará,* 1890–1963 (Vol. 1), edited by Paulo Lamarão. Belém, Brazil: Grafisa, 1977.

Mesa-Lago, Carmelo, ed. *Cuba in the 1970's: Pragmatism and Institutionalization.* 2d ed. Albuquerque: University of New Mexico Press, 1978a.

———. *Social Security in Latin America: Pressure Groups, Stratification, and Inequality.* Pittsburgh: University of Pittsburgh Press, 1978b.

———. *The Economy of Socialist Cuba: A Two-Decade Appraisal.* Albuquerque: University of New Mexico Press, 1981.

Middlebrook, Kevin Jay. "Land for the Tiller: Political Participation and the Peruvian Military's Agrarian Reform." B.A. thesis, Harvard College, 1972.

Mijeski, Kenneth J. "Costa Rica: The Shrinking of the Presidency?" In *Presidential Power in Latin American Politics. See* Dibacco, 1977.

Montes de Oca, Rosa Elena. "The State and the Peasants." In *Authoritarianism in Mexico. See* Reyna and Weinert, 1977.

Moran, Emilio. *Developing the Amazon.* Bloomington: Indiana University Press, 1981.

Needler, Martin C. *An Introduction to Latin American Politics: The Structure of Conflict.* 2d ed. Englewood Cliffs, N.J.: Prentice-Hall, 1983.

North American Congress on Latin America. "Chile: The Story Behind the Coup." *Latin American and Empire Report* (8) (1973).

O'Donnell, Guillermo. "Reflexiones Sobre las Tendencias de Cambio en el Estado Burocrático-Autoritario." *Revista Paraguaya de Sociologia* 12 (May-August 1975):111–158.

———. "Corporatism and the Question of the State." In *Authoritarianism and Corporatism in Latin America. See* Malloy, 1977.

———. "Reflections on the Patterns of Change in the Bureaucratic-Authoritarian State." *Latin American Research Review* 1 (78) (1978):3–39.

Oficina de Asesores del C. Presidente. *Sistema Alimentario Mexicano: Primer planteamiento de metas de consumo y estrategia de producción de alimentos básicos para 1980–1982.* Mexico: Unpublished manuscript, 1980.

Owens, R. J. *Peru.* New York: Oxford University Press, 1963.

Packenham, Robert A. "Plus Ça Change . . . : The English Edition of Cardoso and Faletto's Dependencia y Desarrollo en America Latina." *Latin American Research Review* 17 (1) (1982):131–151.

Padgett, L. Vincent. *The Mexican Political System.* 2d ed. Boston: Houghton Mifflin, 1976.

Palmer, David Scott. *Revolution from Above: Military Government and Popular Participation in Peru.* Cornell University Dissertation Series, Ithaca, N.Y., 1973.

_____ . "Social Mobilization in Peru." In *Chile and Peru: Two Paths to Social Justice*, edited by Leila A. Bradfield. Kalamazoo: Institute of International and Area Studies, Western Michigan University, 1974.

_____ . "Peru: Authoritarianism and Reform." In *Latin American Politics and Development*. See Wiarda and Kline, 1979.

PARA. *Diario Oficial do Estado*. Belém, Brazil: Imprensa do Estado do Pará, November 9, 1976.

Pease Garcia, Henry. *El Ocaso del Poder Oligárquico: Lucha Política en la Escena Oficial, 1968-1975*. Lima: DESCO, Centro de Estudios y Promoción del Desarrollo, 1977.

Pellicer de Brody, Olga. "Mexico in the 1970s and Its Relations with the United States." In *Latin America and the United States: The Changing Political Realities*, edited by Julio Cotler and Richard R. Fagen. Stanford, Calif.: Stanford University Press, 1974.

Penniman, Howard R., ed. *Venezuela at the Polls: The National Elections of 1978*. Washington, D.C., and London: American Enterprise Institute for Public Policy Research, 1980.

Pereira, L. C. Bresser. *Estado e Subdesenvolvimento Industrializado*. São Paulo, Brazil: Brasiliense, 1977.

Perez Alfonzo, Juan Pablo. *Petroleo: Jugo de la Tierra*. Caracas: Editorial Arte, 1961.

Pérez, Carlos Andres. *Acción de Gobierno*. Caracas, n.p., 1973.

_____ . *Mensaje de Nacionalización a la República*. Caracas: Imprenta Nacional, 1976.

Philip, George D. E. *The Rise and Fall of the Peruvian Military Radicals, 1968-1976*. London: Athlone Press, 1978.

_____ . *Oil and Politics in Latin America: Nationalist Movements and State Companies*. Cambridge: Cambridge University Press, 1982.

Pike, Frederick B., and Stritch, Thomas. *The New Corporatism in Latin America: Social-Political Structures in the Iberian World*. Notre Dame and London: University of Notre Dame Press, 1974.

Pinelo, Adalberto J. *The Multinational Corporation as a Force in Latin American Politics: A Case Study of the International Petroleum Company in Peru*. New York: Praeger, 1973.

Portes, Alejandro. "Housing Policy, Urban Poverty, and the State: The Favelas of Rio de Janeiro, 1972-1976." *Latin American Research Review* 14 (1979):3-24.

Powell, John Duncan. *Political Mobilization of the Venezuelan Peasant*. Cambridge, Mass.: Harvard University Press, 1971.

Purcell, John F. H., and Purcell, Susan Kaufman. "Mexican Business and Public Policy." In *Authoritarianism and Corporatism in Latin America*. See Malloy, 1977.

Purcell, Susan Kaufman. "Decision-Making in an Authoritarian Regime: Theoretical Implications from a Mexican Case Study." *World Politics* 26 (1) (October 1973):28-54.

Quijano, Anibal. *Nationalism and Capitalism in Peru: A Study in Neo-Imperialism*. New York and London: Monthly Review Press, 1971.

Rabe, Stephen G. *The Road to OPEC: United States Relations with Venezuela, 1919-1976*. Austin: University of Texas Press, 1982.

Ray, Talton F. *The Politics of the Barrios of Venezuela*. Berkeley and Los Angeles: University of California Press, 1969.

Reckord, Barry. *Does Fidel Eat More Than Your Father?* New York: Praeger, 1971.

Redclift, M. R. *Agrarian Reform and Peasant Organization on the Ecuadorian Coast.* London: Athlone Press, 1978.

———. *Development Policymaking in Mexico: The Sistema Alimentario Mexicano (SAM).* Center for U.S.-Mexican Studies Working Paper no. 24, University of California, San Diego, 1981.

Remmer, Karen. "Evaluating the Policy Impact of Military Regimes in Latin America." *Latin American Research Review* 13 (2) (1978):39–54.

República de Venezuela. Congreso Nacional. *Proyecto de Ley de Nacionalización.* Caracas: Imprenta Nacional, 1975.

Reyna, Jose Luis, and Weinert, Richard S., eds. *Authoritarianism in Mexico.* Philadelphia: Institute for the Study of Human Issues, 1977.

Reynolds, Clark W. *The Mexican Economy: Twentieth-Century Structure and Growth.* New Haven, Conn., and London: Yale University Press, 1970.

Ripoll, Carlos. *The Cuban Scene: Censors and Dissenters.* Washington, D.C.: Cuban-American National Foundation, 1982.

Ritter, Archibald R. M. *The Economic Development of Revolutionary Cuba.* New York: Praeger, 1974.

Roett, Riordan. *Brazil: Politics in a Patrimonial Society.* Boston: Allyn and Bacon, 1972.

Rojas Bolanos, Manuel. *Lucha Social y Guerra Civil en Costa Rica: 1940–1948.* San José, Costa Rica: Editorial Porvenir, 1980.

Ronfeldt, David. *Atencingo: The Politics of Agrarian Struggle in a Mexican Ejido.* Stanford, Calif.: Stanford University Press, 1973.

Rosenberg, Mark B. "The Politics of Health Care in Costa Rica: Social Security Policymaking, 1941–1975." Ph.D. diss., University of Pittsburgh, 1976.

———. "Social Security Policy Making in Costa Rica: A Research Report." *Latin American Research Review* 14 (1) (1979):116–133.

———. *Las Luchas por el Seguro Social.* San José, Costa Rica: Editorial Costa Rica, 1980.

Rouquie, Alain, 1973. "Military Revolutions and National Independence in Latin America, 1968–71." In *Military Rule in Latin America. See* Schmitter, 1973.

Ruscoe, Gordon C. 1977. "Education Policy in Venezuela." In *Venezuela: The Democratic Experience. See* Martz and Myers, 1977a.

Sanders, Thomas G. "Human Rights and Political Process." In *Military Government and the Movement Toward Democracy in South America,* edited by Howard Handelman and Thomas G. Sanders. Bloomington: Indiana University Press, 1981.

Sanderson, Steven. *Agrarian Populism and the Mexican State.* Berkeley: University of California, 1981.

Santos, Roberto. "Sistema de Propriedade e Relacoes de Trabalho no Meio Rural Paraense." NAEA, Belém, Brazil, 1977. Mimeo.

Sawyer, Donald. "Peasants and Capitalism on the Amazon Frontier." Paper presented at the meeting of the Latin American Studies Association, Houston, November 1977.

Schmitter, Phillipe C., ed. *Military Rule in Latin America: Function, Consequences and Perspectives.* Beverly Hills, Calif.: Sage Publications, 1973.

Schneider, Ronald M. *The Political System of Brazil: Emergence of a "Modernizing"
Authoritarian Regime, 1964-1970.* New York and London: Columbia University
Press, 1971.

Schwartzman, Simon. "Back to Weber: Corporatism and Patrimonialism in the
Seventies." In *Authoritarianism and Corporatism in Latin America: See* Malloy, 1977.

Scott, Robert E. *Mexican Government in Transition.* Urbana: University of Illinois
Press, 1964.

Segal, Aaron. "Cuba and Africa: Military and Technical Assistance." In *The New
Cuban Presence in the Caribbean. See* Barry B. Levine, 1983.

Seligson, Mitchell A. "Agrarian Policies in Dependent Societies." *Journal of Inter-
american Studies and World Affairs* 19 (2) (1977):201-232.

Shapira, Yoram. "Mexico: The Impact of the 1968 Student Protest on Echeverría's
Reformism." *Journal of Interamerican Studies and World Affairs* 19 (4) (November
1977):557-580.

Shaw, Royce Q. *Central America: Regional Integration and National Political Development.*
Boulder Colo.: Westview Press, 1978.

Sigmund, Paul E. *Multinationals in Latin America: The Politics of Nationalization.*
Madison: University of Wisconsin Press, 1980.

Skidmore, Thomas E. "Politics and Economic Policy Making in Authoritarian Brazil,
1937-1971." In *Authoritarian Brazil. See* Stepan, 1973.

Sloan, John W. "Bureaucracy and Public Policy in Latin America." *Inter-American
Economic Affairs* 34 (4) (Spring 1981):17-47.

Smith, Nigel J. H. *Rainforest Corridors.* Berkeley: University of California Press,
1982.

Smith, Peter H. *Labyrinths of Power.* Princeton, N.J.: Princeton University, 1979.

Smith, T. Alexander. *The Comparative Policy Process.* Santa Barbara, Calif., and
Oxford: ABC-Clio Press, 1975.

Solis, Leopoldo. *La Realidad Económica Mexicana: Retrovisión y Perspectiva.* Mexico
City: Siglo XXI, 1971.

Sorkin, Alan L. *Health Economics in Developing Countires.* Toronto and London: D.
C. Heath, 1976.

Soto, Oscar David. *La Empresa y la Reforma Agraria en la Agricultura Venezolana.*
Mérida, Venezuela: Talleres Gráficos Universitarios, 1973.

Stepan, Alfred. *Authoritarian Brazil: Origins, Policies, and Future.* New Haven, Conn.,
and London: Yale University Press, 1973.

———. *The State and Society: Peru in Comparative Perspective.* Princeton, N.J.: Princeton University Press, 1978.

Stevens, Evelyn P. *Protest and Response in Mexico.* Cambridge, Mass.: MIT Press,
1974.

———. "Mexico's PRI: The Institutionalization of Corporatism?" In *Authoritarianism and Corporatism in Latin America. See* Malloy, 1977.

———. "Mexico's One-Party State: Revolutionary Myth and Authoritarian Reality."
In *Latin American Politics and Development. See* Wiarda and Kline, 1979.

Stewart, Frances. "The New International Economic Order and Basic Needs: Conflicts and Complementarities." In *Development Strategies and Basic Needs in Latin
America. See* Brundenius and Lundahl, 1982.

Stewart, William S. 1977. "Public Administration." In *Venezuela: The Democratic Experience. See* Martz and Myers, 1977a.

Stone, Samuel. *La Dinastía de los Conquistadores: La Crisis del Poder en Costa Rica Contemporanea.* San José, Costa Rica: EDUCA, 1975.

Tannenbaum, Frank. *Peace By Revolution: Mexico After 1910.* 2d ed. New York: Columbia University Press, 1966.

Taylor, Charles Lewis, and Hudson, Michael C. *World Handbook of Political and Social Indicators.* New Haven, Conn.: Yale University Press, 1972.

Thompson, John K. *Inflation, Financial Markets, and Economic Development: The Experience of Mexico.* Greenwich, Conn.: JAI Press, 1979.

Tugwell, Franklin. *The Politics of Oil in Venezuela.* Palo Alto, Calif.: Stanford University Press, 1975.

––––––. 1977. "Petroleum Policy and the Political Process." In *Venezuela: The Democratic Experience. See* Martz and Myers, 1977a.

UNESCO. *Statistical Yearbook.* Paris: UNESCO Press, 1981.

Unidade Regional de Supervisao Norte. *Plano Anual do Setor Público Agrícola: Consolidação da Regiao Notre,* Belem, Brazil: 1977.

Valdés, Nelson. "Revolution and Institutionalization in Cuba." *Cuban Studies / Estudios Cubanos* 6 (1) (January 1976):1–24.

Vallenilla, Luis. *Oil: The Making of a New Economic Order.* New York: McGraw-Hill, 1975.

Vega Carballo, José Luis. "Etapas y Proceso de la Evolución Socio-Político de Costa Rica." *Estudios Sociales Centroamericanos* 1 (1) (1972).

Velasco, Juan-Agustín. *Impacts of Mexican Oil Policy on Economic and Political Development.* Lexington, Mass.: Lexington Books, 1983.

Velho, Otavio Guilherme. *Capitalismo Autoritario e Campesinato.* São Paulo, Brazil: Difel, 1976.

Vernon, Raymond. *The Dilemma of Mexico's Development.* Cambridge, Mass.: Harvard University Press, 1963.

Villanueva, Victor. "Peru's 'New' Military Professionalism: The Failure of the Technocratic Approach." In *Post-Revolutionary Peru. See* Gorman, 1982.

Warman, Arturo. *We Come to Object: The Peasants of Morelos and the National State.* Baltimore: Johns Hopkins University Press, 1980.

Weaver, Jerry L. "Assessing the Impact of Military Rule: Alternative Approaches." In *Military Rule in Latin America. See* Schmitter, 1973.

Webb, Richard Charles. "Trends in Real Income in Peru, 1950–1966." Research Paper in Economics, Woodrow Wilson School, Princeton University, Princeton, N.J., 1974.

––––––. "Government Policy and the Distribution of Income in Peru, 1963–1973." In *The Peruvian Experiment. See* Lowenthal, 1975.

––––––. *Government Policy and the Distribution of Income in Peru, 1963–1973.* Cambridge, Mass.: Harvard University Press, 1977.

Whitehead, Laurence. "The Economic Policy of the Echeverría Sexenio: What Went Wrong and Why?" Paper presented at the meeting of the Latin American Studies Association, Pittsburgh, April 5–7, 1979.

Wiarda, Howard. "Toward a Framework for the Study of Political Change in the Iberic-Latin Tradition." *World Politics* 25 (2) (January 1973):206–235.

Wiarda, Howard, and Kline, Harvey F., eds. *Latin American Politics and Development*. Boston: Houghton Mifflin, 1979.

Wiarda, Ieda Siqueira. "Approaches and Strategies of Population Policy-Making in a Democratic Context: The Case of Venezuela." In *Dynamics of Population Policy in Latin America*, edited by Terry McCoy. Cambridge, Mass.: Ballinger Publishing, 1974.

Wildavsky, Aaron. *The Politics of the Budgetary Process*. Boston: Little, Brown and Co., 1964.

Wilkie, James W. *Measuring Land Reform: Supplement to the Statistical Abstract of Latin America*. Los Angeles: University of California, 1974a.

———. "Recentralization: The Budgetary Dilemma in the Economic Development of Mexico, Bolivia, and Costa Rica." In *Fiscal Policy for Industrialization and Development in Latin America*, edited by David T. Geithman. Gainesville: University Presses of Florida, 1974b.

Williams, Edward J. *The Political Themes of Inter-American Relations*. Belmont, Calif.: Duxbury Press, 1971.

Williams, Edward J., and Wright, Freeman J. *Latin American Politics: A Developmental Approach*. Palo Alto, Calif.: Mayfield, 1975.

Wionczek, Miguel. "The Rise and Decline of Latin American Economic Integration." In *Contemporary Inter-American Relations*, edited by Yale Ferguson. Englewood Cliffs, N.J.: Prentice-Hall, 1972.

Wolf, Eric. *Peasant Wars of the Twentieth Century*. New York: Harper and Row, 1968.

Wolfe, Marshall. "Social Security and Development: The Latin American Experience." In *The Role of Social Security in Economic Development*, edited by Everett Kasalow. Washington, D.C.: Government Printing Office, 1968.

Womack, John. *Zapata and the Mexican Revolution*. New York: Vintage Books, 1968.

Wood, Charles, and Schmink, Marianne. "Blaming the Victim: Small Farmer Production in an Amazon Colonization Project." Presented at the annual meeting of the American Association for the Advancement of Science, Washington, D.C., February 1978.

World Bank. *World Tables*. Baltimore and London: Johns Hopkins University Press, 1980.

Yates, P. Lamartine. *Mexico's Agricultural Dilemma*. Tucson: University of Arizona Press, 1981.

Periodicals

Business Venezuela, Caracas, Venezuela, May-June 1979

Financial Times, 25 October 1978

Granma (Cuba), 6 January 1980

Journal of Commerce, various issues

Latin America Economic Report (LAER), London, various issues

Latin America Annual Review (LAAR) and the Caribbean. Essex, England: World of Information, 1979

Latin America Regional Report (LARR), London, various issues
Latin America Weekly Report (LAWR), London, various issues
New York Times (NYT), various issues
Quarterly Economic Report (QER), London, 1977
Resumen (Caracas), various issues
SIC (SIC) (Caracas), May 1981, p. 231
Statistical Abstract of Latin America (SALA), University of California at Los Angeles, Latin American Center, 1980, 1981
Washington Report on the Hemisphere, 6 September 1983; a biweekly publication of the Council on Hemispheric Affairs, Washington, D.C.

Acronyms

AD	Democratic Action
ADEX	Association of Exporters
AID	Agency for International Development
ANAP	National Association of Small Peasants
ANFE	National Association of Economic Development
APRA	Popular Revolutionary Alliance for America
ARENA	National Renovating Alliance
BA	bureaucratic-authoritarian (state)
BAP	Agricultural and Livestock Bank
BCV	Venezuelan Central Bank
CACM	Central American Common Market
CAEM	Center for Higher Military Studies
CARIFTA	Caribbean Free Trade Area
CDR	Committee(s) for the Defense of the Revolution
CDS	Sandinista Defense Committees
CIA	Central Intelligence Agency
CM	Council of Ministers
CNA	National Agrarian Confederation
CNC	National Peasants' Confederation
COAP	Presidential Advisory Committee
CONASUPO	National Company of Popular Subsistence
CONCAMIN	Confederation of Mexican Chambers of Industry
CONCANACO	National Confederation of Chambers of Commerce
CONINDUSTRIA	National Council of Industry
COPEI	Social Christian Party
COPLAMAR	Coordinating Program for Marginal Zones
CORPOMER-CADEO	Agricultural Marketing Corporation
CS	Council of State
CTC	Cuban Labor Federation
CTM	Mexican Workers' Confederation
CTV	Venezuelan Workers' Confederation
CVF	Venezuelan Development Corporation
CVG	Venezuelan Guyana Corporation
DASP	Administrative Department of the Public Sector

243

ESG	Superior War College
FAO	Food and Agriculture Organization
FDA	Agricultural Development Fund
FEDECAMARAS	Federation of Chambers of Commerce and Production
FENEGAN	National Federation of Livestock Raisers
FMC	Cuban Women's Federation
FSLN	Sandinista National Liberation Front
FSO	Fund for Special Operations
GDP	Gross Domestic Product
GNP	Gross National Product
IADB	Inter-American Development Bank
IAN	National Agrarian Institute
IMF	International Monetary Fund
INCRA	National Institute of Colonization and Agrarian Reform
IPC	International Petroleum Company
ITT (or IT&T)	International Telephone and Telegraph
IVP	Venezuelan Petrochemical Institute
LAFTA	Latin American Free Trade Association
MDB	Brazilian Democratic Movement
MEP	People's Electoral Movement
MNC	multinational corporations
OAS	Organization of American States
OFIPLAN	National Planning Office
OPIC	Overseas Private Investment Corporation
PAN	National Action Party
PCC	Cuban Communist Party
PDA	Plan for the Development of the Amazon
PDVSA	Petroleum of Venezuela
PETROVEN	Venezuelan Petroleum
PIC	Integrated Colonization Projects
PIDER	Integrated Rural Development Program
PIN	Program for National Integration
PLN	National Liberation Party
PRI	Institutional Revolutionary Party
PRIDA	Unified Program of Agricultural Development
PSD	Social Democratic Party (also PDS)
PSP	Pre-1959 Communist Party (Cuba)
PTB	Brazilian Labor Party
PUN	National Unification Party
PVC	Communist Party (Venezuela)
SAM	Mexican Food System

SICARTSA	Lázaro Cárdenas Steel Production Center
SINAMOS	National Social Mobilization Support System
SNI	National Information Service
SUDAM	Superintendency for the Development of the Amazon
UDN	National Democratic Union
UIR	Revolutionary Insurrectionist Union
URD	Republican Democratic Union

About the Case Study Contributors

Juan M. del Aguila has a B.A. in political science from the University of Florida. He was awarded both the M.A. and the Ph.D. by the University of North Carolina at Chapel Hill. Since 1979, he has been teaching at Emory University and is also serving as the associate director of the university's International Study Center. He has done field research in Venezuela and Costa Rica and is the author of *Cuba: Dilemmas of a Revolution* (Westview, 1984).

Merilee S. Grindle is a graduate of Wellesley College. Her M.A. and Ph.D. degrees are from Brown University and M.I.T., respectively. She has taught at Brown University and Wellesley College and is currently a research associate at the Institute for International Development at Harvard University. She has written extensively on processes of public policy formation and the Third World. Her publications include numerous articles and books. Her book *Bureaucrats, Politicians, and Peasants in Mexico: A Case Study in Public Policy* (1977) is the basis for her essay in this volume.

Cynthia McClintock holds a B.A. from Radcliffe College, an M.A. from UCLA, and a Ph.D. from M.I.T. She is currently an associate professor of political science at George Washington University. She has done extensive field research in Peru and has published widely, including her books *Peasant Cooperatives and Political Change in Peru* (1981) and *The Peruvian Experiment Reconsidered* (1983).

John D. Martz, professor and head of political science at The Pennsylvania State University, received his Ph.D. at the University of North Carolina at Chapel Hill where he also taught for many years. He is the author or editor of more than a dozen books and scores of articles and book reviews, concentrating his efforts on the Bolivarian states, with special attention to campaigns, elections, parties, and ideological movements. He also served as the editor of the *Latin American Research Review* from 1974 to 1980.

Mark B. Rosenberg is associate professor of political science and director of the Latin American and Caribbean Center of Florida International University.

He received a Ph.D. from the University of Pittsburgh and has conducted research in Costa Rica, Nicaragua, Bolivia, Peru, and, as a Fulbright Research Scholar, Honduras. He has published numerous articles and a book on social security policy in Costa Rica that serves as the basis for his essay in this volume.

Stephen G. Bunker holds undergraduate and graduate degrees from Harvard College and Duke University, respectively. He has undertaken extensive field research in several countries of Latin America and in Uganda, and has published numerous articles on his research findings. Professor Bunker has taught at the University of Illinois at Urbana-Champaign and served as a visiting professor at universities in Brazil and Guatemala. He is currently an associate professor in the Department of Sociology at Johns Hopkins University.

Index

249